How to Typeset
from a
Word Processor

The Bowker Graphics Library

The Bowker Design Series

The Book of Graphic Problem-Solving
by John Newcomb

Designing for Magazines
by Jan V. White

Editing by Design
by Jan V. White

Mastering Graphics
by Jan V. White

Photographing for Publication
by Norman Sanders

Using Charts and Graphs
by Jan V. White

Bowker's Composition Series

Book Design: Systematic Aspects
by Stanley Rice

Book Design: Text Format Models
by Stanley Rice

How to Typeset from a Word Processor
by Ronald Labuz

The Interface Data Book for Word Processing / Typesetting
by Ronald Labuz with Paul Altimonte

The TypEncyclopedia
by Frank J. Romano

Other Related Titles

Bookmaking
by Marshall Lee

Visual Communication and the Graphic Arts
by Estelle Jussim

How to Typeset

from a

Word Processor

An Interfacing Guide

Ronald Labuz

R. R. Bowker Company
New York and London, 1984

To Carol,
for all the time

Published by R. R. Bowker Company
205 East Forty-second Street, New York, NY 10017
Copyright © 1984 by Xerox Corporation
Printed and bound in the United States of America

Library of Congress Cataloging in Publication Data

Labuz, Ronald, 1953–
How to typeset from a word processor.

Includes index.
1. Computerized typesetting. 2. Word processing.
3. Phototypesetting. 4. Computer interfaces. 5. Typesetting. I. Title.
Z253.3.L33   1984   686.2'2544   84-11143
ISBN 0-8352-1899-6

Designed by Traci Churchill

Contents

Preface, *xi*

1 The Essentials of Interfacing

■ Computer Communications, *1*
■ Data and Word Processing, *2*
Networking, 2
Telecommunications, 2
■ Interfacing, *3*
Why Should You Interface?, 5
■ The Word Processor/Typesetter Interface, *5*
■ Word Processing and Typesetting, *8*
Early Memory Systems, 8
The Beginnings of Word Processing, 8
Computing without Owning a Computer, 10
■ Word Processors Today, *11*
Mainframes, 12
Minicomputers, 12
Microcomputers, 13
■ Typesetting, *13*
Paper Tape versus Magnetic Memory, 15
Is the Time Right for WP/TS Interface?, 15

2 Checkpoints and Checkmates

■ The Interface Decision, *17*
Research, 17
Self-Education, 18
■ Developing a Rationale, *18*
Economics, 18
Final Steps in the Interface Decision, 22
■ Four Ways to Interface, *22*
Optical Character Recognition: The First Indirect Route, 22
Media Conversion: The Second Indirect Route, 25
Hardwiring: The First Direct Route, 27
Telecommunications: The Second Direct Route, 28
■ Electronic versus Paper Manuscripts, *31*

3 Input Decisions for Type Buyer and Typesetter

■ Analyzing Needs and Requirements, *33*
■ The Typesetting Company, *33*
  The Type House, 34
  The Printing Company and Book Manufacturer, 35
  The Quick Printer, 36
■ The Typesetting Customer, *37*
  The Interfacing Criteria, 37
■ The In-House Graphics Facility, *38*
  Should You Move In-House?, 39
■ The Three Universes of Typesetting Users, *40*
■ Two Input Methods, *41*
  Typewriters as Input, 42
  Computers as Input, 42
■ Word Processing: Text versus Technical Matter, *44*

4 First, Software—Then Hardware

■ Buying Software: A Primer, *45*
■ Word Processing Software Basics, *45*
■ Purchasing Considerations, *46*
■ Necessary Software Features, *46*
■ Which Package Should You Buy?, *51*
■ What Micro Software Is Available?, *51*
  The Most Popular WP Program: WordStar, 52
  WordStar's Competition: Winners, 52
  WordStar's Competition: Losers, 53
■ What Mini Software Is Available?, *53*
  MASS-11, 54
■ Buying Hardware: A Primer, *54*
■ Choosing an Operating System, *55*
  The MS-DOS Option, 55
  The CP/M Option, 56
  Other Operating Systems, 56
■ The Machines, *57*
  IBM PC, 57
  Kaypro 4, 57
  Apple Lisa, 58

5 Purchase and Installation of Word Processors

■ Support, *61*
■ Minimum Technical Specifications, *63*
■ Vendor Considerations, *66*
  Professionals: Computer Stores and Manufacturers, 67
  Mass Marketers: Mail-Order and Department Stores, 67

■ Installation, *68*
Phase One: Before, 68
Phase Two: Installation and After, 69

6 Choosing an Interfacing Method

■ Analyzing Requirements, *75*
The Totals: Should You Interface?, 78
■ Media Conversion, *79*
Black Boxes versus Programmable Converters, 79
■ The Interface: Direct or Indirect , *81*
The Media Conversion Market, 81
Reviewing Media Conversion: Should You Buy?, 86
■ Optical Character Recognition (OCR), *86*
WordCom SI and Kurzweil: The Old and the New, 86
OCR from the Type Buyer's Point of View, 87
■ Hardwiring, *88*
Parallel versus Serial Transmission, 88
RS-232 Serial Port and S-100 Bus, 89
Communications Cables: Null Modem, 90
Hardwire Applications, 90
■ Telecommunications, *91*
Translation Software, 91
Why Choose Telecommunications?, 92
■ Choosing Equipment, *92*
Where Should the Type House Buy?, 92
Where Should the Type Customer Buy?, 93

7 Output Devices: The Typesetters

■ The Market, *95*
■ Direct Entry Typesetters, *95*
■ Systems, *97*
Super Systems, 98
■ The Machines, *98*
Mergenthaler, 99
Compugraphic, 101
Itek, 103
AM Varityper, 105
The Rest of the Field, 106
■ The Choices: Which Should You Buy?, *106*
For In-House Only, 107
For Type House Customers Only, 107

8 In-House Typesetting

■ Do You Want It, and Is It Worth It?, *109*
■ Three Organizational Concerns, *109*
■ Dollar Costs, *111*

- Other Organizational Costs, *113*
- Four Benefits of In-House Graphics Shops, *113*
- Questions for Equipment Purchase and/or Rental, *116*

9 Establishing Telecommunications

- Protocols, *119*
  Code Sets, 119
  Asynchronous and Synchronous Transmission, 123
  Baud Rate, 124
  ACK/NAK, 125
  Parity, 125
  Number of Stop Bits, 126
  Number of Data Bits, 126
  Mode Transparent or Nontransparent, 127
  Paced or Continuous Transmission, 127
  The Remaining Protocols, 130
- Sign-On Document, *130*
- Modems, *131*
  Connections, 131
  Type of Transmission, 131
  Baud Rate, 132
  Modulation, 132
  Line Types, 132
- Buying Modems, *133*
- Testing Modems, *134*

10 Building Translation Tables

- Mnemonics: How Do They Work?, *135*
  Saving Keystrokes, 135
  Keying Typesetting Codes, 136
  Four Steps in the Translation Process, 136
- Word Processing Input: A Troubleshooting Guide, *136*
  Coding Deletions, 137
  Word Processing Conventions, 137
- Typesetting Problems: The Troubleshooting Continues, *140*
  Code Insertions: The Critical Decision, 140
  Using Your Word Processing Operator: Pros, 140
  Using Your Word Processing Operator: Cons, 140
  Using the Typesetter: Pros, 141
  Using the Typesetter: Cons, 141
  Who Should Code?, 142
  Technical Parameters in Typesetting, 143
  Technical Type versus Straight Matter, 143
- Writing the Translation Tables, *144*
  What Codes Should Be Used?, 144
  The Proposal, 144

■ Writing the Tables, *148*
  The Equations, 149

11 For Type Buyers Only

■ How to Select a Typesetter, *151*
  Which Type Houses Interface?, 151
  Costs, 152
  Interfacing Quality, 152
  The Contract, 153
■ The In-House Shop, *153*
■ Alternative Applications of In-House, *154*
■ Implications of Universal Interfacing, *155*

12 For Typesetters Only

■ Using the Technology: New Opportunities, *157*
■ Marketing the Technology, *158*
  Debugging Your Interface, 158
  Announcing the Services, 158
  Finding the Market, 159
  Marketing Strategies, 159
■ Pricing the Type, *162*
  Professional Pricing Guidelines, 163

Appendix I: Computer Basics, *165*

Appendix II: Typography Basics, *195*

Glossary, *199*

Index, *213*

Preface

IF REVOLUTION IS RADICAL CHANGE, then information processing has undergone a true revolution in the last 15 years. The explosive computer market reflects this revolutionary condition. Microcomputers and standalone word processors have joined forces with mainframes and minicomputers. Many of us, faced with the army of computers now on the market, are still timid about whether or how to join the computerized information handling movement. Yet, we all know that we will be changing our methods of handling printed information. It is a fact: Word processing is taking over as the way we create our documents.

Along with word processing has come the opportunity to create typesetting from a word processor—with *interfacing* being the facilitating link. If you are not now moving documents electronically, you will be soon. Interfacing is a major publishing technology of the 1980s. Book publishers, associations, colleges and universities, corporations, government bodies, and nonprofit organizations are all making the move to electronic manuscripts. Why? Mainly, it is to save time and money.

Many people are asking, How do you do it? This book and its companion, *The Interface Data Book for Word Processing/Typesetting*, are plain-speaking guides to both the procedures and the technology of interfacing.

How to Typeset from a Word Processor is organized and written to enable you to make the smartest decisions for your publishing situation—whatever it is. The *Data Book* offers specific product and technical information for implementing the WP/typesetting interface. Neither book is biased for interfacing as a cure-all for every type buyer's or typesetter's needs.

How to Typeset from a Word Processor is for type buyers, typesetters, printers, and students of the graphic arts. All four groups are learning to interface now.

Type buyers find themselves in one of three categories: (1) those who are not now word processing, (2) those who are word processing but not interfacing, and (3) those who are already interfacing. If you are a member of the first group or your "computerese" is rusty, start with Appendix I, Computer Basics. After you have been through the basics, the information presented starting with Chapter 1, The Essentials of Interfacing, should be easily comprehensible.

The second group includes typesetting customers who are already partially computerized. If you are in this category and you have a large typesetting budget, you are probably interested in the new interfacing methods. Chapters 1 and 2 will give you the basics, and beginning with Chapter 6, you will find first an introduction and then an in-depth look at how interface works. Chapter 8, In-House Typesetting, will be of value for those who are thinking about establishing their own typesetting facility.

Finally, there are type buyers who are already interfacing—either commercially with a typesetter or in-house with their own graphics facility. Chapter 6, on interfacing methods, and Chapters 8 through 12 will be of most interest; but do not neglect the earlier, more basic information. Many organizations have made mistakes at very early phases and then find that those mistakes cause problems later on. A fundamental understanding of *how to interface* and *who should interface* is essential.

Typesetters now have to face the fact that word processor interfacing is no longer a frill; it is a competitive necessity. Typesetting executives may find the most useful information in Chapter 6, where there is a full discussion of interfacing hardware on the market today. If you are already interfacing with your word processing customers, Chapters 9 through 11 give you some idea of what to expect from the other side, your customers. Chapter 12 has been written specifically for typesetters. The days of simply getting by through offering interfacing are over. Tomorrow's—and today's—interfacing customers will demand more from the type house.

There are, of course, several subgroups in the huge printing and information processing industries. If you are a printer interested in typesetting, you might study Chapter 7, an analysis of the many phototypesetting options available. The *Data Book* will also be of help for printers and typesetters in the market to buy output phototypesetters.

The *Data Book* also contains information applicable to everyone involved in interfacing: information on modems, word processing software, and a number of translation tables. The Interfacing Yellow Pages will prove useful to both customers and typesetters. The last section of the *Data Book* is a list—as complete as possible—of those typesetters who are now capable of interfacing. Subsequent editions of the *Data Book* will contain updates of information as it is received.

There are several distinctive features in *How to Typeset from a Word Processor*. Practical decision making is aided by the inclusion of checklists for self-evaluation and comparison of word processing and typesetting hardware and software specifications; work sheets and financial formulas help in determining costs and savings in interfacing. Useful terms in the text are highlighted in italics and defined in the Glossary. In addition to Appendix I, Computer Basics, there is a short discussion of typesetting practices in Appendix II, Typography Basics.

Any book is a collaboration. There are several individuals who were particularly helpful in the preparation of this book. Julie Moore is to be thanked for her advocacy and ideas. The graphics work of Don Dempsey began as my rough sketches; his skillfulness and care in interpretation are very much appreciated. The Staff Development Committee of Mohawk Valley Community College, Utica, N.Y., made resources available. The efforts of Bill Gladstone, Paul Doebler, Theresa Barry, Iris Topel, Thomas Maneen, William Houze, Cheryl March, and Paul Altimonte were essential. My thanks to them all. The illustration sources are identified throughout the text; the cooperation of all the companies who helped in supplying photographs and translation tables is gratefully acknowledged.

CHAPTER 1

The Essentials of Interfacing

INTERFACING IS SUCCESSFULLY moving information from one computer to another. The most familiar "interface" is two people talking to each other. Computers can do the same.

But, just like human beings, computers "understand" in different languages. While people need translations, dictionaries, and courses in languages to communicate in "foreign" languages, computers move information because of a spontaneous translation facility. But that capability is not innate. People have to build it into machines. That is one reason for this book. Specifically, this book tells why and how to make two kinds of computers—word processors and typesetting machines—talk to each other.

Unfortunately, communications between computers has as many complications as communications between humans. But whatever the problems, interfacing is now necessary. Accelerated changes in information handling have made the computer as common as pens and pencils. Computers are now at the heart of the printing and publishing process.

Computer Communications

Because computers don't speak in English—or in any spoken language, for that matter—interface translations must be created on the computer's own terms. But creating translations is not as difficult as, say, learning a computer language. There are no magical or mystical skills involved. Rather, computer communications is a practical skill that is not difficult once it is understood. What do you need to understand in order to use a computer to communicate?

To begin any discussion of how computers communicate, terms have to be defined. Technical jargon is often a problem. If you're a bit shaky on computer basics, take a look at Appendix I.

Data and Word Processing

Two major functions of the computer are *data processing* and *word processing*. Data processing involves the manipulation of numbers—often called "number crunching"—to achieve a desired result. The simplest data processor is the hand-held calculator capable of addition, subtraction, multiplication, and division. More complicated machines do accounting, inventory control, billing, and list management.

Word processors manipulate words. The computer used to write this book edits sentences, transposes characters, deletes words, and corrects misspelled words without retyping. With word processors, electronic manuscripts can be retrieved, edited, and saved.

The computer works by allowing us to put words and data on a screen. Depending upon what the machine has been directed to do by the instructions called *programs,* jobs are either stored, printed, or manipulated to produce the desired results. But how does one computer communicate with another? And how do we communicate with them?

■ Networking

The first step in computer communications is networking. A *network* is a collection of interconnected electronic devices capable of communicating with each other. We have all networked. Common examples are airline reservation networks and the long-distance direct-dial telephone network. Computer networks allow powerful *mainframe* and *minicomputers* to serve as hosts for dozens and at times hundreds of computer terminals (keyboards connected to video display screens).

There are two major types of networks: *point-to-point* (Figure 1-1a) and *multiplexer* (Figure 1-1b). Point-to-point networks connect terminals directly with computers through connectors, known as ports, located at the back of the computer. Multiplexing networks are much more powerful and much larger. These systems first connect terminals to intermediaries called multiplexers, which in turn are connected to the host computer. The advantages of multiplexer systems include the capability to construct huge networks and to reduce the cost of establishing the network. The disadvantage is that when communication is interrupted in a multiplexed system, many terminals are affected. Because of the reliability of current equipment (and because of backup systems), that problem is rare.

■ Telecommunications

A capability implicitly necessary for networking is *telecommunications.* There are several ways to establish communications between computers, but telecommunications is the most commonly recognized. Telecommunications, along with electronic circuitry, are technologies that existed before computer communications was possible. By picking up a phone, dialing a number, and talking to a friend, you have telecommunicated. Like humans, computers are capable of communicating over telephone lines, either with other computers or with terminals. Unlike humans, computers do not use verbal messages to communicate—they use numerical codes.

Those numerical codes are the basis and, indeed, the reason for this book. Although some computers have a very limited command of spoken language, computer voice capability has not been perfected enough to allow any substantive communication to take place.

Computers transmit information by telephone through devices called *modems* (an acronym for modulator-demodulator) that translate numerical codes the computer understands into audible sounds telephones can use. But computer communications is not quite that simple. Although all computers use numerical codes to transmit information, different computers use different codes. Just as some people speak French and some speak Urdu, computers have different languages.

The first step in establishing communications is to make certain that translations are available. If translations can be made, communication is possible. Bridging gaps in computer communications is called *interfacing*.

Interfacing

Simple interfaces occur between computer terminals and computer printers. Information is sent directly from a terminal to a printer to produce paper copies, or printouts. More complicated interfaces are the building blocks of networking.

Stated very simply, *interfacing is making two computers talk to each other*. The connection between humans and computers is simpler because computer programmers have allowed us to "speak" with computers in our language. When we use a computer, we communicate in words; the com-

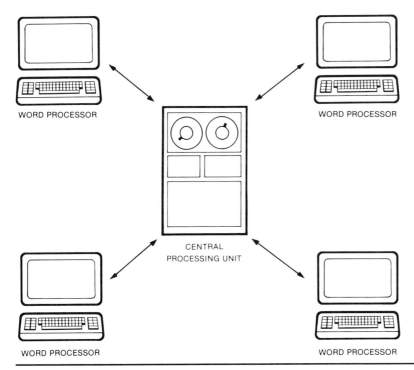

WORD PROCESSOR

WORD PROCESSOR

CENTRAL
PROCESSING UNIT

WORD PROCESSOR

WORD PROCESSOR

■ **FIGURE 1-1a. Point-to-point network.**

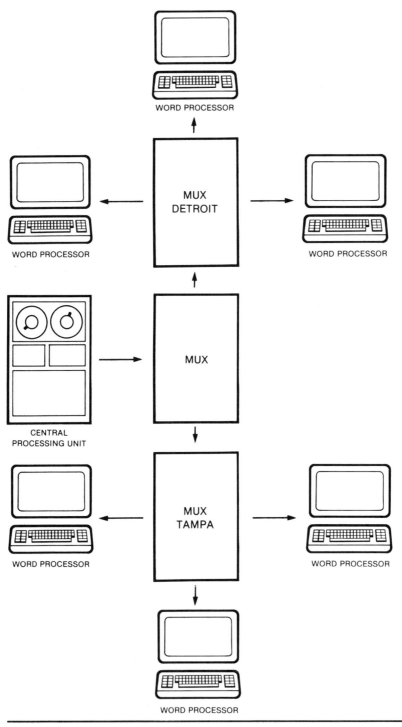

■ FIGURE 1-1b. Multiplexer network.

puter translates the words into a form (numbers) that it can understand. Because these translations take place at the somewhat mysterious level of computer languages, many first-time interfacers are intimidated. But interfacing is no more complicated than translating any language.

■ Why Should You Interface?

We have all been interfacing for some time: travel agency reservations, electronic mail, orbital satellites that allow electronic signals to become cable television, and library information networks are all common examples. Today any computer can talk to another. The challenge is to make certain that once talking has started, communication follows.

Within a very short time, most of us will be using word processors to record information. Today the price of computers capable of word processing is nearing the cost of the more expensive electronic typewriters. When costs are comparable, the obvious choice will be the computer over the typewriter. Beyond the editing advantages of word processing, these new tools are also capable of accounting, billing, and dozens of other functions necessary for any profession.

Book publishers, printers, advertising and public relations agencies, professional societies, and newspapers are among the most obvious candidates for word processing, but there are many other, less obvious segments of the business community that will benefit from using word processors. Currently, information networks are available for securing data important to pharmacists, attorneys, doctors, engineers, stockbrokers, and librarians. When these professionals purchase a computer to tap into important information sources, word processing gives them a competitive edge.

One of the most significant advantages of computerization is that a computerized document is a stored document—it is saved on memory and can be recalled. Because it can be recalled, it can also be sent to other computers. For sharing printed information with large numbers of people, this offers incomparable communication opportunities.

The Word Processor/Typesetter Interface

Many professions require material to be typeset: to be produced on machines that create proportionally spaced characters common to all quality printing. For newspapers, books, journals, magazines, and newsletters, typewriting isn't sufficient. Typesetting is a must.

If you're like most people, your material is prepared on a typewriter. It is then sent to the printer or typesetting company, which re-creates the job by hand or by machine to produce typesetting. Duplication of effort has been the typical production flow for the last 525 years (Figure 1-2). In the last five years, that production flow has changed dramatically—and for the better.

With the new way of doing things, you prepare your documents on a computer capable of word processing. You write and edit your manuscript on the screen until you are satisfied. So far, the process has not changed very much. The computer terminal is simply a new tool used to produce writing. You are now ready to send your writing out for typesetting. This is where tradition gives way to the future, which began in the 1970s.

Because your manuscript is electronically stored, as the manuscript is retrieved from memory, you send your words to any computer with which an interface has been established (Figure 1-3). You thus make perhaps your most important *interface*—the interface with your printer's typesetting machine. Today's typesetting machines are computerized and can communicate directly with your word processor.

Why is this the most important interface? Remember those expensive typesetting bills? Roughly 30 percent of the cost of typesetting is accrued in retyping manuscripts. If your manuscript is electronic, and if it is sent directly to your printer or typesetting company's typesetter, then retyping can be eliminated. Keystrokes have been captured. Although there are

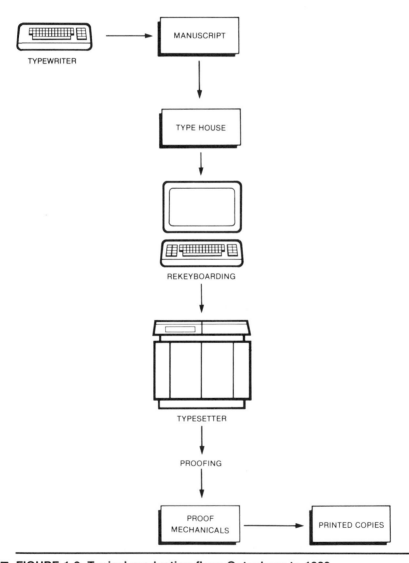

TYPEWRITER

MANUSCRIPT

TYPE HOUSE

REKEYBOARDING

TYPESETTER

PROOFING

PROOF MECHANICALS

PRINTED COPIES

■ **FIGURE 1-2. Typical production flow: Gutenberg to 1980.**

many advantages beyond a 30 percent savings in costs, 30 percent is a persuasive beginning argument. A printing industry projection indicates that by 1993 more than 80 percent of all typesetting will be interfaced.

Interfacing word processors and typesetters presents some special problems. Because each machine is a technical tool, each requires an understanding of a different technical vocabulary. Efficient and professional operation of either one of these workhorses calls for a basic grounding in prerequisite skills.

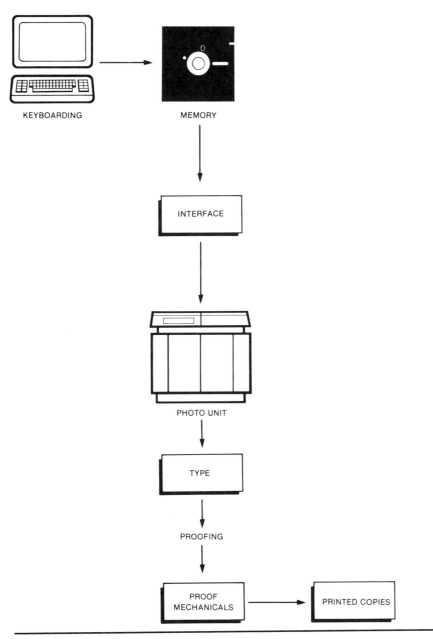

KEYBOARDING

MEMORY

INTERFACE

PHOTO UNIT

TYPE

PROOFING

PROOF
MECHANICALS

PRINTED COPIES

■ FIGURE 1-3. New production flow: interfacing.

Interfacing sounds very simple. But when you know something about the technical genealogies of these two curiously interrelated technologies, you'll begin to understand that typesetting is not quite as simple as you may have thought and that word processing is not quite as complicated.

Word Processing and Typesetting

Word processing is a technical term that has made its way into our standard vocabulary. In simple language, word processing is working with words, and working with words has a long history. From the first "word processors"—the stylus, then pen, then pencil—through the first manual typewriters to today's electronic typing systems, technology has meant increased input speed. But the newest technology, interfacing, takes technology a step further. Speed is increased, not by making typing easier or simpler, but by saving keystrokes.

■ Early Memory Systems

Of course, to save keystrokes it's necessary that characters be stored for retrieval. The critical breakthrough in word processing was memory. By the mid-1960s, machines were on the market that permanently stored jobs on magnetic memory.

The first method available to store documents was magnetic tape. Operators store information on magnetic tape similar to that used in video- and audiocassettes. Errors can be eliminated simply by typing corrections over mistakes. More expensive machines allow actual editing of complete tapes. But the most important advance was memory.

The next step toward modern word processing was the magnetic card (or mag card) system (Figure 1-4). Instead of tapes, these machines use cards that magnetically store large amounts of information. Cards are portable and can be "read," edited, and sorted into various sequences.

Along with the mag card systems of the late 1960s came the electronic typewriters. These machines look and act much like today's word processors, but their memory is volatile. When the machine's power is turned off, memory is erased. Today, for word processing, these machines are dinosaurs. Computers with the same capabilities and permanent storage are less expensive and easier to use.

■ The Beginnings of Word Processing

The first computers to process words were the comparatively cumbersome *standalone systems,* work stations that are totally independent. They do one thing and they do it well. Called *dedicated word processors,* they can only word process, but they are very simple to use and very easy to master. They are also rather expensive in today's market. Some systems cost more than $10,000, or about twice as much as a sophisticated microcomputer capable of word processing.

Standalones were not manufactured to interface. Although makeshift interfaces have been successful, they were manufactured, rather, to be easy to use.

■ **FIGURE 1-4. IBM Mag Card Composer, a typesetter that uses the magnetic card media. Photo courtesy International Business Machines Corporation.**

Terminals. By the mid-1960s, word processing computers as we users know them became available. There are many options for computerized word processing. All of those options are centered around one piece of equipment: the terminal. The *terminal,* the *input device,* the *CRT* (cathode ray tube), and the *video display terminal* (VDT) are all terms describing the same device: a television screen connected to a keyboard.

Computers with terminals for word processing allow writers to compose and edit manuscripts without a pencil or typewriter. Once a document is perfect—without typos, grammatical mistakes, and factual errors—a printout is produced and a letter-perfect page is the result. There are many types of terminals, and what the terminal does is determined by the equipment running it. Some computers allow the operator to view one or even two full pages at one time; others permit a half page. But editing tends to be very simple.

The CRT (the television screen) or the VDT (the screen connected to a keyboard) are run by various computers. Therefore, the user has choices.

The standalone computer is the first option, but there are several others, all of which are more powerful than the standalone. If you want to interface, the standalone system is an outside choice. But what are the other options?

■ Computing without Owning a Computer

Shared-Logic Systems. After the standalone is considered, another alternative is the *shared-logic system*. Your terminal will share memory and computer power with other terminals (Figure 1-5). That is, you will be part of a network. The advantage of shared logic is that as a user you will not have to purchase outright the expensive "brains" of the computer, the *central processing unit* (CPU). Rather, the use, and cost, of the CPU are shared with other users. Shared-logic systems are usually powerful mainframe or minicomputers. By sharing resources, each operator need not purchase printers, CPUs, and a host of other peripheral equipment. The major disadvantages are downtime and response-time degradation.

Downtime refers to that irritating computer condition, breakdown. When the computer is "down" in a shared-logic system, all users are down. Since today's computers have excellent downtime ratios (the percentage of time they do not work), this is a minor annoyance. But the second problem is a greater obstacle. When there are many terminals being used in a

■ FIGURE 1-5. Wang VS 25 word processing system. Photo courtesy Wang Laboratories, Inc. © Copyright 1982.

shared-logic system, the entire system is slower. Computers are fast, efficient processors of information, but they all have limits. When limits are reached in a shared-logic system, processing of information can be frustratingly slow. Many computer professionals own personal computers in order to avoid the problem of *system degradation,* because one user and one machine may mean faster results.

Time-Sharing. If you do not wish or cannot afford to purchase a computer, there is also the *time-sharing* option. Time-sharing is simply buying computer time on someone else's computer. After purchasing a terminal, you join a time-sharing plan and pay for computer processing time on a per-second basis. Because time-sharing computers tend to process quickly, charges for time-sharing may be a wise alternative if your computer usage does not warrant a purchase.

Unfortunately, because many time-sharing computers do not permit their customers to interface with typesetters, this option may be infeasible. Also, the combination of time-sharing and interfacing, when it is possible, can create cash flow as well as technical problems. In some interfacing situations, the typesetter requires long communication sessions with the word processor. This can become quite expensive on a per-second basis. Figure 1-6 provides a comparison of four word processor options: the stand-alone word processor, the microcomputer, shared logic, and time-sharing.

Word Processors Today

Let's assume that you do wish to purchase a computer capable of word processing. What are your choices? The most popular word processing packages are centered around two types of computers: the minicomputer and the micro-, or personal, computer. These are not the only options—you can word process on a mainframe or a *supercomputer* costing millions. Computers still come in different shapes and sizes, but they're all much smaller than they once were.

	Cost	Equipment Required	Necessary Environment	Ease	Support and Documentation	Interfacing Utility
Dedicated standalone WP	$5,000 to $15,000	System	None	Simple	Excellent	Moderate to impossible
Standalone computer	$1,500 to $7,500	System	None	Simple	Fair	Variable
Shared-logic minicomputer	$30,000 to $300,000	System	Air condition-ing, humidity control, com-puter center	Moderately difficult	Good to very good	Variable
Time-sharing	Computer time purchased on per-second basis	Terminal and modem	None	Moderately difficult	Good	Usually impossible

■ **FIGURE 1-6. Comparison of word processing hardware options: standalone, shared-logic, and time-sharing systems.**

■ Mainframes

The first computer was ENIAC of the early 1940s. Designed for the Army, it used 18,000 vacuum tubes to do 300 multiplications per second. For 15 years and three generations of computers, the *mainframe* dominated the market (Figure 1-7). Technology moved from vacuum tubes to solid state in the IBM System/360. Some mainframes occupied entire buildings; the 1958 UNIVAC II used a central processing unit that occupied more than 1,300 square feet.

Today's mainframes are the descendants of these giants. Much more powerful and still expensive, they are used mostly by very large corporations and government agencies. For most of us, the mainframe power is unnecessary.

■ Minicomputers

Digital Equipment Corporation's PDP-8 of the mid-1960s was the first smaller, and cheaper, alternative. These machines were named *minicomputers* because they were smaller than their gigantic mainframe forebears. Today the minis are more powerful than the original mainframes, and they too are expensive. Although there is no agreed-on price structure, computers that cost more than $30,000 and less than $300,000 are usually regarded as being in the mini class.

■ **FIGURE 1-7. ENIAC, developed by IBM in the early 1940s. Photo courtesy International Business Machines Corporation.**

The minis are the systems of choice for many business applications. They are powerful enough to permit many users, are capable of performing many functions well, and are efficient data and word processors. Along with the microcomputers, the minis are the word processors most often interfaced with typesetters.

■ Microcomputers

The 8088 microchip created a new type of computer called the *microcomputer*. Variously known as the "personal computer," "home computer," and the "micro," these machines cost anywhere from $50 to $30,000. For a few thousand dollars, a micro can word process, prepare lists, do accounting, and generally perform all the functions any individual would need. There is no strict boundary between minis and micros. Both use the same sort of technology for the CPU, the *microchip*.

The first microchip CPU measured $\frac{1}{10}'' \times \frac{1}{10}''$. It was more powerful than the 1958 UNIVAC that required 1,300 square feet. Today, smaller and smaller chips are continually being produced. In early 1984, a chip was produced that could process 1 megabyte, or 1 million characters, at one time. The chips are now so small and can process information so quickly that computer power is simply a matter of degree. Cheap, quick word processing is readily available (see Figure 1-8).

Typesetting

The skills required to produce type, the characters that make up professional printing, are seldom simple, and much of typesetting vocabulary is arcane. Terms such as *leading* and *quads* are used in a profession that no longer uses metal to set type. Hundreds of years of technological progress are behind today's electronic typesetting.

From the monk scribes of the Middle Ages to Gutenberg's discovery of movable type in 1456 to the Industrial Revolution, typesetting moved slowly, remaining a hand-assembly process. Mechanized typesetting was perfected at the end of the nineteenth century after many unsuccessful attempts. By 1886, metal lines of type were cast as the machine operators typed at a keyboard.

	Cost	Number of Users	Ease	Support and Documentation	Interfacing Utility
Microcomputers	Under $7,500	1	Fair	Simple	Telecommunications or media conversion required
Minicomputers	$30,000 to $300,000	Dozens	Good	More difficult	Telecommunications possible; excellent media conversion via 9-track tape
Mainframes	$250,000 +	Hundreds	Good	More difficult	Excellent via 9-track tape media conversion

■ **FIGURE 1-8. Comparison of computer hardware options: microcomputers, minicomputers, and mainframes.**

FONT DRUM   FONT STRIP

■ **FIGURE 1-9. Font drum and photo negative.**

Radical changes away from metal type did not occur until after World War II. The first successful phototypesetter, the Fototron, was installed at the U.S. Government Printing Office in 1946. The first generation of phototypesetting was mechanical. In general, photo negatives simply replaced metal molds. Each negative was transported through a series of trays and channels by a system of levers and pulleys.

The mechanical phototypesetters were a hybrid. They were indeed photographic, but in all other respects they were traditional machines. The revolution in phototypesetting would wait until the 1950s.

The new electromechanical typesetters scrapped individual letter negatives in favor of the *font drum,* which is still commonly used today (Figure 1-9). To cite one typical scheme, font drums revolve in the phototypesetting photo unit at tremendous speeds. Attached to the drums are photo negative strips, which contain not one letter but up to four complete styles of alphabets. As the font drum revolves, the typesetting machine—now a computerized, electronic, intelligent machine—flashes light through the font strip at appropriate times to expose whatever letter is demanded. The technique is not unlike that which occurs when a film is shown on a screen, with light flashing through each individual frame of the film to produce, over time, a complete motion picture. In the case of typesetting, complete *galleys* or pages rather than pictures are the result. By the 1980s, more than 95 percent of all typesetting in the United States was produced photographically.

Some machines are capable of producing type at a rate of more than 1,000 lines of classified ad type per minute. Up to 40,000 characters are flashed and photographed in 60 seconds! That speed is the contribution of electromechanics. Electronic sensing within the typesetter's computer permits an accurate abandon that a typesetter even in the 1950s could not have imagined.

But phototypesetters have yet another capability. They have memory. Beginning with paper tape and progressing to magnetic memory, the computers of the second generation have revolutionized typesetting, not only through their speed, but through the *way* in which type is set. It is no longer necessary to actually sit at a keyboard with direct ties to a photo unit. Several keyboards, at independent work stations, can be used to supply information that the phototypesetter's computer digests and sets. Memory is the key.

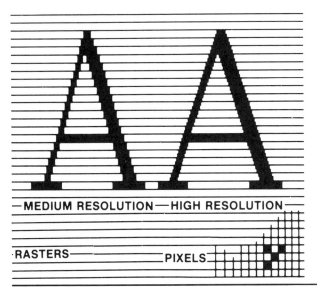

■ FIGURE 1-10. Digital typesetting forms letters by using either pixels or rasters.

■ Paper Tape versus Magnetic Memory

The first form of memory was paper tape, strips of paper perforated in specific patterns to encode information readable by a paper tape reader connected to the computer. An evolutionary analog to the magnetic tape of primitive word processing, paper tapes were replaced by magnetic memory in the early 1970s. The most popular form of magnetic media for typesetting is the *diskette,* that amazing agent that holds vast amounts of information and looks like an entombed 45 rpm record. Once typesetters had magnetic memory, they joined the ranks of the new applications for computers—calculators, microwaves, cars that talk, and satellites that send photographs back to earth from other planets.

Typesetting has come a long way. Computers have replaced lead molds; keyboards have put cases of handset type into museums. The technology continues to improve. The third generation of typesetters is completely electronic, doing away even with the moving font drum. Rather than photographing from a negative, letters are produced as digital patterns stored in magnetic memory by the typesetter's computer (Figure 1-10). Digital typesetting enhances the speed of the second-generation composition machines, and the fourth generation, laser typesetting, promises to replace photographic film or paper with laser scorching.

■ Is the Time Right for WP/TS Interface?

The most significant changes in typesetters occurred in the second generation. The third and fourth generations of typesetting are basically refinements in applications. Today virtually every typesetter in America is a computer that uses computerized memory.

By 1979, some forward-thinking people realized that a phototypesetter's computer was capable of some complex operations beyond setting type faster than you can speak. Word processors had evolved—and word processors shared a common feature with typesetting machines: They both used memory to store information.

The logical questions were: Could the information be transferred? Could an interface be established between the two very different yet curiously complementary functions? The answer: Yes. By the beginning of the 1980s, interfaces had been established. Word processors were "talking" with phototypesetters. The electronic manuscript began to replace traditional paper copy. Many type houses accept manuscripts through telecommunications, typeset the jobs, and send out galley proofs the next day. Keystrokes are being saved, or captured, and retyping of manuscripts by typesetters is quickly becoming an unnecessary expense.

Today is the right time to interface. The technology is in place. But hazardous choices are still possible along the way. Knowing how interfacing works is the first important step toward a harmonious marriage of possibilities and practical results.

CHAPTER 2

Checkpoints
and Checkmates

IN ORDER TO DISCOVER THE RIGHT technology, your first job is to determine, in your own terms, what you need the technology for. The first step toward a computer should not be "We need a computer!" Rather, the first step is self-analysis. Perhaps because of our Mercury/Apollo/Space-Lab, first-man-on-the-moon consciousness, we see the computer as a solution. It is—but not for everything. If you're having trouble with your writing tools, maybe it's because you need to sharpen your pencil. You don't necessarily need a word processor that costs thousands of dollars.

The Interface Decision

The first step is analyzing what you have and what problems need solutions. Those solutions might well require computers. Or they may simply demand a restructuring of internal management processes or perhaps the purchase of noncomputerized equipment.

■ Research

After you've looked at your needs, then you can start the second step: research. Ordinary methods may not be productive here. Researching equipment that has been around for 30 years is much easier than learning about equipment being developed today. A book about computers published in 1978, for instance, is probably out of date. To determine efficiently your needs now and in the future, you must glean information from current periodicals and contemporary book-length publications.

There are dozens of magazines that publish the latest word about what is happening in today's technology. Some books and magazines specialize in the particular area of interfacing and telecommunications technology; others have a more universal application. For example, periodicals like *The Typographer, TypeWorld, The Word,* and the *Dippy/Vippy* combination (for Compugraphic and Mergenthaler users, respectively) offer information specific to advances in typesetting or word processing. *Byte, Dr. Dobbs, Interfacing Age, InfoWorld,* and a dozen others are of value for a broader spectrum of information. These kinds of magazines give an indication of where the industry is going and where you might consider going as well.

■ Self-Education

After you've become reasonably familiar with what is "out there," you can then decide whether to move on to the next step. Does it seem feasible that computerized equipment is actually what you need? If the answer is yes, than you must begin a self-education process. The language of "computer-ese" must be mastered. Capabilities such as hardwiring, interfacing, tele-communications, bussing, hexadecimal coding, and mnemonics have to become part of your vocabulary.

Reading a book such as this one is a good start toward developing an educational strategy. And there are other, very valuable options that should be considered. Try the several industry trade shows and seminars through which you can gain both technical expertise and general computer awareness. Trade groups such as Printing Industry of America, Typographers International Association, and National Composition Association produce special technological reports available to both members and nonmembers.

As you become aware of what you need and what is available to satisfy those needs, you'll probably want to get your hands on the equipment. There are many training options open to the computer buyer. If you decide that interfacing *will* be a valuable technique, some vendors offer free training for several operators at your location, while others charge fees.

Developing a Rationale

During your education process, what should you find? The single most important thing you must discover before proceeding with interfacing is a *sensible reason for interfacing.* The industry literature will give you 42 reasons why you should interface. But there really are only about four major reasons that should be important enough to convince you that interfacing is a good decision. Let's examine each reason.

■ Economics

Interfacing is most often incorporated into the traditional production flow when it saves money. Whether you are affiliated with a Fortune 500 company, a small newsletter, or a health care association, interfacing may make sense on economic grounds alone. But even if you're a real computer fanatic, you shouldn't proceed into interfacing if it puts your cash flow situation in the red after the first year.

The reasons why interfacing is a money-saver are obvious. It captures keystrokes—your job does not have to be retyped by the typesetter because you send the typesetter keystrokes instead of manuscript. Moreover, the keystrokes that you capture can be cheaper keystrokes; rather than paying typesetter rates of $50 and up per hour for the relatively easy job of keyboarding, you can buy cheaper keyboarding by employing word processing personnel at $6 or $7 per hour. Then pay the typesetters to do what they do best: make keystrokes become typeset pages that are correctly positioned, spaced, and designed.

Interfacing can save you anywhere from 10 to 60 percent on your current typesetting bill. But 10 percent of a total typesetting cost of $400 a year is not a significant savings. At that rate, it will take you 20 years to pay off your capital investment! If you anticipate spending more for equipment than you do for a year's worth of typesetting, you're making a fiscally punishing decision.

The Break-Even Point. In general, if you do not currently spend at least $5,000 per year on typesetting, interfacing is not for you. (Some would put that figure even higher.) Interfacing is not free; it's just less expensive. In order to reap the savings, you will have to pay for equipment, training, software, and appropriate personnel. Those costs, given a relatively small typesetting budget, are simply not warranted today.

How much is it possible to save? A National Composition Association (NCA) report on interfacing breaks down the typesetting job into six areas (Figure 2-1). When interfacing, it is possible to cut costs in all of those areas except makeup (putting the job together mechanically, in order to reproduce it). Keyboarding is the most significant savings, as well as the most expensive area for the customer. Proofreading and correcting are greatly affected by interfacing; you save money in typesetting and materials simply by *not* setting second and third proofs.

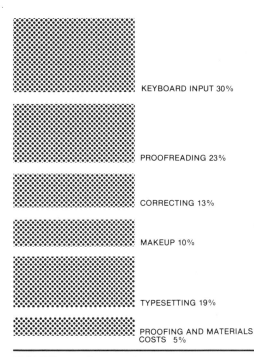

KEYBOARD INPUT 30%

PROOFREADING 23%

CORRECTING 13%

MAKEUP 10%

TYPESETTING 19%

PROOFING AND MATERIALS
COSTS 5%

■ **FIGURE 2-1. Typesetting cost breakdown.**

When the totals are added up, the NCA predicts that it is possible to save up to 57 percent through interfacing. Of course, a perfect document sent to the typesetter with no corrections and proofreading required nets savings in keyboarding (30 percent), proofreading (23 percent), and correcting (13 percent), or a total of 66 percent over your current costs.

Those predictions are not realistic, especially when you first enter the interfacing arena. A more conservative and reliable estimate of anticipated savings is from 20 to 30 percent of your current typesetting bills. Costs may come down in the future as more and more jobs are interfaced. Typesetting companies looking for your business may offer training programs, equipment loans, and free software. But in today's market, if your decision must be justified by economics alone, a minimum typesetting budget is required. Remember that $5,000 will buy only about 500 pages or less of typesetting.

The Price of Cheaper Hardware. Beyond the possible savings in the overall typesetting budget another reason for interfacing is savings in particular areas. Typesetting terminals dedicated to typesetting systems often cost $5,000. The MDT input terminal, for instance, can be used in connection with Compugraphic's Trendsetter phototypesetter. When additional keyboards are needed, they're relatively expensive. A solution? Interface with cheaper, quite serviceable keyboards manufactured as computers rather than with typesetting keyboards. It sounds unlikely, but typesetting keyboards without "brains," called *slave keyboards,* are actually more expensive than many microcomputers with "brains."

The obvious shortcut, then, is to purchase micros as input stations. You save on your installation costs as you increase your computer power. The micros can serve as word processors, data base managers, telecommunicators, information processors, and a dozen other things that a dumb slave terminal cannot do. So, over and above the monetary savings in producing type, you can generate a savings in capital investment for equipment—if you interface.

Type Quality. Investing in interfacing could be valuable aesthetically for those who are interested in typesetting documents that were formerly typewritten. Company reports, technical documentation, corporate directories, and price lists are commonly stored in data base management systems. These documents are often printed on letter quality printers and then duplicated. Many organizations are discovering the value of typesetting—now that interfacing has made it less expensive. There are several good business reasons for choosing typesetting quality over typewritten copy (Figure 2-2).

TYPEWRITING

TYPESETTING

■ FIGURE 2-2. Typesetting versus typewriting.

situations typically encountere
obtaining information from clie
gical or legal problems.   Candi

situations typically encountered in working wit
obtaining information from clients and explorir
gical or legal problems. Candidates will be req

■ FIGURE 2-3. Proportional spacing.

First, typesetting obviously makes a better impression. A sales force trying to close a deal or a grants officer trying to convince a foundation director are both making impressions. When typesetting is used, the process of selling ideas is made more professional.

Second, typesetting is easier to read. The type styles currently used by typographers to design pages are the same type styles used to typeset interfaced documents. Those styles have been developed for more than 400 years to make them easy to read. Typefaces are clearer, crisper, and bolder than typewritten letters. Written communication requires readability.

Third, for those who are still looking for economic reasons, there is a hidden advantage of typesetting over typewriting in "compaction." The actual numbers depend on how large you set your type, but overall, 40 percent less paper often is used with typesetting than with typewriting. Typeset letters are smaller and are proportionally spaced. For example, an "l" in typesetting, unlike typewriting, takes up less horizontal space than an "m" (Figure 2-3). What this means is that if you are producing a job that is 100 typewritten pages, that same document will be only 60 typeset pages. If you print 1,000 copies of a technical report, an in-house procedures manual, or a company price list, you save those 40 pages 1,000 times. The material costs of 40,000 saved sheets of paper add up. If you are using even the cheapest of xerographic bond papers, 40,000 sheets of paper will cost at least $400. Then add the costs of labor, ink, and press time. If you produce several jobs a year of that length, interfacing will pay for itself in saved materials costs.

Speed. When deadlines are a factor, interfacing can make a difference. If you're putting out a weekly magazine or working in an advertising agency with frequent deadlines, jobs that are already typewritten on a word processor need not be retyped. Rekeyboarding takes time. So even if the costs of rekeyboarding are not important to you, the saving in time provides clear advantages. If you're passing on current typesetting costs to your customers, for example, computerization of your input may not be critical for your own economic survival. But no one wants to be the real-life character that's seen in a popular typesetter's cartoon: "But this typesetting charge is more than we billed the customer for the whole account!" Interfacing helps to beat deadlines and therefore decreases the number of last-minute rush jobs for which typesetters charge so dearly. If turnaround time is important to you, interfacing might help—as long as you don't interface at the last minute!

But, remember, there are printing companies that are still handsetting jobs with individual letters of metal type, and they are still making money the old-fashioned way. The jobs come in, the customers are happy, and the business keeps on rolling. So if you are going to interface, you have to have a valid reason—a rationale beyond the fact that the equipment can do it.

■ Final Steps in the Interface Decision

The decision-making process of whether to interface should be accomplished in two stages. First, examine your current production flow. If you find something wrong, look for alternatives. Interfacing is certainly one of the high-tech glamour solutions these days, but there are less ostentatious solutions. Another, cheaper typesetting vendor may be your answer.

Will interfacing make sense? The answer depends largely on your individual circumstances. You must determine *why* you want to interface. If slashed type costs are your major motivation, an investment work sheet should provide the right answers. Figure 2-4 gives step-by-step instructions for preparing such a work sheet; you will probably need to do several, one for each option you consider. Once you have chosen the best option you should do a full financial analysis to see what all the economic implications of the project are. If the bottom line doesn't spell out a purchase, don't buy. If turnaround or aesthetics is most important to you, you should still complete the work sheet—you should know how much convenience will cost you.

Second, once you have determined that interfacing makes sense because of monetary, marketing, aesthetic, or time-saving advantages, then decide on the interface method you'll use.

Four Ways to Interface

There are only four possible choices for interfacers. The options are quite clear. Of the four routes from which to choose, two methods are *indirect* interfacing—meaning that computers do not actually communicate directly with each other—and two are *direct* interfacing—involving direct lines of communication. Indirect routes have been available longer and are less complicated for the consumer. They also save you less money. Direct interfacing offers the only access to that possible savings of 57 percent and more that everyone hears so much about (but so few of us actually experience). Direct interfacing does have greater rewards, but it is also more difficult to establish and maintain.

■ Optical Character Recognition: The First Indirect Route

Using a technology known as *optical scanning* or *optical character recognition*, optical character readers (OCRs) are capable of reading typewritten copy. These machines, the first form of interfacing, have been around since

1. Compute gross annual savings to be generated by equipment purchase.

Hard Savings = Dollars actually saved as profit
- Typesetting charges
- Office operating costs:
  labor, supplies, space, utilities
- Other supplies and services
- Other values*

Soft Savings = Dollars released for other uses
- Employee time
- Space, utilities, etc.
- Other values

Other Benefits = Unquantifiable advantages
- Typesetting vs. typewriting quality
- Turnaround of typesetting
- Service

*An example: A price list revision that would have formerly required six weeks is accomplished in two weeks through interfacing. The additional revenue generated from the new prices over the old ones during the four weeks is a hard gain under "Other values."

2. Compute annual operating cost of the system being considered. Include *only* additional costs incurred in:

- Personnel
- Supplies
- Utilities
- Services
- Equipment maintenance agreements
- Training and education

3. Compute the one-time investment cost of the system. Depreciation is not included here—this analysis provides only an initial indication of the equipment payout. A financial analysis, including depreciation, should be done for the final system chosen. For the payout analysis, include:

- Machinery (hardware)
- Software
- Site preparation: wiring, air conditioning, plumbing, construction
- Training: reference materials, courses, etc.
- Research
- Consultant's fees

4. Compute net annual savings and payout as follows:

Gross Annual Savings	$ XXX
– Annual Operating Costs	XX
Net Annual Savings	$ XXX
Investment Cost	$ XXXX
÷ Net Annual Savings	XXX
Payout (Years to Recover Investment)	X.XX

For projects involving purchases in the computerized word processor and typesetter markets, assume a five-year life for the system. The system will probably last much longer, of course, but it will most likely be technologically viable for only about five years. Here is the payout picture:

Payout in less than one year	Terrific investment
One to two years	Very good
Two to four years	Good to satisfactory
Four to five years	Questionable. This project is not high priority, although other, nonfinancial factors may make the purchase desirable.
More than five years	Financially unattractive. There must be other very strong reasons to justify purchase.

■ FIGURE 2-4. How to prepare an investment work sheet.

the late 1960s. The process as proclaimed by OCR enthusiasts seems quite simple. You type out your manuscript on a typewriter or a word processor. Then bring your manuscript either to your own OCR or to a business offering OCR services. The manuscript is "fed" into the optical character reader, which "reads" the manuscript and converts the typewritten letters into digital codes (Figure 2-5). The codes are usually produced in the form of electronic impulses, which are then sent directly to the typesetting machine by means of a cable. Thus, the manuscript has been typed on a typewriter, and, through an intermediary device, is not retyped. The typesetting machine has the keystrokes, and the typesetting operator can now produce typeset copy.

Optical scanning *is* a valuable technique under given circumstances, but you should approach OCR cautiously. To begin, you have two options in optical character recognition. You can purchase the service from an outside vendor or from your typesetting company, or you can buy your own optical scanning device. Whichever method you use, there are problems.

First, most scanners are not capable of reading every typeface. Rather, they can read only specifically created type styles called OCR-readable faces. In addition, documents read by optical scanners must be formatted correctly; that is, there must be no mix of single and double spacing, no underlining, and certainly no smudged characters. Furthermore, if corrections have to be made, full pages must be retyped. Penciled additions are definitely out. Worst of all, if you are considering a purchase, optical character readers are the most expensive of the interfacing options. Prices start at more than $30,000, and it's not unusual for an optical character reader to cost as much as $100,000. There are scanners, notably the Kurzweil, that are able to read any typeface. But those tend to be priced at the high end of the scale.

The advantages of scanning for the interfacer are, first, that there is no

■ FIGURE 2-5. Kurzweil OCR scanner. Photo courtesy Kurzweil.

need to translate word processing documents. If you have a "golf ball" element typewriter, you can use the correct font in your typewriter and begin interfacing with OCR today, as long as you are willing to produce typewritten documents that are perfectly uniform, page after page after page. That process is not as easy as it sounds, especially if you're not using a word processor that allows you to edit quickly, easily, and without visible erasures or insertions on the typed page. Theoretically, however, no additional equipment is necessary.

The second major advantage is that OCR operation is easily understood. The operator simply feeds pages of copy into the machine.

Typical applications include megabuck typesetting users who are willing to produce every document with the same typewriter style. The jobs are sent to their in-house typesetting department for optical scanning. Another application is the book publisher or other major typesetting user that purchases OCR services from one of the many typesetting companies that offer the service. In general, optical scanning is primarily for the high-volume buyer that produces straight matter (simple text). Complicated technical material filled with equations and tables is much more difficult to scan than simple paragraphs.

■ Media Conversion: The Second Indirect Route

Everyone who read printing and typesetting magazines in the 1970s read about this alternative. Referred to as the "black boxes," media converters solve the problem of media inscrutability. Computers use magnetically stored digital codes to retain information. Although most computers use similar methods to store information, the stored codes are, unfortunately, not immediately transferable from one computer to another. Each machine understands and stores information in its particular way. The media converters do the job of translation (Figure 2-6). Media conversion is discussed at length in Chapter 6.

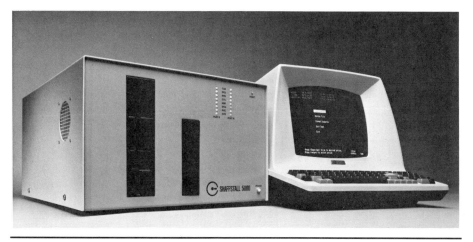

■ FIGURE 2-6. Shaftstall 5000 media converter. Photo courtesy Shaftstall Corporation.

These machines are theoretically able to read the magnetic media (usually diskettes) used by any computer. After the media is "read," information is converted into a format understandable by a typesetter. In most cases, the media converter is wired to the typesetter and transmits documents using telecommunications cable. So typesetting is produced from computerized word processing documents contained on diskettes.

This sounds too good to be true, and it probably is. There are about 20 typesetter manufacturers and dozens and dozens of word processor manufacturers. Although the diskettes can be formatted in a limited number of ways, that limited number still adds up. The worst part of the situation is that the media converter must be programmed (i.e., software must be written) to permit each connection to work. For instance, in order to facilitate interfacing with a Mergenthaler typesetter in a large metropolitan area, a typesetting company with a media converter must have a program to interface Apple with Mergenthaler, another to interface Kaypro with Mergenthaler, another for IBM with Mergenthaler, another for Altos with Mergenthaler, Radio Shack with Mergenthaler, Digital with Mergenthaler, and on and on and on. Figure 2-7 lists the most popular microcomputers in the United States.

When a typesetting company wants to be able to interface with all possible customers, it is faced with a tremendous capital outlay. The most popular media converter in the 1980s, the Shaftstall, requires a $1,200 surcharge for each program application. Add up all the programs needed,

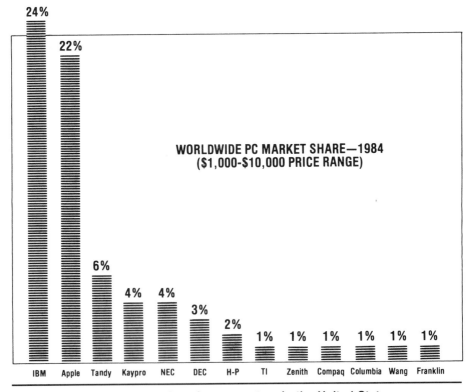

FIGURE 2-7. The most popular microcomputers in the United States.

and the price for a well-equipped media converter can run up to $40,000 or more. The machines themselves cost from $6,000 to $25,000. The programs are additional.

For the customer, the advantage of media conversion is that there is no out-of-pocket cost. The type house pays for the converter, and the customer simply uses the service. But, of course, the typesetter's investment costs must be reclaimed in higher typesetting costs. In the long run, interfacing customers save less money with media conversion than with direct interfacing methods.

For the typesetter interested in establishing interfacing, the cost of purchasing a well-equipped media converter will become increasingly prohibitive as more and more companies enter the microcomputer and word processing equipment markets. AT&T and Sperry joined the fray as late as 1984—another two software packages that media converting type houses must purchase (at $1,200 each). Other methods are available that are better—and cheaper.

The question for typesetters is whether to participate in a universal interface, keeping all its vendor or customer options open, or focus on a limited group of companies using one machine, the equipment-specific interface. Media conversion is an excellent option for typesetters that are certain of never interfacing with a large and varied universe of computer users. If, for instance, all of one's seven largest type customers use Apples, media conversion could be a wise choice.

■ Hardwiring: The First Direct Route

Hardwiring is the system of choice for any company that sets its own type in an in-house graphics shop. For anyone else, hardwiring is impossible. *Hardwiring* is simply wiring together a typesetter and a word processor with communications cable. Jobs are sent directly from the word processor to the typesetting machine by the cable. Hardwiring does have limits. Some manufacturers specify that cabling cannot exceed 25 feet (others say 125 or even 150). Boosters and signal amplifiers are available, but boosting can cause problems. The longer the wire, the less reliable are the signals sent through the hardwiring cable. Cabling the two machines is fast and efficient, but does require the purchase of both hardware and software.

The hardware required is a *null modem,* which is the cable that basically emulates telecommunications. The word processor and typesetter react as though telecommunicating, but the process is simplified because you, as user, have total control over the interface. The advantages of hardwiring are its simplicity and cheap installation costs. The very obvious disadvantage is that unless you're a *very* big customer just across the hall from a typesetter, you'll need to purchase your own typesetting equipment in order to hardwire. That investment, if you do not currently have an in-house graphics shop, will usually be cost-justified only if you spend more than $50,000 per year on typesetting. An adequately equipped typesetting operation with hardwiring capabilities requires a minimum investment of $40,000 the first year.

Several inexpensive alternatives are on the market these days, but as you look at ads selling rebuilt typesetter packages for under $7,000, be careful to remember that typesetting does not come cheaply. An effective typesetting machine, together with processing unit, fonts, and paper, will cost at least $25,000. When you add paste-up facilities, salaries, and office space, $40,000 in start-up costs is actually a conservative figure.

One more cautionary note: *Beginning typesetting and beginning interfacing at the same time can be a disastrous first step.* Typesetting and interfacing are two different technologies. To attempt to establish two new technologies at the same time borders on recklessness. If you do have a hardwiring application, implement it in two stages: typesetting first and then interfacing.

For commercial typesetting shops, the only meaningful hardwiring application is in wiring word processor terminals as input stations to an existing typesetter. It's simply impossible to hardwire with your customers—distance cannot be overcome.

■ Telecommunications:
The Second Direct Route

As the name suggests, *telecommunications* is communications with the telephone. Special equipment is necessary, but in terms of possible savings the equipment cost is a minor concern. *Acoustic couplers* and *modems* are telephone devices that, first, understand the electronic signals generated by the computer and then convert the signals into tones similar to those we use in speaking over the telephone (Figure 2-8). The signals are sent over telephone lines (or by telecommunications satellites) to a second modem or acoustic coupler, which then converts the tones it "hears" back into the electronic signals understandable by the second computer (Figure 2-9).

Modem, an apt description, is an acronym for modulator-demodulator. Acoustic couplers differ from modems in that they require a handset from a standard telephone to be fit into the coupler created for that purpose. Modems simply connect to a port at the back of the computer and require no telephone. Prices for the acoustic couplers start at about $100; modems loaded with extra features cost more than $1,000. The two devices are basically variations on a theme.

Using modems to telecommunicate, a word processor can send documents to a communicating phototypesetter directly. For the customer, that's where the saving is. If your document is properly prepared, it is

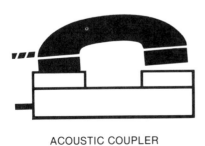

ACOUSTIC COUPLER

■ FIGURE 2-8. All acoustic couplers have send-and-receive coupling devices.

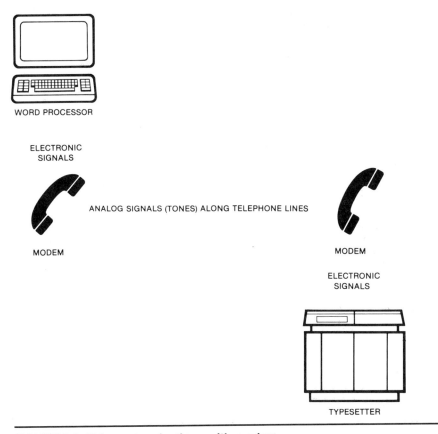

WORD PROCESSOR

ELECTRONIC
SIGNALS

ANALOG SIGNALS (TONES) ALONG TELEPHONE LINES

MODEM

MODEM

ELECTRONIC
SIGNALS

TYPESETTER

■ **FIGURE 2-9. Telecommunications with modem.**

possible for personnel at the type house to send the job directly to a photo unit without further keyboarding.

The word processing document is sent to a typesetter using the RS-232 connector, one of the few standards of the typesetting industry. Most machines use this "plug" to allow jobs to be moved over cable. Other standard "plugs" are the IEEE Standard and GPIB Standard. All work similarly to create a *serial interface*.

Serial Transmission. One bit (binary digit, or 0 and 1) at a time data transmission is called *serial transmission*. Because the RS-232 is a standard in typesetting, data sent from one machine using the serial interface are understandable to the second machine using the RS-232. It's possible to send jobs directly, without intermediary devices. For the cost of a telephone call, you've sent your electronic manuscript to the typesetter.

The advantages of telecommunications are plentiful. It's cheap, reliable, and easy to install. Telecommunications does not require a huge investment in either hardware or software. It is fast, and it offers a tremendous savings in keystroke charges. Best of all, it is the one workable *universal* communications method. When you have telecommunications working, you can telecommunicate with anyone who has telecommunications facilities. You are not limited by geography or by equipment, either in your selection of typesetters (if you're a type user) or in your selection of customers (if you're a typesetting company).

Of course, there are some requirements to tap into telecommunications. You will need phone lines. Even if you have a WATS line or use MCI or any of the other long-distance telephone options, long-distance phone charges add up. But that's the price you pay for the elimination of geographic restrictions on your business choices. More important, serial communications is only one of the many ways to telecommunicate.

Translation Tables. Serial communications works most of the time. But because different keyboards are being used, and different keyboards understand a specific key in two different ways, serial communications interfacing is not enough for typesetting interfacing. You must design translations of those characters that are out of the ordinary, including such things as em spaces, quad left keys, and the like. These translations are created in documents called *translation tables,* and this software requires some development time. It is possible, again, to simply send serial, but serial will not enable the word processor to encode typesetting information into the word processing document. The word processor will be able to send only letters and numbers. As any typesetter will tell you, the simple letters and numbers that are keyboarded are by far the simplest part of typesetting. If you send characters only, you are leaving the hard part for the typesetter. That is not the way to 57 percent savings.

To make interfacing with telecommunications work best for you, translation tables are a must. It will take some time to learn, first, how translation tables work; second, how to write translation tables; and, third, what you want to include in your tables. This book, and its companion volume, *The Interface Data Book for Word Processing/Typesetting,* will show you how to build and use translation tables.

The most important advantage that telecommunications offers is its universal communications capability. Telecommunications, unlike media conversion, OCR, and hardwiring, does not limit the user. As in many other industries, typesetting has found that telecommunications is indeed the wave of the future (Figure 2-10).

	Equipment Cost	Equipment Required	Limitations	Ease for Customer	Ease for Type House	Interfacing Utility
OCR	$25,000 to $100,000	OCR hardware	Special OCR-readable font required	Very difficult	Difficult to establish; simple after establishment	Outdated
Media conversion	$12,000 (hardware only)	Converter hardware; additional programs	Specific software required for each conversion	Fair to moderate	Moderate	Major type houses
Hardwiring	Under $2,000	Null modem; software, RS-232 port	In-house applications only	Moderate	—	In-house only
Telecommunications	Under $5,000	Software, modem, RS-232 port	None	Fair to moderate	Simplest to establish	The only universal interface

■ **FIGURE 2-10. Comparison of interfacing options.**

Electronic versus Paper Manuscripts

In the next ten years, most of us in the typesetting industry will become interfacers. By 1993, 80 percent of all typeset jobs will be interfaced. So by the 1990s, we will no longer be using paper manuscripts. The change in production flow, however, will not be radical. What we'll be doing, and what we've actually been doing since 1970, is substituting electronics for paper. After the telecommunicated document is transmitted, the production process remains the same. Yet for a slight change in the overall flow of things, you save 50 percent.

Word processors will continue to be a tremendous bargain. Even now many companies are retrofitting their secretarial pools. Intelligent computers are replacing electric typewriters. In the publishing field, many authors have already converted. Much of the computer literature being written today is sent to publishers, not as 500 pages of paper, but as a couple of diskettes. The electronic manuscript is here.

Why will telecommunications be the choice for most typesetting customers? The marketplace has something to say here. There are dozens of computer manufacturers. Which one should you choose? Which one is best for interfacing? If you decide that media conversion or OCR is a preferred technique, then you have to make certain that you purchase a word processor capable of producing media that can be converted cheaply or can produce OCR-readable typefaces. If you choose telecommunications, your word processor (or your typesetter) choice *does not matter*. A computer that can telecommunicate can telecommunicate with any other communicating computer. In today's market, that's an important factor.

A shakeout among computer companies, so long promised, has begun, and that very fact weighs the choice in favor of telecommunications. Undercapitalized and poorly managed companies are dropping out of the market.

Media conversion services will probably not purchase hundreds of dollars worth of conversion programs for the one user of an anachronistic word processor. But if you choose telecommunications, you can communicate with anyone. You don't necessarily need your manufacturer for interfacing, although you should be careful to purchase from manufacturers that will be around for service and updates.

There is no communications standard in the industry, but telecommunications is the closest thing there is to a standard. Scores of machines with dozens of types of disks are with us today. The shakeout will leave us with more than a dozen manufacturers and force us to deal with as many translations. Still, telecommunications is a cheaper way to communicate with more vendors' equipment than any other. The modem will likely be the machine of the 1990s.

CHAPTER 3

Input Decisions for Type Buyer and Typesetter

CAPTURING KEYSTROKES IS NOT SIMPLE. After you've made the decision to join the boom in communications and keep that cash flow healthy, what will you use to create keystrokes?

Analyzing Needs and Requirements

Before you begin talking to computer hardware sales reps, look at your organization and analyze what you need. Avoid unnecessary capital investments for equipment that's not needed.

These days, it isn't necessary to spend six months at hard labor creating a working interface (Figure 3-1): support is better, documentation is available, and we are generally better informed about the ways of computers. But there are hidden costs that can be organizationally disruptive and monetarily painful. The payoffs, of course, should make those prices worth paying.

There are three types of organizations interested in interfacing: the *typesetting company*, the *typesetting customer*, and the *in-house graphics facility*. All should meet some minimum requirements before taking the plunge into interfacing. To be blunt, if you don't meet the provisions below, proceed at your own risk. Interfacing is not for everyone. There are occasions when interfacing a job is simply nonsensical.

The Typesetting Company

The typesetting business is a disjointed group of entrepreneurs doing things in several ways. There are major type houses whose only job is professional typesetting, full-service commercial printers and book manu-

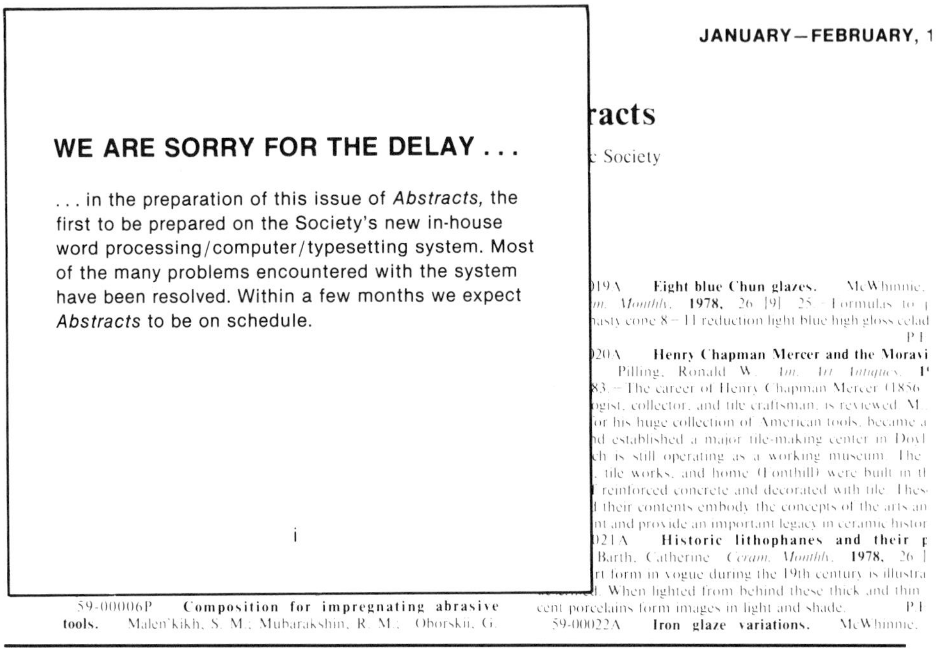
JANUARY—FEBRUARY, 1
racts
Society
WE ARE SORRY FOR THE DELAY . . .
. . . in the preparation of this issue of *Abstracts*, the first to be prepared on the Society's new in-house word processing/computer/typesetting system. Most of the many problems encountered with the system have been resolved. Within a few months we expect *Abstracts* to be on schedule.
Eight blue Chun glazes.
Henry Chapman Mercer and the Moravi
Historic lithophanes and their
Composition for impregnating abrasive tools.
Iron glaze variations.

■ **FIGURE 3-1. The problems of pioneers.**

facturers that typeset jobs for their printing customers, and smaller, quick printers that do a small amount of typesetting as a sideline.

■ The Type House

In the late 1970s and early 1980s, several major typesetting job shops (such as Al Heeg's Mercury Typography of San Francisco and Jim Reidy's County Photo Composing of Jefferson, Massachusetts) dedicated themselves to word processing and data base typography. After painful beginnings, interfacing offered those typographers a competitive edge that paid off. Heeg estimates that seven months and more than $45,000 were spent on salaries, hardware, and research before a working interface was established. Within two years, billings for WP typography were up to $30,000 and more per month.

Today type houses everywhere are interfacing. If you are a major house in your area and you are not yet interfacing, your competitive situation will soon be hurting (and perhaps already is). Interfacing is not just a competitive edge anymore; it is a competitive necessity. If you are not able to offer your customers a facility to capture keystrokes, your customers will find type houses that will.

Interfacing has collapsed whatever geographic restrictions there once were in typesetting. Even if you are the only type house in your city, customers can pick up the phone and dial a typesetter in the next town. As customers become more aware of the opportunities for savings, interfacing will be standard practice. To be short and sweet: Type houses *have* to interface to survive. On the face of it, it's not a particularly good deal. You buy expensive hardware that must be adapted to your present organization and in return you offer your customers a savings of 20 to 50 percent. That's a slice of your income. But the alternative may be economic suicide.

■ The Printing Company and Book Manufacturer

Decisions are not as easy to make here. Depending on how large a typesetting operation you have, interfacing may or may not be required. Large printing companies and book manufacturers that regularly print jobs exceeding 200 pages are finding that their customers are beginning to demand interfacing services. If typesetting is typically offered to such customers, you should expect more and more such requests. If the invoice for your typesetting equipment shows a price tag greater than $20,000, it's likely that interfacing is for you. If it's less, then you are probably doing service typesetting: logos, letterheads, and brochures for which interfacing is simply not worth the effort.

The costs of design and implementation of your service make the establishment of an interface *only* a possibility. But that possibility should be surveyed cautiously. The overriding factors are how important typesetting is to your business and what sorts of typesetting you do. For any operation that grosses in double-digit millions, interfacing is an obvious choice. For book manufacturers that regularly take a manuscript from typesetting through binding, capturing keystrokes provided by publishing companies will increasingly become an economic imperative.

Satellite Keyboarding. For printers or type houses that are interested in maximizing the benefits of interfacing, there's yet another possibility. *Satellite keyboarding* is an offshoot of interfacing that's a winning technique for both typesetting vendors and in-house shops. Satellites are easy-to-use keyboards used to churn out keystrokes. They are the impetus behind one relatively new phenomenon in typesetting these days: cottage labor. Employees key at home. The typesetting company saves overhead costs. The satellite keyboards are equipped with interfaces and the employee "delivers" information to a powerful minicomputer (known as the front end) that processes the keyboarded information. These satellites can be housed at the typesetting company or, in the case of cottage labor, at the home of the typesetting personnel. The interface is in-house instead of between customer and vendor. Easy input, total control over keyboarding, and smaller overhead are the advantages.

Satellite keyboarding is a good way to enter the world of interfacing feet first. After establishing themselves in-house, some companies go one step further. They take the commercial plunge by creating satellite interfaces with the equipment used by several major customers (see Figure 3-2). Assume you have an IBM Personal Computer (PC) in your plant. If seven of your customers are using IBM PCs for input, you can accept typesetting jobs as magnetic diskettes, load the disks on your IBM PC, and then interface the job to your own typesetting machine whenever you wish. That control goes a long way toward making an interface work successfully. The obvious hurdle, of course, is that in order to offer widespread service,

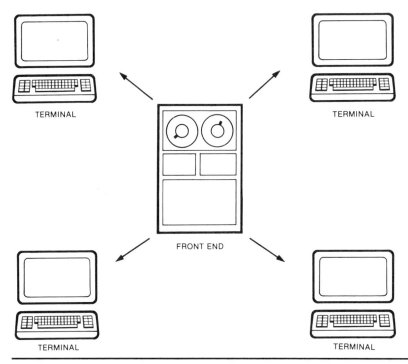

■ **FIGURE 3-2. Satellite networking is another interfacing alternative.**

dozens of microcomputers have to be bought and then mastered. There are cheaper, and better, ways to go.

The printing company should look at its own operation. If you bill more than $100,000 per year in typesetting, then there is no question that you should be interfacing. If you have seven customers a week who ask if you're interfacing, again, there's no problem. But the real situation is often less clear.

Are there subtle, telltale signs to look for before interfacing? Examine your current work flow. Do you want to retain typesetting as a service to your customers, or does it cost more than it's worth? Do you often typeset jobs that are hundreds of pages long? Most importantly, are you interested in expanding your work flow toward typesetting? Interfacing will require both time and effort and may change the relative importance of typesetting to your overall profit picture.

■ The Quick Printer

Fast and easy answers come quickest to the quick printer. Interfacing is probably not appealing for the small duplicating job shop. Capturing keystrokes will not change your customer base. Interfacing cannot generate customers who want 20,000 copies of a 64-page bulletin next week, and it will not give you the equipment necessary to produce that sort of work on short turnarounds. Your customers will not change, and neither will their typical jobs.

Interfacing is a technique that is best used when many pages are being typeset. Small jobs can be profitable as well, but those jobs should fit into a standard format. If you are dealing with many customers who have monthly reports of a dozen or so pages, interfacing could be worthwhile. But if the majority of your jobs are résumés, business cards, fliers, and brochures that join your work flow on sporadic schedules, capturing keystrokes is technological overkill.

If a quick printer interfaces, the appropriate hardware choice is usually telecommunications. It's the least expensive of the three options available (media conversion, OCR, and telecommunications), and it is the method most likely to allow communications with a wide pool of relatively small accounts. Because of a fluctuating group of customers, however, interfacing is usually not advised.

Interfacing does supply the quick printer with a new alternative, however. In recent years, several large printers and typesetters around the country have created printer networks. R. R. Donnelly, the largest printer in the United States, has created a Chicago-area network serving small printers. If you have a word processor, Donnelly (and its competitors elsewhere) will accept your word processing documents and convert them into typesetting at bargain rates. The quick printer thus has a typesetting capability to sell to its customers—and an inexpensive way to increase the value of the Apple computer being used for accounting.

The Typesetting Customer

Should you interface? Interfacing is and will continue to be a widely used technology, but it has limits. Those limits are placed by the training and development time necessary to interface successfully.

First, look at your type requirements. How many input keyboards, including typewriters, do you have now? If you have one electronic typewriter used mainly for invoicing, then interfacing is not warranted. If your type budget does not contain several monthly items billed at more than $200, interfacing is probably not financially valuable. But remember that there are reasons other than monetary to interface.

Second, are you the typical interfacing customer? Book and magazine publishers, professional societies that produce membership directories, advertising agencies, corporations with technical manuals and annual reports, colleges and universities with catalogs, and dozens of other major typesetting users are the core of the interfacing public. If you spend more than $25,000 per year on typesetting and you are not interfacing, you are losing money today.

■ The Interfacing Criteria

What sorts of guidelines are there to determine whether interfacing makes sense? There are several criteria that make interfacing a workable alternative (see Figure 3-3). It's simpler, for instance, if you are already word processing. One obvious fact of capturing keystrokes is that you have to be producing enough keystrokes to make them worth capturing. Unfortunately, there is no magic formula for determining whether interfacing will be an asset in your individual case. But here are some guidelines.

Checklist: Before You Consider Interfacing

Annual type budget—Over $5,000. ☐

Are area vendors capable of interfacing? ☐

Do you have word processing established in-house? ☐

With well-trained WP operators? ☐

Is your staff technologically enthusiastic? ☐

Do you have the time? ☐

Do you currently have an in-house graphics facility? ☐

■ **FIGURE 3-3. Checklist: Before you consider interfacing.**

You *should* be spending a minimum of several thousand dollars annually on typesetting. The clearest cases are those that are spending very little money for typesetting or are spending tens of thousands. For example, if your annual type costs are more than $25,000, a savings of 30 percent can generate $7,500 in savings every year. On the other hand, if you are spending $500 a year on type, interfacing can save you only a few dollars. Those in the middle have the biggest problems in justifying the interface decision. If you are spending $5,000, for instance, the first year's savings *may* pay for the equipment necessary to telecommunicate. Under those conditions, is an interface worthwhile? The answer will depend upon your own financial analysis.

You *should* be willing to invest time rather than capital expenditures in the new technique. There *should* be typesetting houses or hardware vendors in your area that are willing to lend support to your technological retrofitting. And, most important to avoid a discouraging experience, you *should* have operators who are well trained on the equipment you will be using for input. One source of much disillusion in the early days of interfacing was that type customers wishing to interface would buy word processing equipment and then immediately expect to interface.

Remember that word processing and interfacing are two technologies that your personnel must learn. Typing and word processing are similar, but actually quite different, kinds of keyboarding. If you don't have word processing now, and you decide that word processing is the way you want to interface, incorporate a two-phase plan into your route to high tech. Have your employees learn word processing and then move on to keyboarding for interfacing.

The In-House Graphics Facility

Large in-house graphics shops provide the ideal situation for the hardwiring interface. But your own typical job will determine whether interfacing can be an asset for you. There are in-house graphics shops that do five pages of design and paste-up a week, and some that print millions of impressions each year. Establishing an in-house interface is comparable to commercial interfaces in that several technologies are at work. But the situation is even more complicated. Chapter 8 is devoted to the in-house graphics facility.

You should consider an in-house interface only after word processing and typesetting technology are institutionally established and functioning smoothly. In that case, the graphics production manager interested in capturing keystrokes need only incorporate one new technology into the job flow. More often, however, interfacing itself has prompted the establishment of the in-house shop. The company that does not now have an in-house facility but is creating a graphics department should at least have word processing in place. If you are contemplating lobbing word processing and interfacing and phototypesetting together in one grand slam organizational rearrangement, you're courting disaster.

The most that can be expected of your employees is two revolutions at once. So, assuming that you have word processing and you want to move the memory in your word processor to a phototypesetter, the first step is in-house typesetting. The production facility is now faced with a double-headed high-tech dilemma: merging both typesetting and interfacing into the production flow at the same time (assuming that your company already has word processing capabilities). This is possible, but not recommended. When problems occur, both vendors point fingers at the other, and problems don't get resolved. What's worse, you often don't know where a problem is occurring—typesetter or interface? The process is simplified if typesetting is already established. If it isn't, move to typesetting first, then on to the word processor interface.

■ Should You Move In-House?

Provisions for in-house and commercial typesetting are about the same. For the in-house situation, remember to include both present and anticipated typesetting in your page count of anticipated work flow. Technical manuals and reports that are currently typewritten will be typeset for a more professional look and use less paper. Figure 3-4 gives a first year's budget for the installation of an in-house graphics shop capable of interfacing. It's not inexpensive, so a minimum annual typesetting expenditure of $25,000 or more is not unreasonable to expect of an organization actively considering the establishment of an in-house shop.

If you're already typesetting in-house, you know the headaches of frequently retyping documents that were originally keyboarded on your organization's word processor. Here interfacing is clearly a solution to rekeyboarding.

In-house interfaces are frequently easier to establish because of the available control. A hardwire interface can capture simple keystrokes. Having a word processing terminal located in your typesetting room is ideal. Production personnel can then send jobs through the hardwire whenever needed. An additional plus is that the word processor may offer features the typesetter does not, such as global search and replace, split screens, editing power, and merging text from two different documents.

Equipment Expenditures (minimum)		
Phototypesetter	$15,000	
Phototypesetting processor (RC)	3,500	
Waxer	250	
Light table	400	
Chairs	400	
Total		$19,550
Supplies Expenditures (minimum)		
Typesetting paper, 8-inch, $40 per roll, 50 rolls	2,000	
(estimate 3 feet of typesetting paper per column foot of type needed)		
Typesetting chemistry	600	
Miscellaneous paste-up supplies	600	
Lettering sheets, 20 sheets, $5 per sheet	100	
Artist's lamp	75	
Glideliner straightedge	75	
Miscellaneous supplies	500	
Total		$3,950
Personnel (minimum)		
Typesetter/traffic manager	14,000	
Mechanical artist	9,000	
Benefits (add one-fourth of salary)	5,750	
Total		$28,750
Grand Total		$52,250

Plus hidden costs of piecemeal estimating, instruction, supervisory time, and aggravation.

■ FIGURE 3-4. The in-house graphics facility: a cost sheet for the first year.

Your typesetting personnel can use cheaper, better word processing terminals for input, send the job through the hardwire, and then use the photo unit of the typesetter as a very high quality printer for output. The typesetting terminal is always available if it's necessary to *massage* (call up a job to the typesetting screen and make changes within a document that has already been interfaced).

The Three Universes of Typesetting Users

Most of us interested in saving money will assign ourselves to one of three groups of users of typesetting.

Universe A. In this universe are those who don't word process with computers now. The residents of this universe are not going to want to invest heavily in a technology that is relatively new. So the $30,000 to $250,000 price tag for a minicomputer is way out of line. You may believe you have a tremendous amount of information passing through the portals, but in fact it's probably a moderate amount. Those with the big work loads moved to computers years ago. But there's certainly enough work to justify scrapping the typewriters and moving into the 1980s.

The recommendation here is to move to microcomputers or standalone word processors. A price tag of less than $5,000 will enable your organization to computerize input. If that price tag is not justified by your work load, you are not producing enough type to justify interfacing. If you do move toward micros, telecommunications will be the least expensive—and best—interfacing alternative.

Universe B. Unlike Universe A, this is a much more specialized group of computer users. Phototypesetting companies have been using micros and minis for years. Minicomputers are used in front-end phototypesetting systems like the Penta, Bedford, and CCI. The minicomputer does the work of justifying, hyphenating, and making end-of-line decisions, while the terminals are simply dumb input stations. The micro? That's a dependable, inexpensive alternative to the typical phototypesetting terminal that sells for about $5,000.

For $5,000, a typesetting company can purchase a sophisticated phototypesetting terminal that "talks" to a front-end minicomputer. But that's an expensive typewriter. More and more typesetters are discovering that the micro is an ideal answer to the problem. The micro, at $2,000 or less, fits the bill perfectly. So micros talk with minis at many large type houses.

Universe C. These are the major word processing users. Either old hands at word processing or new kids on the block, the minicomputer users with a Wang VS or a Digital VAX are usually experienced, well-educated users. Because telecommunications and other interfacing methods are now established technologies, members of this universe who are not now interfacing will be soon. Rising printing costs and slashed equipment prices have meant more terminals, more interfacing, and more in-house graphics shops.

These users are the ideal interfacers. They have heavy-volume typesetting requirements and the cash flow necessary to make equipment purchase decisions easy. Because of the microcomputer, however, this universe is continually growing in size. Inexpensive but sophisticated equipment, and a now established technology, have combined to create a huge population of potential interfacers. Those who don't already own a minicomputer have moved toward the micro in the 1980s. When this universe, and any other, decides to capture keystrokes, one of its first decisions is to determine how those keystrokes will be created.

Two Input Methods

After determining that interfacing has potential in your organization, the next step is deciding how you will keyboard your jobs. The method chosen will go some way toward pinpointing the available methods of capturing keystrokes. In very general terms, you can use a computer or you can use a typewriter. If you choose the typewriter, you will be handicapped in making choices; the computerized word processor offers wider flexibility, but at the cost of new technology. Of course, if you are already using word processors, as millions of organizations are, your choice will be obvious.

■ Typewriters as Input

You can only do one thing: optical character recognition (OCR). Because of the prohibitive cost of optical scanners, if you're interested in interfacing using typewriters as input, you will need to establish a relationship with a type house offering optical character recognition interfacing. Except for huge operations, in-house OCR is economically out of the question. The pros and cons of OCR are touched on in Chapter 2 and are given in more detail in Chapter 6, but OCR is much more complicated than simply putting keystrokes on paper and then feeding pages into a box that looks like an intelligent paper shredder.

The most significant advantage that OCR affords the typesetting house is that, with a powerful scanner like the Kurzweil, you can read virtually any typeface from any word processor—but *not* from any typewriter. Documents that are optically scanned must be produced specifically with OCR in mind. Care must be taken to avoid smudging, differences in spacing, and several other possibly explosive problems.

There are so many potential problems with typewriter interfacing that it's hardly worth the trouble. One exception is large type houses that use typewriters for input. Rather than buying expensive input terminals, some superhouses and book typographers have dozens of typists producing copy that is fed into optical scanners. For a large corporation or any other institution using or producing large amounts of type, it can be worth the trouble to establish efficient OCR input standards and then teach your employees to use those rigorous standards when producing pages on electric typewriters. For the rest of us, the 95 percent who don't have 50 employees keyboarding type, OCR is an expensive input and output technique. For the customer, savings are less; for the type house, initial investment is greater.

■ Computers as Input

Most users will decide on word processors as input devices. Prices for inexpensive word processors and intelligent typewriters are about the same. If interfacing capability were the only criterion when making hardware judgments, word processors would win every time.

If you are going to use a word processor and you don't have word processing capability now, you are forced to analyze your input requirements. There are two groups of computers that are most often used for word processing, the minis and the micros. Which is better for you?

Minis versus micros. If you now have or anticipate requiring less than five input stations in the future, standalone microcomputers are probably the solution to your needs. They are comparatively inexpensive, easy to use, and not dependent on other terminals. If one microcomputer crashes (a euphemism for a dying computer), then your other micros will keep working. For a greater number of typing stations, you may have to upgrade your equipment to the more expensive micro systems or a minicomputer.

Be careful if the price tag is under $1,500. The hardware at that very low end of the market is usually game-oriented and not intended for word processing. (But, to make a case for inexpensive computers, the Kaypro 4, used in writing this book, is quite satisfactory and sells for under $2,000 as a complete package: terminal, software, and documentation.) The minicomputers, like Digital's VAX and Data General's Eclipse, are powerful machines capable of faster, cheaper, and easier to use word processing than the micros. They are also much more expensive—compare $5,000 with $30,000 and up as a general figure. There are very few machines that sell between $10,000 and $30,000. The Osborne Executive, priced at $16,000, did not sell well, in part because micro users thought it too expensive and mini buyers thought it not powerful enough.

Poised between that line are the multiuser micro systems like the Altos and the Ithaca Intersystems. They allow up to six terminals to be networked together. Above $10,000 but well below $30,000, these micro systems allow users to share files with each other without cumbersome exchanges of magnetic media.

Making the Mini versus Micro Decision. Avoid the common mistake of many computer browsers. Your first thought should not be, "How much can I afford?" More often than not, what you can afford is probably more than what you need.

First, determine what you need in order to do your current and future jobs. Don't project ten years from now. Remember, *a computer should pay a complete return on investment within a year or two.*

Second, what types of raw materials will you be using for input? Are your jobs scientific or technical? Some computers, like the Hewlett-Packard series of micros, are designed for a certain type of user (in H-P's case, the scientific and engineering markets). When examining hardware, be careful to price software along with equipment costs. Some computers are sold as functional systems (like the Eagle PC or the Kaypro), with software included in the base price. Others are sold dumb, with no programs included. Compare apples to Apples. After you've done the research to discover what you are buying, start considering dollar figures.

What do you want to do? Are you willing to spend what the market dictates to get the job done? Don't try to convince yourself to dismiss the peripherals, that bevy of devices that let you get information in and out of the computer easily. You may budget without them, decide after implementation that you do need them, and thereby start the budgetary spirals. After you've done the legwork on your budget, if the numbers don't spell out a purchase, then don't buy.

Whichever computer you choose, interfacing techniques and possibilities are the same. Both minicomputers and microcomputers will support media conversion (usually through either diskette or nine-track tape), OCR (by producing OCR-readable type styles with a computer printer), hardwiring, and telecommunications. The interfacing principles are the same regardless of type of word processor. Once you have purchased a word processing computer, your interfacing choices are open.

Word Processing:
Text versus Technical Matter

Word processing isn't as simple as putting words on the terminal. There are various types of material with corresponding variations in suitability for word processing. *Straight matter* is uninterrupted text such as you find in your favorite novel. Typical *tabular material* are the charts and tables you find in the *Wall Street Journal. Technical matter* is scientific and technical notation, the stuff of which research reports on the ceramic structure of silicon-based cements are made.

If you're doing straight matter, interfacing and word processing are much simpler. Any word processing package will handle straight matter, and most interfacers specialize in this area. But if you're anticipating tabular or technical material, the going gets rougher. Take a second look at what you're doing and make certain that your equipment, and your interfacer's, will work for your particular type of job. It is more difficult to interface with complicated material, but, as many accomplished interfacers have shown, it's certainly possible.

CHAPTER 4

First, Software–
Then Hardware

WHAT'S THE FIRST STEP IN picking out a computer? The first step is not picking out the computer. The first step, *for everyone,* is picking out the software. *Find a word processing program that works well for your application, and then find the hardware that will run that software.* The word processing hardware is the nuts and bolts; the program, the software, runs the show.

Buying Software: A Primer

All word processing software does the same thing, in theory. But discovering the best word processing software is a subjective pursuit. Some die-hards using the most antiquated, difficult, and downright rude programs will speak of their software in golden tones.

Word processing "architecture" is aptly named. We all expect word processing programs to be similar—a common misconception. There are lean and mean Bauhaus programs that do the job quickly and well; there are Art Deco programs that are elegant stylizations: and there are the shacks without floors that nobody wants to live in. The hovels of the word processing world are programs without documentation, the manuals that explain how the program actually works. Programs without good documentation are cheap, and deservedly so. They don't shelter you from those cold blasts of ignorance when you don't know how to store a job, delete a sentence, or even make a correction. You're on your own.

Word Processing Software Basics

What do you want your word processing program to do? The first and most important function of any word processor is to forgive us our trespasses. For years, using our first word processor, the pencil, we rubbed down the important end as we erased our mistakes. After progressing to a typewriter, we used white paint to hide errors. With luck, the typewriter was self-correcting.

All word processor programs make it easier to correct mistakes. You call the offending word to the screen and simply type over the mistake. Connected to a printer that produces paper copies, a computer becomes an instrument for avoiding errors. That's the basic role—easy input and easy correction of errors. But a word processing program does much more than allow you to look perfect all the time.

Purchasing Considerations

Can the software actually do what the ads claim? Most programs will do the basics. The questions to ask when surveying available software are similar to considerations you'd have when anticipating the purchase of any equipment.

Many of us, normally skeptical about promises from other vendors, are wide-eyed optimists when it comes to computer purchases. Advertising will obviously feature the most impressive aspects of a program; you'll find the weaknesses later—on the job—if you don't research products carefully. Use the checklist in Figure 4-1 as you assess software features. Here is what to look for.

1. Can the software perform as promised without major inputting miracles? The fewer keystrokes it takes to perform any given function, the better. Many programs require the user to perform alphanumeric calisthenics before inserting a misplaced word. If it takes four keystrokes to make an insertion, then there's something very wrong.

2. How clear are the operating instructions? You should not expect to be able to master a word processing package in one afternoon at Computer-Land. But be careful to avoid word processing software that is not menu-driven. *Menus* are lists of available activities displayed on the screen like a table of contents. They are very helpful, especially when you are beginning to learn a system, because they display the codes for the various operations possible within the package. You therefore don't have to learn immediately that the sequence "control, K, D" means *something* in the software package. You simply follow the prompts on the menu. Without a menu, you're on new roads without a map.

3. Perhaps most important, does the software seem easy to learn and comfortable to you, the user? When first using software, the command structure and sequence should seem logical. If you seem to know what to do next without consulting a manual, the software is doing its job. Experiment and shop around. Selecting WP software that fits your expectations and your personal work habits is as important as any other consideration. You will be using the system. Find something that you, and any other reasonable person in your organization, will be happy using.

Necessary Software Features

The options seem endless. One word processing analyst has prepared a comparison chart listing 224 available options.

Checklist: Word Processing Software Options

The Necessities:

Menu-driven ☐

File length: More than 10K ☐

Character display: 80 characters ☐

24 lines ☐

Block and file moves ☐

Word wrap ☐

Global search and replace ☐

Documentation: Available ☐

Understandable ☐

Friendliness ☐

Options:

UDK ☐

Printer commands ☐

Headers and footers ☐

Autopagination ☐

Other desired options _____

■ **FIGURE 4-1.**

Options are easily divisible: There are the necessary features, and there are the extras. Word processing software prices range from nothing to more than $500 for microcomputers; minicomputer packages can cost $15,000 and more. Although there are some exceptions, free software is usually worthless. The major risk involved in choosing software is not losing a few hundred dollars, it is losing days and hours of time invested in a program that's simply too unwieldy to do you any good. Also, buying and trying to learn the wrong package can discourage you from continuing in word processing. Splurge on software! It's inexpensive and definitely not the place to cut corners.

Necessity 1: File Length. A *file* is a job or a document. *File length* is the maximum number of characters that a document can contain. Just like the overstuffed drawers of your file cabinet, there's a saturation point. Characters are usually measured in K, short for kilobytes, or thousands of bytes. A *byte* is a letter, number, space, asterisk, or any other character that appears on the terminal screen. Thus, 5K is about 5,000 characters. (Actually, it's 5,120, because each K is really 1,024 characters—2 to the 10th power.)

The file length governing documents typeset on the Compugraphic MDT/Trendsetter phototypesetting system is about 2½K. That's too short for most word processing applications, although fine for typesetting. *Word processing software should allow documents to be at least 10K*. To convert K into some common denominator, each K is about one-half of an 8½″ × 11″ double-spaced, typewritten page. So 10K is about five pages.

The minimum specification for WP file length, then, is 10K. For longer documents, it's awkward and unwieldy to use multiple files to hold the job in anything less than 10K segments. Editing is much easier if the entire job can be brought to screen memory at one time. You should not have to search through several files in order to edit. It's frustrating and time consuming. There are several fairly popular software products that limit the size of documents to a relatively microscopic five or six pages, or 1,300 words. These packages sell for under $75 and they're not worth the price.

The best word processing programs allow you to create jobs that are limited in size only by your *disk capacity* (for microcomputers) or user memory (for minicomputers). Disk capacity is the amount of information that can be stored on your magnetic media (usually diskettes); user memory is the maximum number of characters you can consume in the memory of the minicomputer used by your organization.

One example: The Kaypro 4 allows a document to be as long as 394K (the disk capacity). The third and fourth chapters of this book required 94K, but there aren't many times when you'll want to create jobs that are that long. This is too much of a good thing—it would take more than a few moments to move through a document that is 394K, or 200 pages long, no matter how fast your computer is. If you need to make a correction on page 117, you have to scroll through those pages. The computer's purpose, speed, is defeated. Documents should be restricted to some manageable size; but if you have the full 394K available, *you* pick the most convenient size, *not* your computer.

Necessity 2. 80-Character Display. Adequate character display is a must. Most programs do not allow the user to control the number of characters horizontally displayed on the screen. The character display is in part determined by the hardware, as in the case of the Osborne portable computer. With its very small screen, 45 characters are the most that can fit on a line without requiring a magnifying glass to see those tiny, tiny letters.

Some word processing programs allow you to decide whether to work with 40- or 80-character screens. Screen widths should be the standard 80 characters wide. Some systems also offer 132 character-wide screens. These are useful when preparing tables or graphs. In order to reproduce these huge images, you'll need a printer capable of printing 132 columns across.

Necessity 3: Block and File Moves. Computer letters in your junk mail are brought to you courtesy of block and file moves. Copy block, delete block, block write, block move, file move, and file insertion are all names for similar facilities. All of these functions allow the user to move paragraphs (blocks of copy) from one document to another without retyping. Blocks can be copied, deleted, moved, or stored without leaving the current document. If you wish to type 20 letters that are all the same except for the addresses, type the addresses and then type the letter onto a separate document. Then use file moves to merge the files. A couple of keystrokes brings the file containing the text of the letter into the address file. You have 20 letters produced much more quickly and much more efficiently than before.

Necessity 4: Word Wrap. With most word processing systems, the program automatically ends lines and then moves to the next line. The operator need not strike the return key, as is necessary in typewriting, because copy is "wrapped around" to the next line. There are no decisions to make about where to end lines. Beware: Some word processing packages do not have this elementary, absolutely necessary feature.

Necessity 5: Global Search and Replace. There are words or phrases that you don't want to have to write out every time you need them in a document. If you are typing a report to justify the purchase of equipment for your organization, you needn't type the organization's name each time. Use a shorthand code instead. After completing the document, you use a search and replace function to make the code become the company's name globally—in all cases, throughout the job. Keystrokes are saved and keyboarding is quicker.

When researching charts, ads, and articles about word processing software, beware the search and replace clauses. Global search is not global search and replace, and a simple search and replace is usually not global. If the program searches globally, it may mean that the software will look for instances of your string of characters but then won't automatically replace them. You're left with a dumb machine that requires you or your operators to manually type in the replacements.

If a program offers you a simple search and replace function, it may search and replace, once. You then key in the search and replace and it does it again, once. And so on. That process actually encumbers you with more keystrokes. Don't buy it.

Necessity 6: Menus. Menu-driven software are programs that display available commands on the screen while you are working. This isn't just a convenience, it's a basic. The alternatives are to try to remember all the commands *before* you start using the program, or constantly refer to manuals or command cards. You can spend so much time fumbling through the documentation that it takes several frustrating sessions just to get started. Menu-driven systems are easier to use, tend to be more expensive, and are worth it.

Necessity 7: Documentation and Friendliness. After all that's been said, easy use remains one of the most critical elements to consider. Buy the manuals from the software manufacturer. If you can understand what is happening before you purchase the programs, you'll probably find the manuals useful later. Does the software seem easy to learn and use? That's what "user-friendliness" is all about. There are no guarantees that the software you purchase will be the best available. But you don't need the best; you need software that you feel comfortable using. If your software works for you, then it's doing the job. Here's a plan that may work.

Look over the list of necessary options and frills. Grade the options you think you need on any basis you wish—0 to 5 or 0 to 10. Mark those features that you believe are critical on the checklist (see Figure 4-1). Eliminate any programs that don't offer what you consider to be critical. Finally, grade the rest of the options using the scale: 10 for most needed, 9 for important, and so on. The word processing software information in the *Data Book* may aid you in computing a "batting average" for some of the most popular programs available. The high scorers will be the most useful programs for you. After determining which software has the most to offer, look at the software in use. When you're convinced by the demonstration that it works the way you expect, keep doing homework. Look at competitive systems and follow through on examining what "extras" you find valuable.

Extra 1: User-Programmable Keys. Many programs allow you, the user, to create new identities for keys that you don't normally use. If you're not a mathematician, the odds are that you'll never use the < key. So you can program that key to mean something that you do use. This feature is sometimes called *UDK,* or *user-defined keys.* After you've created a UDK with the < sign, simply type the < keystroke every time you need the word or phrase you have defined. The word appears on the screen immediately. The UDKs are valuable but are not indispensable because block and file moves can perform similar tasks.

Extra 2: Printer Commands. Boldface, strikeover, subscripts and superscripts, overstrikes, strikeouts, and underlining are just the beginning of the list of options available for your printer.

Boldface is achieved by a software command that automatically prints the desired letters twice. But the letters are very slightly (imperceptibly) typed apart from each other. When the ink strikes the paper, the two printed letter images combine to create one darker, bolder image.

Strikeovers are similar in that they require the printer to type material twice, but in this case the material is not bold, it's just a bit darker. As typographers realize, bold letters are thicker than regular letters, not just darker. So the strikeover gives a better impression, but not a bold one.

Subscripts and *superscripts* are another feature used in mathematics and scientific typing. They are the numbers above and below the normal characters on your lines of typewriting.

Overstrikes, on the other hand, are used for scientific notation or foreign-language typing. If you anticipate that you will be needing the accent grave for French typing, you'll need the capacity to strike the accent over the "e."

Strikeouts are generally worthless, both in baseball and in word processing. Striking out, unlike striking over, commands the printer to print a solid line of hyphens through your nice, clean word processing. So strikeouts make your work illegible. The advantages of *underlining* capability are self-evident.

Extra 3: Headers, Footers, and Pagination. For authors who are contemplating an assault at long manuscripts, automatic pagination will be important. If you're interested in lengthy reports, page numbering can be automatic as well. If footnotes are included, the software should format the page so that footnotes are printed intact as desired at the bottom of each page. Many programs also permit users to key in headers for identification. Some automatically place single-line headings at the top of printed pages; others allow multiple-line headers.

Extra 4: The Extra Extras. There are hundreds of other features. One of them may be the one obscure item that you need. Multicolor printing, changes in type font selections, manuals on diskette, edit traces that make it impossible to mistakenly destroy deletions forever, printer queuing that lines up jobs to be sent to the printer, and, of course, automatic centering. The list goes on and on, but the most important options outlined in Figure 4-1 have been covered here.

Which Package Should You Buy?

When you have compiled your shopping list of the features you need, you can then attempt to find the perfect software to fit your situation. But what is actually available?

This book is not a buying guide to the hundreds of packages on both the minicomputer and microcomputer markets. But highlighting the features of some of the best known programs will arm you for your informed assault on the software.

There are definitely two marketplaces. The microcomputer software explosion is dominated by those machines that use *CP/M* (Control Program for Microcomputers, developed by Digital) and variations of *MS-DOS* (MicroSoft's Disk Operating System).

At the minicomputer bazaar, the situation is much less stormy. Economics and population are the two causes. Micro software nearly always sells for under $500, while mini word processing packages, which are fewer in number, can cost up to $15,000. The typical word processing software for the Wang, Digital, Data General, and IBM minicomputers are provided by the hardware manufacturers. Competitive packages are available, but again, at a high price. Whether that software is worth the fare will largely depend upon how well you get along with the resident software on your mini system.

What Micro Software Is Available?

Volkswriter, Easywriter, Scripsit, ScreenWriter, Perfect Word, Word Perfect, Perfect Writer, Wordhandler, Wordvision, Kitchen Editor, Palantir, Star Edit, PeachText, The Final Word, WordNet, Write-On, Disk Edit, Final Copy, Forthwrite, Bank Street Writer, Megawriter, PFS:Write, The Creator, VisiWord, Friendly Writer, Microsoft Word, and WordStar—these are just a few. The *Whole Earth* people received an advance in the millions of dollars to produce a *Whole Earth* catalog of available microcomputer software. Small wonder!

■ The Most Popular WP Program: WordStar

There are no startling revelations to be made here. WordStar is the most popular word processing program. It allows you to stretch and move and twist a word any way you wish. But it's not the simplest software to learn, nor is it the cheapest, at $495. Some complain that WordStar commands are unusually obscure. The sequence "control, K, D" stores a job and then allows you to continue to start another document. Buy why K D?

It does take time to learn WordStar and its idiosyncratic command structure. However, the software is well documented. There are more than a half million users of WordStar, so if you have any contacts with computer literati, someone will know WordStar. The program offers easy editing features, is menu-driven, and has a powerful repertory of more than 150 commands. If you decide on WordStar, you haven't made a mistake. Best of all, because so many people already use the software, more typesetters have already interfaced with WordStar than with any other word processing program.

One warning: WordStar is available for nearly every word processing machine on the market, including all the major hardware sellers. If the computer you are looking at *does not* accept WordStar, you may be making a hardware mistake. WordStar requires a minimum 64K system with one disk drive. A 64K computer is a machine with 64K (roughly 64,000 bytes) of internal memory. If your computer is less than 64K, you may have a toy; if the micro does not have disk drive capability, you can play games but you won't be able to process information effectively.

■ WordStar's Competition: Winners

It really is unfair to group the rest of the software under the uncharitable rubric of "WordStar's competition." While WordStar is a front-runner in the word processing race, it certainly does not own a controlling share of the market.

There are major competitors to WordStar, effective performers that require very little sophisticated training. To concentrate on the highlights, Microsoft Word is representative of the new generation of word processing software. It offers such advantages as splitting the screen into as many as eight "windows" to allow you to compose from computerized notes or to merge files. It's also possible to write documents in columns automatically. Microsoft Word sells for $375, but is available only for IBM and IBM-compatible computers. IBM-compatibles are clones of the IBM Personal Computer that use the same (or very similar) operating systems and can therefore use much the same software. Hyperion, Compaq, BMC, Sage, Hitachi, and Eagle are among the rapidly increasing population on this block. (Franklin is the most familiar of the Apple-compatible clones.)

Volkswriter, from Lifetree Software, is inexpensive ($195), but offers most of the features of the higher priced programs. Written for the IBM operating system, Volkswriter is quickly becoming a cult favorite among aficionados. Perfect Writer, on the other hand, has proliferated throughout the industry. Nominally priced at $495, few seem to *buy* Perfect Writer because so many hardware manufacturers offer the program free to their customers. The manual is simple but thorough, and the program allows you to share documents with other members of the Perfect series (such as Perfect Calc). The Perfect programs will run on either IBM or CP/M machines, so the Perfect Writer universe is quite large.

Apple users have less latitude. Probably more software (more than 15,000 programs) has been written for Apples than for any other specific computer, but numbers can be deceiving. Many of those programs are games (Apples have superior graphics capability, so many games are written for them). In addition, there are 100 CP/M-based machines; there's only one company making Apples. Apple Writer is available at $195. There are many inexpensive word processing programs dedicated to the Apple, including Bank Street Writer, at $70, and Megawriter, at $60, but both of these limit the user to a maximum document size of five to six pages (many such programs were originally written to teach children how to word process).

The heavy-duty programs written for the Apple include ScreenWriter ($130) and Wordhandler ($199). ScreenWriter will automatically produce an index from a list of keywords specified by the writer. One solution that any Apple user can fall back on is to simply purchase the Apple version of WordStar for $375—not a very creative solution, but one that will solve the problem.

■ WordStar's Competition: Losers

There are programs you should not use. These are the losers in the word processing competition.

Cheap software is not worth the price. When you're ready to buy software, look for advice, but don't accept it unthinkingly. If someone is using an incredibly difficult package, he or she may still recommend it. Before you purchase, test it. Neighborhood computer stores are often happy to demonstrate software. But be careful: There are always people at stores who can demonstrate the program, but can you use it?

Avoid having word processing software custom-made for your application. There are so many packages available that one will fit your needs. Creating your own is both more expensive and requires programming contortions that are time consuming and ill advised.

Finally, suppose you've done the homework, and your program doesn't work the way you expected. After an honest try at using the software, if it doesn't work as well as it should, throw it out. The purchase price of software is not the largest risk involved. Being driven away from word processing by defective programming is a far more costly price to pay.

What Mini Software Is Available?

Minicomputer decisions are much fewer and easier. Each software package tends to be manufactured for specific hardware, and most users employ the software they purchase with the machine. There are, however, alternative packages available for most minicomputers. A good example is MASS-11, created by Microsystems Engineering for use on Digital Equipment Corporation's superstar VAX series of minicomputers.

■ MASS-11

The Wang VS series and Magna and other minicomputers that are designed as word processors need no extra software. The resident software on this sort of machine is powerful enough to satisfy any user's needs. But despite its best-selling position in the mini market, not all of us are using Wangs.

Many organizations have a VAX or Eclipse or IBM minicomputer in accounting or records. That mini can be converted into a word processing demon if you have appropriate software. This is where packages like MASS-11 join the fray.

MASS-11 is a college favorite these days. The package is being used on many campuses because Microsystems Engineers, the creator of the software, offers MASS-11 free to many schools. A new marketing strategy has developed to sell both hardware and software: Educate students to use your product. When programmers leave school, they recommend that product to their employers.

MASS-11 sells for $15,000 in its latest version. That price is a package. The user receives both word processing and data processing software, along with the necessary utility programs to allow for printing, interfacing, and display.

Why consider a package like MASS-11? Suppose you have a minicomputer. You can buy three well-equipped micros for the price of the MASS-11 software. The rationale for minicomputer software is based on the information already contained on your mini. If you are typical of mini users, there are lists of customers, members, or clients already on your minicomputer. If you want to use that extensive data base to do a mass mailing, you will need a word processing program. The alternative is to retype the lists onto the microcomputer memory. For large organizations, the retyping costs will far exceed $15,000.

These software packages, then, allow you to tap into your latent resources. In addition, if you do not use an integrated system for input, it's quite possible that information you store today on the new microcomputers will be needed tomorrow on your minicomputers. Your options are then to either interface or retype. Again, either alternative will entail expenses in time and money.

Another argument for spending the $15,000 is that if you do buy micros, you are sacrificing the power of the minicomputer. All computers are similar to each other, but there's a reason why a minicomputer costs more than $30,000 and you can buy a stripped-down micro for under $2,000. The minicomputer is capable of manipulating greater amounts of text more quickly and more efficiently than a smaller computer. If you have the power, use it.

Buying Hardware: A Primer

The new shakeout of computer manufacturers began in the early 1980s and it continues. The major problem that the elimination of computer competition causes for the computer user won't be higher prices. There will always be a dozen or so hardware giants fighting for our dollars. The real riddles will be for those organizations that purchase machines that cease to be produced. Nobody is going to create software for hardware that isn't made. Parts won't be available, and service agreements will be expensive or impossible to obtain.

The first shakeout occurred in the 1970s. Several large corporations toying with the computer industry took their losses on the mainframe and minicomputer markets and figuratively went home to their more basic pursuits.

Computer experts are now telling customers to buy from established companies. The promise of the computer guru is a self-fulfilling prophecy. Clients are told not to buy from smaller companies, which, we are told, may go bankrupt and leave us with no support. Based on that master advice, clients don't buy from those companies. Those companies get no orders. They do go bankrupt. All the experts congratulate themselves on predicting their demise.

Whatever the reason, computer hardware companies are disappearing. It is a time to be optimistically prudent. If a computer will pay for itself in six months, what's the harm in buying a computer from a company that won't be here in two years? The hardware has already paid you a fine return on your investment.

If preparing jobs for an interface is the only function for which you will use your computer, then the shakeout is cause for minor inconvenience without major trauma. Penalties will be paid by those who use the computer as a number cruncher or a long-term data base. If your inventory records, billings, bibliographic information, or directory of clients is stored on a computer, then you must be certain to keep that computer alive. The shakeout could cause big problems.

Choosing an Operating System

For interfacing, it is important for the interfacer to choose hardware that is capable of communicating easily. There are four operating systems that together account for the great majority of microcomputer use: MS-DOS, CP/M, TRSDOS, and AppleDOS. The latter two were created specifically for Radio Shack and Apple computers, respectively, and each allows users to buy CP/M as an option.

Assuming that interfacing is all you will ever want to do with your microcomputer, recommendations are easy.

- Buy MS-DOS if your computer is a 16-bit machine.
- If you purchase an 8-bit computer, buy CP/M. A 16-bit machine processes 16 bits (binary digits) of information at one time. They are naturally faster than their 8-bit cousins. In the world of micros, the IBM PC uses the 8088 chip, which is rapidly becoming the industry standard. There are, however, plenty of 8-bit machines using Zilog's Z80 chip.

■ The MS-DOS Option

The expensive option is an MS-DOS, 16-bit, Intel 8088 chip computer (a variant is the 8086 chip, which is slightly faster than the 8088). In alphabetical order, this world includes the Columbia MPC, Digital Rainbow, Eagle PC, Heathkit H100, IBM PC, NEC APC, Seiko Series 8600, Tele-Video 1603, Texas Instruments Professional, Toshiba T300, Victor 9000, Wang PC, and Xerox 16/8. There also are the portables: the Compaq, Computer Devices Dot, Hyperion, Otrona Attache, Seequa Chameleon, and Sharp PC-5000. This is IBM territory. Many of the machines here are IBM-compatibles, meaning that they are capable of using *some,* but not all, of the software created for the IBM PC. A thorough list of features and prices for each machine is available in the *Data Book.*

■ The CP/M Option

The less costly decision is to buy a Z80, 8-bit, CP/M-based computer (CP/M-86 is the upgraded, 16-bit version of CP/M that is available to run some systems). The list is almost as long: the Basis, BMC if800, Coleco Adam, Epson QX-10, Franklin Ace 1200, Fujitsu Micro, Morrow Micro Decision 3, North Star Advantage, Onyx Sundance, Radio Shack Model 4 (with optional CP/M), Sanyo MBC 1000+, Sony SMC-70, Toshiba T100, and Xerox 16/8 (taking no chances, Xerox—like IMS, North Star, and Seequa—allows the user a choice between Z80 or 8086, CP/M or MS-DOS). The portables on this market are the Access Matrix, Kaypro series, ModComp Zorba, Osbornes, STM, and Teleram T-3000. Again, check out the *Data Book* for a complete picture.

■ Other Operating Systems

There is the third world—the computer counterculture. These are computers made by computer companies that decided to go off on their own and use *neither* standard. There are some good reasons for unorthodoxy. Apple's Lisa, for instance, uses the 68000 chip and the Xenix operating system because Xenix is a favorite among computer programmers. Originally priced at $10,000, Lisa won't be used by home hobbyists very often. Further down the line, the Apple IIe and its later incarnations were constructed to be used with the AppleDOS operating system. Apple is one of the few companies that has a powerful enough market position to use its own operating system, but even Apple has included both CP/M and MS-DOS as options.

Another company that can dictate operating systems with authority is Radio Shack. Its TRSDOS is, again, an operating system dedicated to one machine. But Tandy and Apple are following the same different drummer: Radio Shack makes CP/M available on its Model 4.

Many of the worst-selling computers, on the other hand, use unconventional operating systems that doom them to extinction. Software is written by the large software houses to be sold in volume. If there is only one machine using a unique operating system, software won't be written. Conversely, as a computer consumer, you should not buy hardware offering very little software.

Interfacers should also be wary of novel operating systems. Typesetters who deal with CP/M and MS-DOS software are most comfortable dealing with WordStar, Perfect Writer, and other word processing programs written for these operating systems. Programs written for eccentric operating systems may or may not be well written, but your choices will certainly be limited. These constraints may mean that you will be forced to use a program with which your typesetter has never interfaced. Your typesetting interface is therefore a new experience for both word processor and typesetter. That's an invitation to frustration.

The Machines

■ IBM PC

The IBM Personal Computer hit the market in 1981 and made microcomputers respectable. But the PC is not a sweeping revolutionary; it's a basic system with several features shared by IBM's competitors. The difference is IBM support and a dealer network that offers quick, confident solutions to problems.

The IBM PC is a good example of the 16-bit computer that should be overtaken in time by the 32-bit machine. For the 1980s, the 16-bit computer is generally the best we can expect from the micro (although Apple has been showing the way recently toward the new 32-bit machines). The IBM Personal Computer is an MS-DOS machine using the Intel 8088 CPU chip (the IBM version is PC-DOS). Internal RAM memory is 64K, which is the standard, but can be upgraded to as much as 640K (expandability is also a common option). Storage on 5¼″ diskettes is 360K, average for the more powerful machines. An 80-column screen display fills out the hardware. Available programming languages include BASIC, COBOL, FORTRAN, LOGO, and Pascal.

With a full package of software and hardware selling for about $5,000, the PC is more expensive than most of its rivals. But excellent support and a huge library of available software are enough justification for users to make the IBM micro a best seller. The PC XT (a PC rigged with a hard disk drive) and the PCjr, nicknamed the Peanut, round out IBM's offerings in the micro market.

■ Kaypro 4

Here's an American success story. In the early 1980s, the Kays were making oscilloscopes for the California aerospace industry. A few years later, the company had to build a circus tent to warehouse all those sheet metal computers it was selling. No beauty-contest winner, the Kaypro computers are transportables; they're not light enough to be considered portable.

Kaypro followed Osborne into the 8-bit transportable market. Using the established CP/M, Zilog Z80 combination, the Kaypro 4 is packaged with the Perfect software series (Perfect Writer, Perfect Speller, Perfect Filer, and Perfect Calc) and WordStar, along with several versions of BASIC. Priced at a hard-to-beat $1,895, this micro offers more than $2,500 worth of software and documentation and then throws in the computer for free.

There are, of course, some problems. An 8-bit computer is obviously aimed at the low end of the business and professional market. Although most of us don't have any problems with it, some word processing personnel aren't ready for the smaller letters displayed on the definitely smaller screen. The 8-bit processing is slower than 16-bit operations. But, like the PC, the Kaypro series is well built, dependable, and selling well.

■ Apple Lisa

The Lisa and its less expensive companion, the Macintosh, may be the machines of the future. Apple has put together the most novel computer architecture of the 1980s and has created something new. It's expensive ($9,995, software included, for the Lisa), but it may be worth it.

Steve Jobs, president of Apple, has said that the Lisa project was a drive to create "the personal computer of the 1990s." This is what we may be using: Your screen has a row of pictures, and you have a mouse. A *mouse* is a hand-held device that allows you to move about the screen without touching a keyboard. You have a flat surface on your desk, and as you move the mouse, the cursor moves on screen.

The row of pictures displayed on screen includes a file, a wastepaper basket, a clipboard, and a calculator. If you want to word process, you "grab" the clipboard from your electronic desk (the Lisa screen) by moving the cursor to the appropriate screen picture. The Lisa supplies you with prompts for word processing. If you want to destroy a job in your electronic files, touch the wastepaper basket on screen.

This professional micro uses the 16-bit Motorola 68000 microprocessor chip. The power of that chip allows the Lisa a tremendous 1,000K of RAM (1 megabyte), as compared to the 8-bit machine's 64K. The 5-megabyte hard disk drive holds thousands of pages of typewritten text.

There are stumbling blocks. Price is the most obvious. For word processors, many of the advantages of the mouse are lost. It's possible to send complicated instructions to Lisa without using the keyboard, but it's still not possible to create text without typing. Compugraphic, long an apostle of interfacing, has used the Lisa as a component in its PCS (Personal Composition System). But overall the Lisa is an expensive alternative not developed explicitly for word processing. However, as competitors create cheaper clones, the Lisa may indeed become the prototype of the 1990s.

Checklist: The Right Word Processor for Interfacing

✔ *First,* do some self-analysis to determine what you want your software to do. What software features are most important to you? Research the market (the comparative information in the *Data Book* will help here) and discover what currently available software best accomplishes your goals. Buy "canned" software; don't write your own.

✔ *Second,* after you find the software you think you want, go to a computer store and ask to see the software demonstrated. Then buy the manuals. Is the information understandable? Remember that the documentation can save or cause a lot of headaches. If possible, use the software at some commercial location. Is it really as easy to use as it seemed in the demonstration?

✔ *Third,* after you've decided on the current software, research hardware solutions and determine which hardware will run the software you have chosen. Always decide on software first. The hardware comparison charts in the *Data Book* will give you a start toward a verdict on hardware.

✔ *Fourth,* be aware of the shakeout. The big four in microcomputers are IBM, Apple, Radio Shack, and Kaypro, in that order. Computers offered by large corporations (and not just the small-fry working out of their garages) have gone under. But don't forget that a micro often pays for itself in a year or less.

CHAPTER 5

Purchase and Installation of Word Processors

AFTER THE DAYS OF SELF-ANALYSIS and research involved in choosing the type of word processing equipment that's right for the job, the natural inclination is to go ahead and buy a machine to get the interface underway. But remember that there is more at stake here than a single computer purchase. Why all the bother for a word processor costing less than $5,000? If you get the wrong machine, you may be in trouble. It's as simple as that. Buy intelligently and you win. This chapter is a guide for the perplexed.

Support

If you do have a word processor in mind, the first step toward a purchase is an assessment of your decision. What you should now look for is *support*. Support comes in four forms: *documentation, service, user groups,* and *training*.

Each of the forms of support should be available and comprehensible. Ask questions of both sales reps and hometown computer shop personnel. If you can't find (or understand) the answers before your purchase, you may be left on your own *after* you buy the computer.

    1. *Documentation.* Clarity and quantity are the important barometers here. If you find that the manuals that come with your computer are unintelligible, there are dozens of independently published handbooks that unravel the mysteries of specific computers. Unfortunately, those books concentrate on the best-selling computers, such as the Atari, Colecovision, and Commodore. Books on business computers like the Monroe and Ithaca are much rarer.

    If the company's documentation is all that's available, buy the manual before you buy the machine. A reading should give you some idea as to how intelligible your major source of information will be. It will also introduce you to the computer.

Manuals should be typeset for easy reading and quick reference. Helpful illustrations and a good index are pluses. Except for any manuals you purchased on your own, all company documentation should be furnished free with the computer purchase.

2. *Service.* Any sales rep worthy of the trade will extol the dependability of the personal computer. As a rule, they are dependable, but chips can be blown and disk drives can die. Your computer will eventually need servicing.

First and foremost, service should be local. (Be wary of the company that instructs you to save the computer box for shipping your wounded machine back to the factory!) The best of all situations is on-site service—repairs made by a service rep in your office. Competition is stiff in the micro market, and many manufacturers are offering on-site repair through their network of dealers. (Check the *Data Book* for service arrangements.)

A local computer store should handle any repairs after the 90-day warranty runs out. Check with local owners of the hardware you are considering. In their experience, has service been prompt, available, and reliable?

If service isn't available within 50 miles in any direction, don't buy that computer. If you are considering the purchase of a machine that's just hit the market, be aware that every service rep must be trained to repair a computer. Some computer companies have sold so many computers, so quickly, that service training has been neglected. If your computer breaks down, *no one* knows how to fix it.

One alternative to company servicing is a new industry subgroup of computer fix-it firms that sell long-term service agreements for individual machines.

3. *User Groups.* Computer user groups are proliferating along with computers. There are clubs and organizations made up of the owners of specific types of hardware and software. Most user groups are openly independent, but some manufacturers have followed the lead of typesetting companies that sponsor user groups for the buyers of their hardware.

If there is a major or even a minor flaw with a particular piece of hardware, you'll hear about it through the user group. When software documentation is obtuse, you'll know before you buy. The user group is the perfect source of information: experienced users who know the problems and can often supply the solutions. Check to see if there is a local user group for the computer you're considering.

4. *Training.* You really shouldn't expect a three-day seminar in your office if you buy a micro for $3,500. Minicomputer users who spend tens of thousands of dollars are buying sophisticated equipment that requires some initial handholding. But micro buyers are much more on their own. Training is taking different forms in the small business computer arena. There may be training available in your own office.

If there is, that's a plus. It should be free. Many organizations, though, are willing to pay for personal service.

Courses in particular applications and overall training programs are offered by many dealers. But after the first few weeks of orientation are over, training goes on. Check to see if there is a dealer in your area who is willing to answer your how-to questions over the phone. Does the manufacturer have a toll-free number to handle those annoying problems that you simply can't resolve? This day-to-day "training" may be more important to you than the number of hours invested by a customer rep during orientation.

Finally, many colleges and high schools in metropolitan areas are offering evening and weekend courses devoted to particular computers and software applications. If you are considering one of the more popular machines, a hands-on, one-on-one introduction to the computer is conveniently and inexpensively available.

Minimum Technical Specifications

If you are satisfied with the support available in your area, company literature and the *Data Book* will describe the computer you have in mind and list its technical specifications. You are going to be doing serious word processing, so there are minimum specs any hardware should meet. Figure 5-1 checks them off. If a WP does not meet these minimum specifications, you will have difficulties in everyday operations.

- ✔ *Processing Speed: 16-Bit or 8-Bit?* The more powerful 16-bit machines are definitely the machines of the future. The 16-bit micros process 16 bits (binary digits) of information at a time as opposed to 8, meaning that they can generally "read" twice as fast (in actual operation, they aren't quite twice as fast). The IBM PC, sold as a 16-bit, moves 16 bits on the bus but does not process as fast as the true 16-bit machines. In a time test, the Hewlett-Packard HP-16, equipped with the Motorola 68000 microprocessor chip that's the heart of many 16-bit machines, finished a problem in 35 seconds. The IBM required 2½ minutes.

  Some manufacturers produce hardware that's capable of both 8-bit and 16-bit operation. The Fujitsu Micro 16, Ithaca, BMC, CompuPro 816, Xerox 8/16, Vector Graphic, and Digital Rainbow are among this group. For real power, the Apple Lisa and the Eagle 1600 are 32-bit machines.

  What do you really need? Computers should not be bought solely for the amount of processing power they provide. More *can* be less. Software that is written for 8-bit machines cannot be used by 16-bit machines (unless, of course, they can shift down to 8-bit operation). Eight-bit software is tested, proven, and reliable.

  The 16-bit machines are impressive. If the software you want to use is available, fine. If not, go with an 8-bit machine, make a return on your investment within a few years, and then upgrade to a 16-bit computer later.

  Don't buy any computer with less than 8-bit processing.

Checklist: Minimum WP Hardware Specifications

Processing speed:	8 bit	☑
	16 bit	☐
RAM:	64K	☑
	128K	☐
Disk drives:	Single	☐
	Double	☑
Ports:	Parallel	☑
	RS-232	☑
Operating system:	Nonproprietary	☑
	Proprietary	☐
Keyboard:	64 + keys	☑
	128 + keys	☐
	Numeric keypad	☑
Minimum screen display:	5 inch	☐
	7 inch	☑
	80 characters	☑
	132 characters	☐
	24 lines	☑
	40 lines	☐

■ **FIGURE 5-1.**

✔ *RAM: 64K or 128K?* RAM is the amount of memory you can use for programming space. How much you need depends on what you will be doing with your computer. Some programs require more than 64K; others do not. The 64K models have enough memory for the majority of WP software. Programs such as VisiWord and Word Perfect require a 128K machine. WordStar, the most popular word processing program for microcomputers, requires a 64K RAM.

Don't buy anything less than 64K. Several portables on the market, like Epson's HX-20 and the Radio Shack Model 100, are expandable to 32K. This is not enough for word processing. Also to be avoided are the recreational computers such as the Commodore VIC-20, Texas Instruments 99/4A (taken off the market in 1983), Mattel Aquarius, Radio Shack Color Computer, and the Timex/Sinclair 2068.

When checking out software packages, remember to note the minimum system size required to run the product.

✔ *Disk Drive.* For micro users who want to edit information quickly and easily, a disk drive system is required. Disk drives are either rigid drives capable of storing megabytes, or floppy disks. If the machine is equipped for use with floppy diskettes, a *dual disk drive* system is a must.

You should always have *backup* copies of every job created. The backup copy will be available if the worst happens and you lose all material on your diskette. If you have an extra copy in reserve, you don't have to start over. Backups are much easier to make with two disk drives. With one drive, the process takes longer, there are more chances for errors, and it's a labor-intensive, inefficient process.

✔ *Ports.* Ports are the plugs in the back of the computer that connect a CPU to printers, modems, and the outside world in general. At least two are needed: a *parallel port* for output to a printer and an *RS-232* (or similar) port for a modem or hardwire. Even if you decide to go with media conversion or OCR, an RS-232 capability is a plus.

A computer without a port is deaf and dumb. There are on-line information data base services, such as The Source, NewsNet, Dialog, and CompuServe, which offer general information, news, and stock reports. Other data bases are more specifically oriented toward one profession: Med/Mail is an electronic mail service offering news to physicians about continuing education and meetings of the American Medical Association; the Computer Technologies Department of the Printing Industry of America has an electronic Bulletin Board to supply members with free programs and computer news.

Data base network services will be a source of expert advice throughout this decade and the next. An RS-232 port, connected to a modem, will link your CPU to that information. Whatever your interfacing decision is, telecommunications should not be ruled out as an information source. A communications port is a necessity.

✔ *Operating System.* Whether you decided on CP/M, MS-DOS, or another standard possibility is not the question here. You should select a *nonproprietary operating system,* an operating system (OS) that is not owned and controlled by the manufacturer.

If you buy a computer with an operating system that is controlled by the hardware manufacturer, you are limited in your choices of software: You can buy only what the computer company makes. Independent software houses are locked out of developing new (and better) software compatible with the operating system and you are locked in to a very limited software selection. That limitation was one of the major reasons for one major corporate failure on the home computer market.

There are many computers on the micro front that have proprietary operating systems. But most manufacturers allow the user the option of purchasing either CP/M or MS-DOS, or both, as a second operating system. You then have the advantages of a specific OS along with the ability to choose from, for instance, the more than 3,000 programs written for CP/M. Apple, Zenith, and Radio Shack also build models that can be made to use CP/M.

Be apprised that a computer with a peculiar operating system, and no CP/M or MS-DOS option, may have an extremely small software library. That eliminates much of your word processing options.

✔ *Keyboard Requirements.* Your word processing operators need a keyboard that looks and acts like an IBM Selectric. Some computers have tiny keyboards with soft rubber keys or membrane keys or keys the same size as an aspirin tablet (called Chiclet keys). No one wants to peck at keys the size of sleeve buttons.

Many connoisseurs demand a keyboard with a full complement of 128 keys, complete with reverse video and search functions. More keys mean fewer keystrokes when doing specific tasks such as storing documents. But they're not a necessity. A 60-key keyboard will do everything that 128 keys do, even though it may require four keystrokes to delete a document rather than one.

✔ *Character Display.* More numerically important is the display on screen. Eye strain, tunnel vision, and downright crankiness can result if you make the wrong decisions. Manufacturers classify screens according to the number of lines that are displayed and the number of characters available in each line. Another measure used is the size of the screen.

A screen should be a *minimum* of 7 inches wide. That leaves enough latitude so that 80 characters filling the screen's width will not be so small as to be invisible. The resulting letters will be close to the size of typewritten characters. Screen display, as you might guess, must be 80 characters or more. Display should be as crisp as possible and must include both upper- and lowercase letters. Equally important is the number of lines displayed on screen at one time. The standard is 24 lines; don't consider anything less than 12.

Those are the seven basic technical considerations when shopping for a word processor. Here are some extra features that are advantageous but not essential.

- Green phospor and amber screens—supposedly easier to read.
- Two RS-232 ports—a plus.
- IBM compatibility—to tap into the huge software library developed for IBM.
- Good graphics—for producing charts and other visuals.
- A numeric keypad—for accounting and engineering mathematics.

Vendor Considerations

The right vendor will vary depending on your own experience and degree of certitude that you've found the right computer. For typesetters, the decision is easy: You buy your phototypesetter from the factory or you don't buy at all. In the microcomputer market there is a far more fragmented set of buyers and sellers. There are four sources of computerized equipment and supplies falling into two separate categories: the professionals and the mass marketers.

■ Professionals: Computer Stores and Manufacturers

The best choice for the consumer who does not know *exactly* what is required and needed is the computer store or the manufacturer.

Big computer chain stores such as ComputerLand with its 500 stores or small individually owned computer stores are staffed by professionals who are quick to supply answers and easy to talk with. There is no hard sell in these places. In fact, most computer salespeople are so downbeat that they rarely seem to notice you the first time you walk in the store. They know you just want to use the machines, so go ahead. It usually takes three trips to a computer store to buy something: the first to see it, the second to really put it through the paces, and the third to use your checkbook. For most consumers, the computer store is the place to buy. You can see hardware and software being used, and you can use it yourself. Hands-on experience is by far the best way to get acquainted with a computer.

Some computers are sold directly by the manufacturers. The largest manufacturers, like IBM and Radio Shack, have stores and offices in many cities. Radio Shack, for example, now has 7,700 outlets.

Before the 1980s, the computer manufacturers' sales force sold *all* computers: micros, minis, and mainframes. Things have changed with the microcomputer retail revolution. Minis and mainframes are still sold through a roving sales force, but the great majority of micros are sold through dealer networks.

Microcomputer sales reps are generally smooth, friendly, and willing to sell you what you really need. Most are also professionals at teaching customers how to use the computers. Micros like the IBM or NorthStar that are sold by a company's own sales force may be slightly more expensive than competitive machines. Many customers feel the personal touch is worth the surcharge. Of course, before making any purchase, it's advisable to check the computer against user groups and minimum specifications.

■ Mass Marketers: Mail-Order and Department Stores

There are two places most of us should not buy computers: large retail stores and mail-order houses. The people selling computers in a department store usually know very little about the equipment and less about your needs. Mail-order houses will take your order and your credit card number, but don't expect help from the selling end, especially if you have problems after the sale. With very little overhead, mail-order firms do sell at rock-bottom prices. Consider purchasing through a mail-order house only if you are knowledgeable about what's available and you know precisely what unit you want to buy.

Word processors are business machines that must be supported. Unless you have thoroughly researched the market, including a test-run on the machine, you should depend upon a computer store. The prices will be higher than through mail-order wholesalers, but you'll be buying an answer to the questions of the first day—and every day after the first day.

When stocking diskettes, computer paper, and other supplies, buy from the wholesalers. They sell the same supplies cheaper than the computer stores, and the quality is the same. Since there's no service necessary on these cheap consumables, good sense dictates buying from the least expensive source.

Installation

■ Phase One: Before

Before the machine is delivered, there are several steps to follow to ensure a successful installation. The groundwork will involve two factors: site preparation and management of employees.

1. *Site Preparation.* Site preparation is much different for minicomputers than for micros. The larger word processors must be housed in a humidity- and temperature-controlled environment. This usually means a small room constructed specifically for the computer. Remote terminals are hardwired to the word processor and placed wherever needed.

   Micros are much less demanding. These smaller machines take up about the same amount of room as a wide-carriage electric typewriter. Some care must be taken to avoid extremes in temperature, humidity, and static electricity.

   Other considerations include adequate electrical wiring, a phone hookup if you're telecommunicating, cables for hardwiring, and making sure the desk is big enough! The size of a computer is listed on its spec sheet.

2. *Management of Employees.* The first rule is to be *patient.* An interface takes time. *Don't be ready to telecommunicate or hardwire the first day.* Some bugs will need to be worked out, and unrealistic expectations invite discouragement.

   A few weeks before the installation, prepare documents to be used as sample interfacing projects. Don't be overly ambitious; start with small, simple jobs and move to more difficult jobs later. Be prepared to allow your operators to learn slowly, and at their own pace. Allow at least a week of short learning sessions, rather than just one massive attack at the new machine. Have the manuals on hand with enough paper, diskettes, and other supplies. Learning is a difficult process; avoid making the initial experience unpleasant.

   Prepare yourself mentally. The computer transition is a major organizational effort—treat it that way. Be well rested for installation day. Do whatever you can to make the installation a *positive* first experience, both for yourself and your employees.

   The investment in equipment is an investment in making people more productive. Let your word processing people know this. Your personnel should also be aware that there are no time limits on training. Don't overdo the training. "Traditional" work interspersed with training sessions will make for a smoother transition.

   New technology *is* intimidating no matter what the sales literature says. Don't expect quick WP keyboarding for typesetting from your personnel. New crafts are not casually learned.

At least one person should be trained before installation. That person can be a source of confidence for the rest of the staff. He or she will be able to answer any of the obvious questions, thereby assuaging some of the inevitable anxieties.

■ Phase Two: Installation and After

Three more things should be taken care of to help ensure a smooth start-up of your interface: professional installation of equipment, debugging of the WP/typesetter interface, and provision of coding guidelines and an interface preparation manual for employees.

1. *Professional Installation.* The computer should be installed by a professional, either from the manufacturer or from a local computer store. Remember, whether it is a mainframe or a micro, this will probably be the first computer your employees have ever used. Setting up properly will make all the difference toward a good beginning.

2. *Debugging.* After the machine is installed and working, the next step is to debug communications. When you first attempt to establish the hardwire or telecommunications, start with a simple document composed of straight text without mathematics or superscripts. *Do not start with complicated jobs.* Failures early on can create a poor psychology that will be difficult to overcome. Avoid them by using simple jobs specifically prepared for the first interface attempt.

The major personnel decision will be to appoint someone to be in charge of communications. That person should be selected from those who will actually be doing the day-to-day work. Software management and upkeep will ultimately be the responsibility of this person in charge.

When an interface works, let it be. Control the urge to over correct small problems. Let the people doing the keyboarding see that the interface *is* working. This will help keep the atmosphere exciting and optimistic. The right psychology goes a long way toward making the interface run smoothly.

3. *Coding Guidelines and Interface Preparation Manual.* A coding chart that visually offers all available special characters should be prominently displayed (see Figure 5-2). Distribute copies to all employees. Along with the chart, a list of word processing codes to use *and to avoid* should be prepared. That list can be augmented with any mnemonic shorthand you will suggest.

In addition, a short description of how the interface works is often helpful. Include a few pages on basic typography along with the nontechnical description of the technology. In general, the coding guidelines are an operations manual.

The interfacing manual is a bit different. Only those employees who actually transmit information will benefit from the interfacing manual. In any interface, there are several screens full of necessary protocols for which parameters must be supplied. The interfacing

	1	2	3	4	5	6	7	8
						Font Number		
	a	*a*	**a**	*a*	a	*a*	^{1}	*a*
	b	*b*	**b**	*b*	b	*b*	^{2}	*b*
	c	*c*	**c**	*c*	c	*c*	^{3}	ð
	d	*d*	**d**	*d*	d	*d*	^{4}	η
	e	*e*	**e**	*e*	e	*e*	^{5}	ϑ
	f	*f*	**f**	*f*	f	*f*	^{6}	x
	g	*g*	**g**	*g*	g	*g*	^{7}	μ
	h	*h*	**h**	*h*	h	*h*	^{8}	o
	.							.
	.							.
	.							.
	.							.
	.							.
	9	*9*	**9**	*9*	9	*9*	^{9}	↕
	0	*0*	**0**	*0*	0	*0*	^{0}	×
	$	*$*	**$**	*$*	$	*$*	{	Ñ
	)	*)*	**)**	*)*	)	*)*	}	Ç
	?	*?*	**?**	*?*	?	*?*	|	Ø
	-	-	-	-	-	-	■	Æ
	‰	•	‰	•	%	•	◄	À
	,	,	,	,	,	,	►	Ü
	;	;	;	;	;	;	'	Ö
	.	.	.	.	.	.	"	Ä
	,	,	,	,	,	,	/	É
	!	*!*	!	*!*	!	!	]	ˆ
	(	*(*	(	*(*	(	(	©	˙
	&	*&*	&	*&*	&	&	¾	˝

Special Coding

	1	2	3	4	5	6	7	8
$ 1	⊓	✓	⊬	÷	⊞	√	∟	⇟
$ 2	☐	…	△	∺	⧻	∼	⌐	↔
$ 3	∓	|	≥	≠	±	∫	⌐	α
$ 4	⌢	#	≤	≐	∓	∞	⌐	☐
$ 5	◇	△	≦	≚	⌣	∓	∪	⊥
$ 6	⊓	ξ	≧	=	⌢	≈	∩	R
$ 7	∛	∫	≅	+	⊘	⊙	⊂	ℒ
$ 8	∜	∮	>	∈	⊙	⊠	⊃	ℒ
$ 9	⊕	⋄	∟	∈̄	⋘	↛	‡	φ
$ 0	∂	◬	<	∴	⋙	⊲	†	ψ

■ FIGURE 5-2. Type font coding chart.

INSTRUCTIONS FOR TRANSFERRING
FILES FROM THE VAX USING THE AM TERMINAL

To move a file from MASS-11 to an output file on VAX, send the file to printer 3. This will form a file called "spool.lst." This file can be transferred to the typesetter.

To move a normal output file from the VAX, substitute its name for "spool.lst" in the instructions below.

Files that have mnemonic codes are loaded using a different program than files that have not been coded. See note below.

1. Turn on COMP/EDIT terminal.
2. Insert communications disk (blue label with "COM" in pencil) into Drive 1 (label facing away from terminal).
3. Initialize with 'tab skip' 'left arrow' (held together) then 'home' 'left arrow.'
4. Put utilities disk (black label with "VAXLOGIN" in pencil) into Drive 2.
5. Run login to VAX with:
   E 2 VAXLOGIN.
6. Log on VAX in normal manner.
7. Insert your disk into Drive 1 to receive file.
8. Assign name to VAX file with command:
   ASSIGN spool.lst DOCUMENT.
9. Load program to AM COMP/EDIT with command
   $ "$/E 2 STDVAX 1 filename" *
10. Wait for file close message (9 lines).
    When finished log off VAX.
11. Remove both disks.
12. Reinitialize COMP/EDIT system with typesetting program (Drive 1) using commands in #3 above.
13. Put your disk in Drive 2.
14. Transfer complete; check file.
15. To check for your file, touch key 'directory' and '2' (first row numeric).
16. To display your file, switch to noncounting mode with 'cmd' 'n' 'c', then 'file' 'read' '2.' Type "filename."
17. File will not display until you touch 'read' key.
18. Carry your disk to the COMP/EDIT typesetter and follow instructions in "AM Typesetter Guidelines" for coding recommendations.

*STDVAX is used for VAX files that have no codes inserted. To move coded files with width information use the program called FROMVAX. For more information refer to the booklets "Welcome to the COMP/EDIT Phototypesetting System: Operating and Reference Manual."

■ FIGURE 5-3. Instructions for telecommunications.

AT THE KAYPRO 4

1. Turn machine on.

2. Insert data disk in Drive A; CP/M disk in Drive B.

3. Type: B:TERM. Return.

4. After prompt, Return.

5. Type: - on numeric keypad.

6. Type: B:STAT LST:=UL1.

7. Type: WS (to call up WordStar word processing program).

8. Type: P (to telecommunicate).

9. Type file name you wish to send.

10. Return until all commands are completed.

AT THE MDC-350

1. Turn machine on.

2. Insert ASCII communications disk in lower disk drive.

3. Type: L.

4. Strike: UTIL key on left keypad of keyboard.

5. Type: 9.

6. Establish following protocols: 1 stop bit, no parity, 8 data bits, and 300 baud.

7. Remove ASCII communications disk and insert data disk in lower disk drive.

8. Type file name.

9. Strike: RVC on left keyboard.

10. Type: 1. Terminal is ready to receive telecommunications.

■ FIGURE 5-4. Synopsis of Kaypro 4 and MDC-350 interface commands.

preparation manual will supply the answers to those protocol questions. (Refer to Chapter 9 for specifics on protocols.)

After you have successfully established the interface, prepare a document that shows a picture of a blank terminal. Make several dozen photocopies of this page.

On the first page, type in the first command necessary to physically order the transmission of a document. Begin as simply as turning the machine on. Assume that the person creating the communications *knows nothing*. At the bottom of this page, tell the operator very simply how to turn on the machine.

On the second page, show what *should* have happened to the screen after the machine was turned on. Drawing expertise isn't as critical as completeness. At the bottom of this screen, type the first command necessary to begin the telecommunications session. Follow this with page 3 showing the screen again, *after* the second command has been completed.

Direction by direction, keystroke by keystroke, the interface manual should visually demonstrate the screen result of *every necessary keystroke*. After a dozen or so communications sessions, your personnel may no longer need to consult the manual, but it will be invaluable in the beginning stages of any new employee's relationship with the interface. The manual also includes a one-page synopsis of all the interface steps—it will be a ready reference for your experienced employees (see Figures 5-3 and 5-4).

Mistakes cause frustration. Making the first-time interfacer comfortable with the new technology will help create a good psychology in the long run. Equally as important, if you write the steps down, they are permanent. It's possible to move information correctly once and then, without writing the steps down in a second attempt, find that you cannot recapture the correct pattern. Interface documentation is a simple, easy way to retaining a winning formula.

The preparation manual may be as long as 30 pages. If you are working in-house, you should include sections on *both* typesetting and word processing.

CHAPTER 6

Choosing an Interfacing Method

YOU HAVE AN INPUT METHOD well established in your organizational structure and you think it's time to use your word processors to set type. You are ready to decide which interfacing technology you should use—or whether to interface at all.

Telecommunications, hardwiring, optical character recognition, and media conversion are the choices (as outlined in Chapter 2). Telecommunications is the method of choice for *most* applications. But you are not most people. Your organization has specific needs, and individualized problems need individualized solutions.

Analyzing Requirements

Any consideration of interfacing options must begin with a clearheaded analysis of whether interfacing is indeed advisable. Every word processor coordinator and type production manager have created (or inherited) a specific work pattern that, presumably, resolves particular problems for the organization.

The nonconformist nature of the word processing and typesetting industries makes simplistic go–no-go advice impossible. Taking the quick test that is presented in Figure 6-1 can be an effective strategy toward getting suitably oriented. Rating your personnel and your needs is an often neglected but very necessary management tool.

- *Your Organization.* Take a look at your organization in terms of long-term needs and goals. What do you want to do now, and where do you want to be several years from now? If computerization of your work flow does not pay for itself in five years or less, you are over-

A Self-Test: Interfacing

Organization, 10 points ☐

The typical job, 15 points ☐

The typesetting bill, 20 points ☐

Area vendors, 10 points ☐

Return on investment, 10 points ☐

Employees, 10 points ☐

Management, 10 points ☐

Control, 15 points ☐

Maximum: 100 points

■ **FIGURE 6-1.**

stepping your needs if you interface. Very honestly, how much does your organization *need* to interface?

It is not impossible to import more than one technology into your current work flow, but it is harder. Using the checklist in Figure 6-1, give yourself 10 points in the "Organization" box if you are already using some form of computer and there is consensus within management that some change is needed (or management is receptive to computerized change). Give yourself fewer points if you are using typewriters and management is satisfied—no points for an Underwood manual; 5 points if you are using electronic typewriters.

- *The Typical Job.* Interfacing works best with straight matter. If your input is in the form of paragraphs, not four-level mathematic equations or short, choppy advertising, the interface will be easier and thus more attractive. Under "The Typical Job," log 15 points if you are a book company specializing in fiction or a magazine publisher using long articles. Give yourself 5 points if the longest document you ever produce is an eight-page brochure.

Don't rule out interfacing if you produce tabular or technical matter. It is possible to transmit; although you will have a more difficult beginning, once the correct translations are made and you have debugged the interface, it is almost as easy as straight matter. Deduct 5 points from the maximum 15 if you have occasional equations interspersed with generous amounts of scientific notation (subscripts, superscripts, Greek letters, math symbols); you get only 5 points if you are interested in transmitting *only* technical material.

Note: Some in-house typesetting shops set the straight matter themselves and then ask type houses to set only the more difficult technical matter that remains. Don't be surprised if you are charged very high rates. Many typesetting companies simply refuse to accept such assignments.

- *The Typesetting Bill.* Capturing keystrokes works *very well* in data base typography, but you need not be a mainframe user typesetting thousands of pages. If you spend more than $10,000 per year on typesetting, assign yourself the maximum 20 points under "The Typesetting Bill." Give yourself 15 points for type purchases under $10,000 and 10 points for less than $5,000. If you spend less than $2,000 a year, you are probably better off sending the job to the typesetter as a traditional paper manuscript—give yourself zero points.

  If you spend only $2,000 a year on typesetting but that covers *one* job that is done once every year (perhaps an annual directory) *or* you produce a periodical job that is always formatted the same (a monthly newsletter, for instance), you rate 10 points. If you spend between $2,000 and $10,000 annually and all your documents tend to be formatted similarly, add 5 bonus points to your score.

- *Area Vendors.* What are the type houses in your area doing? If many typesetters and type customers around you are telecommunicating or converting media, it is time to join in. Give yourself 10 points under "Area Vendors." If you are a typesetter, the time is right because you are now operating at a competitive disadvantage. If you are a typesetting customer, use the knowledge easily at hand to aid you in your communications retrofit. Take only 5 points if you can't find a typesetter within 25 miles that is ready to interface. It is possible to interface long distance, but you won't be able to depend on ready advice if you cannot interface with a nearby type house.

- *Return On Investment (ROI).* Your major expenses will be computer hardware and software, interfacing hardware, and software development costs. Miscellaneous charges include documentation (manuals), storage devices (diskettes), and training sessions. If the ROI for your expansion takes less than 18 months, your score is a 10 in this category. For every six months beyond a year and a half, deduct 5 points. After three years, your score is zero.

- *Employees.* What sort of personnel do you have today? Are they open to learning the new technology, or will they be a hindrance to development? When interfacing is first established, those who deal with it daily—the typists and typesetters—must be willing to learn and grow. If they are unwilling, the wrenches they throw will have a tremendous and perhaps lasting effect on your interface. Your choices present a dilemma. You can either expend time and effort in convincing employees that it is time to learn the new technology or you can hire new employees who will have to be trained. The latter option is not inviting at any time and is particularly disastrous when contemplating the use of new technology. If you have a corps of eager (or even complacently accepting) employees, you score a 10. For every 25 percent of your work force who are unwilling, deduct 5 points from the maximum 10 in the "Employees" category.

- *Management.* What sort of management does your organization have? Will management allow you to spend the time, money, and personnel necessary to make the technology work? You get zero points if the answer is no. If the answer is yes, are they (or are you) professional enough to allow other professionals to implement the technology without meddling?

If your management is positive but obtrusive, your days will be frustrating. Occasional tours to see how things are doing are fine. The real problem is with those who think they know more than they do about computers. Management must let the interface work, and that means keeping hands off while production is working on the interface. If you think your company's management can be unobstructively supportive, take 10 points. If your executive director (or you) will be meddlesome, subtract 5 points from the maximum score of 10.

- *Control.* There should be one person in charge of and responsible for the interface. That person should have enough organizational power to be able to control the situation. Making a production head the nominal chief of an interfacing team and then undermining that person's authority is no way to interface successfully. If you have severe organizational authority problems, assign yourself only 5 points as a score in the "Control" category.

  Does the person in control have enough computer savvy to make the development work? If not, is that person interested enough to be able to learn quickly? If your answer is yes to either question—and interface management is possible—you score 15 points. If there is no one on board (including you) who is capable of taking charge of the interface, hire someone and credit yourself 10 points. If you don't hire anyone, your interface will founder; you score zero points.

■ The Totals: Should You Interface?

Adding up the points on your checklist will give you a raw total. But, just as important, you should have answered several important questions as you graded your potential. How will you be using the interface? How much will you use it? How much typesetting do you now do? What is the potential for employee satisfaction and retention? What are your management strengths and weaknesses? All of these considerations will become important as you make decisions about interfacing.

Here's what your score means:
- From 90 to 100: You should have been capturing keystrokes long ago. Your organization meets all the critical criteria to begin to interface today.
- From 75 to 89: You can save money through interfacing, but you should be careful about investing in the more expensive interfacing methods. A technological or organizational overhaul may be necessary before you move to telecommunications.
- From 60 to 74: You should definitely have second thoughts about the interface potential. The promise is there, but you have identified problems that may make an interface difficult and perhaps unwise.
- Below 60 points: There are serious problems with beginning any sort of communications. You either have too little work to make an inter-

face worthwhile or too many organizational problems to attempt any systematic changes. Solve the internal problems first and then reassess your interfacing potential.

If you decide to interface, then there is a new series of questions to answer. Which method should you choose? What's available on the market? Chapter 2 gave a short introduction to the various interfacing methods. The *Data Book* offers comparison charts that supply detailed technical information. But what are the right answers? *How should you interface, and what machine should you use?* The rest of this chapter is an interfacing buyer's guide.

Media Conversion

Media conversion is the transfer of magnetic data from a format not understandable by a computer into a form that is intelligible. The magnetic data are converted from magnetic jibberish into meaningful sentences.

For the type customer, a *conversion service* is a spin-off of the word processing environment. If your organization decides to scrap one word processing system for a competitive system, how do you convert the years of data you have stored on the first system? You use a conversion house's service. It is not unusual for hundreds of diskettes to be converted from Wang configurations to Xerox, or IBM to Wang, or scores of other possibilities.

The technology employed by the conversion service has been neatly packaged into a media converter that a type house can purchase for a hefty price tag of more than $10,000. Media conversion is expensive for both type buyer and typesetter. It may supply solutions that no other possibility offers, but those solutions don't come cheap. Beyond expense, media conversion packages are also intrinsically based on translations available *now*.

Typesetters: If your media conversion vendor does not promise delivery in two weeks or less, be on your guard. Delivery in 60 days? Chances are the company will be frantically trying to create a brand-new conversion program to fit your order—and it could take a long time to get right. Conversion programs are supplied on disk; it only takes a couple of minutes—not 60 days—to make copies of programs that already exist.

Both type house and type customer should be on guard for vendor vocabulary. "Media conversion" has different meanings in different interfacing contexts. Because paper is a medium, some services offering both magnetic and paper conversion sell their services as media conversion. In that sense, media conversion can be synonymous with OCR.

Also confusing are the several typesetter/word processor combinations manufactured by the same company. AM, a major producer of typesetting equipment, had manufactured word processors as well; Wang, a huge word processing company, offers a phototypesetter as an option. Both Wang and AM refer to their offerings in terms of media conversion.

◼ Black Boxes versus Programmable Converters

A type house interested in purchasing media conversion equipment has two choices. First, there are the descendants of the "black boxes." These machines are not programmable by the typesetter and are bought with a specific interface in mind—one word processor to one phototypesetting machine. The second, much more costly, class of media converters are intelligent machines that can be programmed by the typesetter to understand (and convert) a wide array of magnetic media.

Black Boxes. Black boxes are at the less expensive end of the media conversion scale (but even the cheapest media converters are more expensive than telecommunications equipment). They range in price from $6,000 to well over $25,000. What do you get for $25,000? The ability to take a diskette from *one* type of word processor and convert the information so that it is understandable by *one* specific brand of phototypesetter. They are expensive and ornery. Inconsistencies in word processing input are often problematic. *Black boxes no longer serve the needs of the typesetter.*

However, some in-house graphics facilities find this type of machine a perfect solution to a perennial problem. Suppose your organization's word processor has been storing information for years. Your phototypesetting department is underutilized; a monthly newsletter, occasional letterheads and brochures, and telephone answer sheets are the standard work flow. There are jobs that you want to typeset, but you can't afford to pay for retyping on the phototypesetting machine. The black box is an answer. You can move information from the word processor to the phototypesetter and put typesetting to work at producing sales lists, directories, and manuals that were formerly produced as computer printouts. You save paper and corporate communications is improved.

But how many such organizations are there? An example from the past is Compugraphic's WordCom. Selling for $5,000, the WordCom allowed users to convert IBM mag cards into diskettes readable by the EditWriter series of phototypesetters. If you have an EditWriter and an IBM, you're in luck. But, like all the black boxes, the WordCom serves a very limited market. Outside of that market, the black boxes belong to history and printing museums.

Programmable Converters. Programmable converters *theoretically* are capable of interfacing between any two computers. This market is dominated by five competitors and dotted by the offerings of several typesetting manufacturers. Shaftstall, purchased by Penta (a major manufacturer of front-end systems—front ends are minicomputers that serve as the hubs of typesetting networks) in 1983, is still the front-runner in the media converter race. Although the oldest is not always the best, Shaftstall has more experience, and has developed more new features, than the other manufacturers. Cromwell, Applied Data Communications, Antares, and Altertext offer enough competition to satisfy any type house shopping for media conversion hardware.

Why would any typesetter want to use a media converter that costs 100 or 200 percent more than telecommunications? Because media conversion is the best available *indirect interface.*

The Interface: Direct or Indirect

Telecommunications is a direct interface. It requires type house personnel to be actively involved, at a given time, with the customer. Media conversion is indirect; a diskette is received in the mail and the type house can convert it at any time. If you are a typesetter who telecommunicates, your schedules are in some measure controlled by your customers. When they call, you telecommunicate. The promise of eliminating short-term, anarchic demands on your equipment may be reason enough to pay the price for media conversion.

The largest type houses have resolved their scheduling difficulties by incorporating both media conversion and telecommunications into their battery of services. Telecommunications capability is a must for typesetters in the 1980s. If you are considering a media converter purchase, you should be aware that the black boxes—with no communications capability—are going the way of the dinosaur.

■ The Media Conversion Market

MediaCom 5000. Shaftstall's MediaCom 3300 was the industry standard for media conversion, as the company literature says, "for years." Introduced in the fall of 1980, the 3300 sold very well—so well, in fact, that the 3300 is the norm that other media conversion manufacturers must meet to be competitive. Shaftstall devices have outsold all other media conversion systems by a factor of 10 to 1.

The Shaftstall 5000, which became available in 1983, is basically a sophisticated version of the 3300. Both machines are hybrid devices. Much more powerful than the black boxes, the new breed of media converters offers both media conversion and telecommunications capability in one unit. Figure 6-2 gives an idea of what this generation can do. Incorporating a disk reader, telecommunicator, and disk writer, the 5000 and its competitors are not taking any chances. If telecommunications is the wave of the future, the MediaCom devices already purchased won't be relegated to the basement.

For media conversion, diskettes are inserted into the MediaCom and "read." After reading is completed, information is either stored on diskette, or telecommunicated, or sent directly to a phototypesetter through a hard-wire interface. This dual off-line and on-line capability is an important advantage: Your typesetter doesn't have to be tied up interminably accepting hardwired data from the converter.

Shaftstall advertises that its media conversion works between any phototypesetter and "more than 50 different kinds of word processors and computers." Therein lies the problem of all media conversion. It is *not* a universal interface.

Assume that you are a typesetter who has spent tens of thousands of dollars on a media converter and a full complement of software. After installation, the hardware is working well at reading Wang and IBM diskettes. But then you receive a telephone call from a major customer who has an oddball word processor, for which you have no available program for media conversion. You can't convert and there goes a major account.

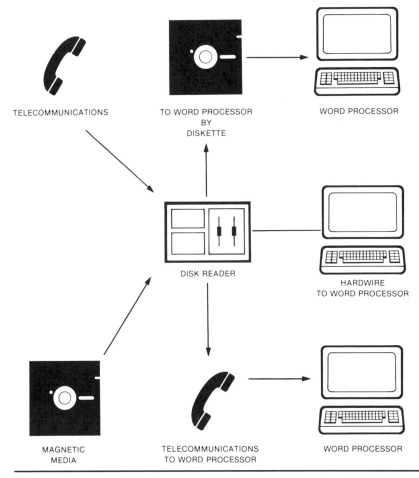

FIGURE 6-2. Capabilities of today's generation of media converters.

After spending tens of thousands of dollars, you have a machine that can't do the job all the time.

The solution that Shaftstall (and all of its competitors) offers, of course, is telecommunications. Type houses can develop translations for odd machines and then telecommunicate. The terminal of the MediaCom allows you to write telecommunications software onto diskettes and then be incorporated into your work flow as needed. But ask yourself: If I'm going to telecommunicate, why spend $20,000 or much more for the interface? Telecommunications is available for $5,000 or less on most phototypesetting systems.

Altertext Disk Reader. Altertext hit the market in August 1982 with its media converter. The device was first developed to be used only by Altertext in-house, which was one of the leading conversion services in the early 1980s. Because of its experience in the word processing business, Altertext still offers a great variety of word processor-to-word processor conversions. Along with telecommunications, on-line and off-line conversions, and a user programmable system, the Altertext offers dozens of options. Altertext Systems I and II can be augmented by IBM bisynchronous hardware, mag tape drives, optional software, and even laser printer interfaces (see Figure 6-3).

Antares. Another company that hit the market in the early 1980s, Antares takes a radically high tech approach to media conversion. A Digital PDP-11/23 minicomputer front end is attached to a 10 megabyte rigid disk drive for storage. The complete collection of software is sold with the hardware as a package. The problem? The base price for the system is $55,000.

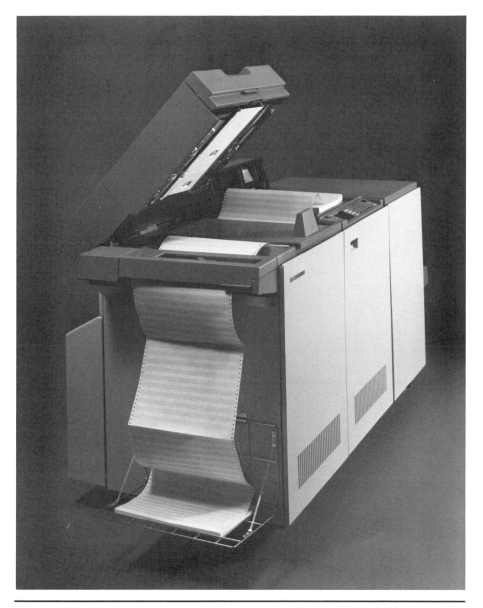

■ **FIGURE 6-3. The newest intelligent copiers have created a new industry, electronic printing. Photo courtesy of Xerox Corporation.**

The translations tend to be very fast (the Antares has been accused of being hardware overkill). As for programmability, the media converter is not user-programmable. Custom software translations are written by Antares as requested by the type house. The all-or-nothing Antares approach (and the resulting high price tag) will appeal only to the largest typesetting companies.

Applied Data Communications (ADC). ADC makes the Trans/Media 500. A typical smart converter with telecommunications user programmability, the Trans/Media also offers a disk drive that accommodates nine-track tapes. Because most minicomputers and mainframes use nine track, this advantage could be important for a typesetter using a direct entry photo unit not equipped with a nine-track drive.

Front-end systems use nine-track tape drives to accept both software and typesetting jobs. In this case, a media converter is unnecessary; the interface is directly facilitated by the standardized nine-track tapes. That option, of course, is available only to those type houses that own a front end, which often costs $200,000 and more.

The Trans/Media has the capability to convert in three different ways: hardwiring to a phototypesetter, writing to a diskette, or writing to nine-track tape. Because of this variety, the converter can be used to make multiple copies of diskettes, move information from mag tape to diskette for distribution, or convert 8″ diskette media to 5¼″ diskettes. This is a high-powered machine.

In its company literature, ADC offers conversions to "a variety of formats," without mentioning specific numbers. The Trans/Media is not an amateur's option. By making the Trans/Media easy to use and comparatively simple to program, ADC has, in effect, reversed the traditional programming role, shifting it to the user. The user does receive six application programs with the basic system and is offered free training in programming the Trans/Media.

If you have computer programming proficiency, you can program the converter yourself to meet any of your needs. Rather than paying a vendor for software, you'll be paying for your own development, labor, and equipment time. But, again, this is what you'll be doing if you choose the less expensive telecommunications route.

Cromwell Context. Cromwell Graphics Systems moved into media conversion with its Context in 1982. The Context is aggressively marketed to typesetters that want to reach a particular segment of the interfacing market: the CP/M word processors.

For $6,995, say recent Cromwell ads, you receive 80 disk formats free. The $25 handling charge for disk updates aside, this seems like a very good deal. The Context offers telecommunications and a terminal for user programmability. The bad news? As of 1984, programs for reading MS-DOS and TRSDOS diskettes are "under development."

For type houses, Context is great for dealing with your CP/M customers. But type buyers who use IBM, IBM-compatible, and Radio Shack computers are neglected, along with anyone who has any of the other unusual operating systems. IBM users could use CP/M-86 (the 16-bit version of CP/M) as an operating system, but are they likely to give up MS-DOS just to use your type house for typesetting?

Itek. Itek is a major supplier of phototype systems that entered the media converter market in 1983. The converter library translates media from 20 different word processors and computers. At $11,500, Itek offers a basic machine at a middle-of-the-road price. It may be a good choice for anyone using an Itek phototypesetter, because the translations between converter and typesetter will obviously be excellent. Unfortunately, user program-mability is *not* an option.

Itek's standard package is equipped with two translation programs; additional programs cost $800 each, so a fully equipped system can cost more than $30,000 (see Figure 6-4).

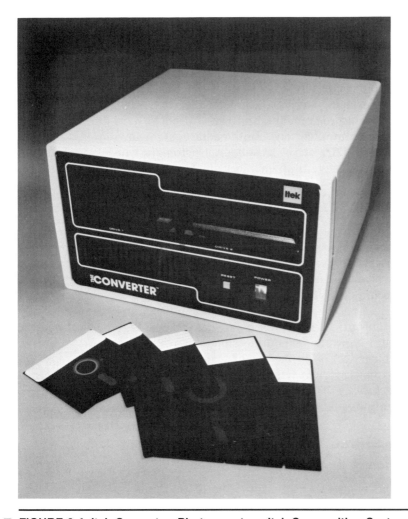

■ **FIGURE 6-4. Itek Converter. Photo courtesy Itek Composition Systems.**

■ Reviewing Media Conversion: Should You Buy?

For type houses, a media converter is worth purchasing if it will pay for itself in increased business within a year. Remember that you will have to buy a truckload of software to communicate with a wide range of computers. But if you are a typesetter with several large customers using the same input device, or if you have a long-lasting relationship with a major customer, media conversion may make sense.

The newest machines are simple to operate and don't require user programming. These turnkey systems are the new wave and will be competitive with telecommunications for some time. In the maniacal atmosphere of the type house, the ability to convert when you want to convert may warrant the purchase price. With media conversion, you're at the mercy of only the mail, not every customer with a telephone.

There are drawbacks to media conversion, not the least of which is the very expensive price of equipment. Beyond the economics, it is frustrating to turn away jobs that you cannot convert. Remember that media conversion is not as universal as the advertisements lead us to believe. One industry expert points out the reality: 90 percent of the time, media converters are used not for conversion but for telecommunications.

For the type customer, media conversion is a real option. If you have a word processor or computer, you need not purchase additional equipment to cash in on interfacing savings. You will have to find a typesetter that is capable of converting *your* media, and you will not save as much money as if you used telecommunications. But media conversion requires no real preparation on the part of the customer. Customers who use uncommon word processors will have problems locating type houses able to interface.

Optical Character Recognition (OCR)

Another indirect method is optical character recognition (OCR). For years, the OCR interface market has been dominated by Kurzweil Computer Products, a division of Xerox. Theoretically, the optical recognition process is marvelous because it is so simple. The material to be interfaced is typed, fed into the scanner, and immediately converted into magnetic data. A hardwire connecting the OCR and a typesetter feeds the memory to the typesetter for output. In 1981, the *Seybold Report,* a high-tech newsletter much relied on by graphic arts professionals, gave us the news: "We have witnessed a sharp decline in the use of scanning equipment."

Technology moves forward and, in this case, beyond OCR. Optical scanning was a technique of the 1970s. Today, there are the better options of telecommunications and media conversion.

■ WordCom SI and Kurzweil: The Old and the New

In 1975, Compugraphic was selling the WordCom SI as an optical scanning package. A UniScan optical character reader was hardwired to a Compugraphic terminal, the EditWriter 1750. Input was produced with IBM Selectrics using special OCR-readable fonts, such as OCR-A, Courier, Letter Gothic, and Prestige Elite. Care had to be taken to avoid smudging and irregular spacing, but errors were conveniently pointed out to the operator. The operator had to handhold the OCR, feeding pages and watching for errors to be corrected on the EditWriter screen.

The interface was expensive in a variety of ways. The SI cost $19,950. Personnel requirements, slow throughput speeds, and high equipment prices combined to create a technology that was begging to be replaced.

The OCR story continues with the development engineers at Kurzweil. A new, intelligent optical scanner was developed for the 1980s that answers all the competitive thrusts of media conversion and telecommunications, except one—the price. Prices for optical scanners begin where prices of other interfacing devices top out. Ranging from $10,000 to as much as $150,000, intelligent optical character readers like the Kurzweil are capable of reading *any* printed or typed letters. Typewriting, word processor printouts, typesetting, and even Cyrillic, from 6 to 24 point in size, can be read and translated into magnetic memory. It's a dependable, well-engineered machine that works.

Optical scanning has a variety of applications. Here are some examples: A law firm uses it to create a data base of reports, depositions, and briefs; two Italian cities convert municipal records to computer storage; a university in Great Britain scans scholarly texts for computerized analysis; a society for the deaf scans printed material and creates synthesized voice output; a typesetter converts the printed pages of hardcover books into memory for setting pages of a new softcover edition; and a legal printer in Chicago scans last-minute jobs for overnight typesetting.

For most type houses that are not in an overnight hurry, OCR is simply too expensive to make economic sense. Who can use it? You must have several major customers who output copy to OCR-readable fonts. Your customers will have to offer you very large typesetting orders to make the Kurzweil, or any of its competitors, worth the price.

If optical scanning is within your economic reach, it works very well. There's still no better technology for rapidly reading printed materials. The point, of course, is that *reading* is a slow, expensive, and labor-intensive process as compared to data stream telecommunications.

■ OCR from the Type Buyer's Point of View

For the type buyer, optical scanning seems trouble free. But the reality, especially with the first OCRs, was quite different. The new generation of scanner has improved capabilities, but there are still some complications. Your material must be well organized—scraps of paper and notes written alongside the edge of dog-eared sheets are definitely unusable. The input must be clean and crisp.

Finding a typesetter near you with OCR capabilities might be another problem. Only the largest type houses tend to have OCR, in part because of the expense and in part because the technology is so labor intensive. If you are interested in optical character recognition services, an interfacing relationship based on OCR will require some preliminary communication regarding formats, sizes, and margins.

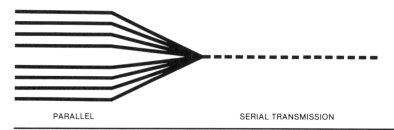

PARALLEL　　　　　　　　　　　　　SERIAL TRANSMISSION

■ **FIGURE 6-5. Parallel and serial transmission.**

The right users for OCR are customers with big jobs who are willing to invest in perfectly typewritten pages. If your organization has not been tempted by OCR yet, that is good de facto evidence that OCR is probably not the correct choice for you. The best jobs for OCR are large conversions existing only in paper formats (such as converting the pages of a hardcover edition to memory for typesetting a paperback version).

Hardwiring

Hardwiring, of course, is connecting two machines together with cables (the hard wire). It is the ultimate direct interface. Any word processor or phototypesetter purchased today must be capable of hardwiring.

Rule: If you are looking for a word processor or a phototypesetter and find one that can't be hardwired, don't buy it. Any input or output device that cannot be hardwired was developed using very old technology. That technology is not worth purchasing at any price.

■ Parallel versus Serial Transmission

There are two types of hardwired communications: *serial* and *parallel.* In order to understand these possibilities, imagine a busy railroad yard. There are eight tracks; each is continually occupied. But this is a strange railroad. The eight tracks coming into the station converge into a single track going away from the station. Furthermore, as the station manager switches the trains onto the one available track, he does so at precise intervals. The space between trains is rigidly controlled.

Coming toward the station, the trains are taking the parallel route; several trains (or several bits of information) move at the same time on different tracks (see Figure 6-5). Going away from the station, the trains (information bits) are carried serially, on one track, with trains (or data) being pulsed out at exact intervals. If all was perfect with the world, eight tracks would be built to carry the trains out of the station as well as in, but that possibility is out of the question because of the expense involved.

The hardwire interface is typically a serial communication. One-way printer cables are usually parallel. Because a 16-track (eight tracks either way) parallel communication channel is very expensive, communications is serial, or one-track. But how does it work? The CPU of your word processor sends and understands signals on parallel tracks. To communicate, the parallel signals must be converted to serial. You need a compu-

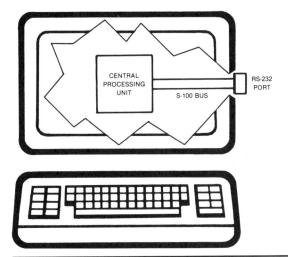

■ FIGURE 6-6. Cutaway view of a microcomputer, showing CPU, S-100 bus and RS-232 serial port.

terized equivalent of the railroad switching device, something that will merge eight tracks of information onto one track.

■ RS-232 Serial Port and S-100 Bus

The *RS-232* port is the switching device that moves eight tracks of information into one channel. But the RS-232 port does not do the job entirely. When hardwiring (and when telecommunicating as well), information is stored as magnetic data and moves through the computer when transmitted.

There is no magic to getting data memory from the CPU to the RS-232 port. The signal takes a bus—the *S-100 bus*—which is a standard of the industry. Originally developed in 1976 to be used in the 8080 microprocessor of the pioneering Altair microcomputer, the S-100 was standardized by the Institute of Electronic and Electrical Engineers (IEEE) to reduce problems of inconsistency in transmissions. Because the S-100 bus is also compatible with the Z80 microprocessor, it is used to move information on most micros.

The S-100 is a set of signal channels that carries data bits to and from the CPU (compare it to the tracks the trains follow on their routes). So the bus is a physical device; it is wire and pins. But, as a user, you never see the S-100 (see Figure 6-6). What you can see, and what you can physically use, is the RS-232 port.

The port is invariably located at the back of the microcomputer; it is equipped with 25 tiny pins. The RS-232 is the visible connector that allows information moved by the bus to be transmitted to other computerized devices. Each pin on the RS-232 plug does a specific job in the transmission. It is standard practice at this point to begin a lengthy discussion about pin 7, pins 4 and 5, and pin 3, but that job is best left to the technical manuals.

What is important to point out here is that the S-100 bus transports the

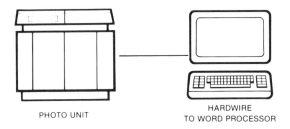

PHOTO UNIT

HARDWIRE
TO WORD PROCESSOR

■ **FIGURE 6-7. Hardwiring.**

data from the CPU to the RS-232 port. Along the way, the parallel signals are converted through the serial port. There are ports that allow parallel transmission, but the serial port is most common. Since both the sender and receiver must be on the same "wavelength" (either serial or parallel), it is usually best to be conservatively serial for telecommunications. If you hardwire in-house to your own devices, parallel transmission is a possibility. In this case, the RS-232 would be scrapped for a unit, such as the Potomac Micro-Magic modem, allowing parallel communications.

■ Communications Cables: Null Modem

The next step in establishing a hardwire interface is to actually send the information somewhere. Getting information to the port at the back of the computer is not enough. Your terminal just hums away while the CPU waits patiently to send data bits somewhere. What you need now is a track to get your messages across to your output device.

A *null modem* is your track. Null modems are cables equipped with an RS-232 connector on either end (see Figure 6-7). The CPU in your word processor sends serial data through an RS-232 plug connected to the cable. Information is transmitted through the cable, terminating with another RS-232 at the output end (the phototypesetter). If the typesetter has been programmed correctly to receive the serial data, you are interfacing successfully.

■ Hardwire Applications

Hardwire interfaces are by far the simplest to establish because the interface is always a controlled translation. The data are moved from one known type of machine to another known type of machine. There is no need to set up translations for dozens of different computers, because only two computers are involved.

The problems with hardwiring are significant. Most manufacturers recommend a maximum cable length of 125 feet (some, like Mergenthaler, suggest maximums as low as 25 feet). Maximum lengths are set because electronic signals deteriorate when pushed longer distances. Boosters can be purchased to move the signal farther, but there are no guarantees of accurate transmissions after boosting. Compugraphic claims that with line drivers and voltage amplifiers, a hardwire of "a couple of thousand feet" is possible.

This technique is clearly dedicated to in-house interfaces. If you can control a production situation and place a typesetter in close proximity to your word processor, the null modem track is suitable for you. Commercial applications are nearly nonexistent.

Telecommunications

If you have a telephone and a computer, the only other things you need in order to telecommunicate are a *modem* and *telecommunications software*. Telecommunications is burgeoning and shows no signs of diminishing. Every week or so somebody offers another telecommunications software package or hardware device. Telecommunications software and hardware sales are booming because telecommunications has two great advantages over other methods. It is the one universal interfacing method, and it is generally less expensive, both for the typesetter and the type customer.

For the type customer, the initial steps in establishing a telecommunications interface are, first, confirming that your word processor has an RS-232 port and serial communications program, and, second, purchasing a *modem* or *acoustic coupler*. These are the telephone devices that connect a computer to the type house. Acoustic couplers cost from $100 to $350; modems, which do not require a telephone, range in price from just over $200 to more than $1,000. Telecommunications software usually costs less than $500.

On the type house end, a modem or acoustic coupler will also be needed, along with a program board and communications program. For the type house, the software/hardware telecommunications package is more expensive. Price tags are from $2,000 up to about $6,000.

■ Translation Software

The reason for the relatively high software cost on the phototypesetter end of telecommunications is that this is where all the work is done. Somewhere between the CPU of the word processor and the CPU of the phototypesetter, a translation of word processing codes must be made. Technical codes such as line feeds, soft returns, and other keystrokes necessary to word processing but alien to typesetting must be eliminated. Simple characters must be translated correctly.

All of these functions, and many more, are the province of communications software. After being installed and fine tuned by type house personnel, the translation software, known as *translation tables*, does all the work. If all works well, the interface can be quick and immaculate. From data base typography and mainframe communications to brochures and newsletters, telecommunications is often the answer.

The most difficult task in the telecommunications interface is creating the translation tables. If you are a customer buying type, the tables that tell the typesetter's computer what your computer is talking about should be readily available from the type house. The typesetter will give you codes to use when inputting the copy to be interfaced. Given the correct translations, these codes will automatically be translated into the typesetting parameters needed to set the job as demanded.

The method chosen to build and use the tables governs the amount of savings possible. Those methods will be discussed in depth in Chapter 10, but savings can run from 10 to 50 percent. It is therefore important to understand *how* you will be telecommunicating. There is room for misunderstanding when it comes time to pay the type bills. If you are expecting (or promising) savings of 50 percent, you'll need to take steps to ensure that that promise is delivered.

■ Why Choose Telecommunications?

Telecommunications offers faster turnaround time, cheaper type, increased readability for jobs that are originally typewritten, aesthetic advantages of typesetting over typewriting, and slashed paper use costs. The price? When compared to benefits received, the costs of telecommunications are persuasively small.

Telecommunications is for almost everyone who uses typesetting. The break-even point can be very low when compared to other methods. *If you have a word processor and you regularly prepare jobs exceeding 16 pages in length, telecommunications probably makes sense.* Unlike other methods, the telephone interface does not require a specialized type of input or a tremendous investment in hardware.

Because of its relatively low investment requirement, nine out of ten customers should probably choose this method. The best test is to look at the other options. If none seems to be indispensable to your way of doing things, then telecommunications is the right choice. It is not accidental that 80 percent of the market will be interfacing in the 1990s. The telephone, that ordinary piece of machinery, is the vehicle that will carry us toward universal (or nearly universal) interfacing.

Choosing Equipment

■ Where Should the Type House Buy?

You will have to purchase some equipment and software. Choices for type houses are easier than for the customers. Because nearly every typesetting manufacturer offers communications packages for its own equipment, buying software and hardware from the same manufacturer usually makes sense, since it knows its own requirements. But just because a telecommunications package is available is no reason to buy it.

There are special features that some manufacturers offer that make their technology attractive. AM, for instance, has created an interface that allows bilateral communications. Documents can be sent from the word processor and then back again by the phototypesetter, creating a true conversational mode. The comparison chart in the *Data Book* furnishes the raw data on the available packages.

Another option for the type house is to overlook the typesetting manufacturer and buy hardware and software from a second vendor. Their packages tend to be more expensive but offer many features a typesetter may find valuable (see the *Data Book* comparisons).

Media conversion systems sold with telecommunications options are also sold by several companies. Competitors in the telecommunications software market include Antares, ADC, G. O. Graphics, Information Design, Intergraphics, Microtext, Phoenix, Shaftstall, and Telesystems. G. O. Graphics has produced more than 70 percent of the more than 10,000 telecommunications systems sold in the U.S. market.

■ Where Should the Type Customer Buy?

Type buyers also need to purchase basic hardware and software. Word processing and computer hardware folks don't offer software to run communications, so in some cases it will be necessary to find it. Fortunately, finding communications software is an easy task. Even more fortunate, some of the best programs are free and available from computer user groups. Unlike word processing software, communications programs are comparatively easy to write and write well.

There are programs, manufactured by software houses, that are not free. This software is usually inexpensive since it is competing with free software. One of the best is MITE, manufactured by Mycroft Labs and sold for $150. Free software is frequently not as well documented (or easy to use) as the licensed software offered for sale, so the price may well be worth paying, especially if you are a first-time interfacer. The software comparison charts in the *Data Book* give names, manufacturers, and features of some of the most popular programs.

In addition to software, a modem or acoustic coupler will have to be purchased. Many cognoscenti extol the virtues of the more expensive modems. Modems do offer faster transmission rates and are purportedly more dependable than acoustic couplers, but the latter are usually reliable.

Modems selling for more than $1,000 are smart machines that can automatically dial and do other dazzling things that will come in handy for large-scale users. If you do not intend to run up gargantuan phone bills by

	Equipment Prices	Typical Job	Ease	Customer's Savings	Breakeven Point
Indirect Methods					
Media conversion					
Black boxes	$6,000 to $25,000	Outdated	Very difficult	—	—
Programmable converters	$12,000 to $30,000	Large documents; over 100 pages	Moderate	Variable	Hundreds of pages
OCR	$30,000 to $100,000	Large documents	Difficult	Expensive input	Thousands of manuscript pages required
Direct Methods					
Hardwiring	Under $2,000	In-house documents; any length	Moderate	20 to 50% savings over commercial typesetting	$50,000 initial investment; minimum annual type budget: over $25K
Telecommunications	Under $5,000	Manuscripts of 10 pages or more	Simple	10 to 50% savings (possible)	As little as $500 of billed typesetting per month

■ FIGURE 6-8. Options: indirect and direct interfacing.

telecommunicating six hours a day, an acoustic coupler is a serviceable alternative. Even the slowest sends data at the rate of 300 baud (or 300 bits per second). At 10 bits per character, that's 30 characters per second, fast enough for most of us.

Beyond the basic hardware and software, you must invest some time in learning the translation codes supplied by the typesetter. If you are dealing with a wise typesetter, the codes will be logical alphanumerics, which are easily understood.

You must also learn something about typesetting and typography before keyboarding for typesetting output. Typesetting and word processing are similar in some ways but very different in critical areas. Terminology will not be the least of your problems when first preparing documents for interfacing. Appendix II gives a few quick lessons in type and typographic terminology.

The last major task for the type customer will be to find a typesetter that offers the service you require (see Figure 6-8). Who should you interface with? The *Data Book* offers a representative list of several hundred type houses prepared to set your interfaced documents. But, before you look at a directory of names, several questions still need to be answered, including basic prices to expect and how the translation tables really work. You'll also have to know something about the machines for sale on the typesetting market these days. These questions will be addressed in the next several chapters.

CHAPTER 7

Output Devices: The Typesetters

THE INTERFACING PROCESS IS NOT impeded by a lack of typesetting equipment. The hardware exists and it is easy to use. Given enough time and a strange sense of economic value, you could probably force even a well-worn linotype machine to produce metal letters from interfaced input. But there are good machines, and there are bad.

Output hardware can make the interface simple—or very complex. The type house interested in offering interfacing services may be best served by the purchase of new equipment.

For type buyers, it is important to discover a typesetting vendor that uses appropriate hardware. Typesetters attempting to interface using antiquated equipment cause problems both for themselves and their customers. In-house graphics facilities interfacing with internal word processors should also carefully scrutinize the capabilities of their present hardware.

The Market

Actually, there are several typesetting markets. Like word processors, phototypesetters are separated into subdivisions according to performance and price. The least expensive machines are the descendants of the first phototypesetters of the 1950s and 1960s.

Direct Entry Typesetters

Called *direct entry typesetters,* the Compugraphic ExecuWriter, the AM Comp/Set 500, and other members of this group lack memory capacity (see Figure 7-1). As lines are typed on the machine's keyboard, they are immediately typeset. Documents are not stored in memory.

It seems logical that some form of memory is necessary to interface. But if you are willing to use the typesetter as a slave printer, it is possible to send data and have them set directly. G. O. Graphics developed the CW/CI

■ **FIGURE 7-1. CompuWriter IV, direct entry phototypesetter. Photo courtesy Compugraphic Corporation.**

interface to be used with Compugraphic's CompuWriter series. The CW/CI feeds input to the CompuWriter, which is set immediately as it is received. The main limitation is the amount of photo paper that will move into the light-tight paper cassette during one interface session. There are several competitors to the CW/CI selling interfaces for less than $2,000.

The main drawback to direct entry typesetters is that technologically they are 15 years old. They are slow and unreliable, but they are very cheap. It's possible to buy a used typesetter of this vintage for $4,000 or even less. Interfacing to this class of machine will work, but there are faster and better ways.

By the 1970s, a second generation of typesetters was developed. Still called direct entry input, this class of machines also connected input and output in one device. But memory was added.

The storage device used in these intelligent standalones was invariably a diskette. Later machines of the 1980s separated input from output, creating the possibility of typesetting networks. But the advances of the 1970s—sharp cuts in prices, versatility, and ease of operation—have been the principal reasons for the explosion of in-house graphics in the late 1970s and 1980s.

The intelligence and adaptability of these second-generation typesetters have often made them the ideal choice for interfacing. There are several major manufacturers of standalones selling at between $15,000 and $30,000 (see the *Data Book* for comparisons of costs and features). Dominated by the big four—AM, Compugraphic, Itek, and Mergenthaler—the marketplace is spotted with manufacturers that positioned themselves in specific parts of the marketplace.

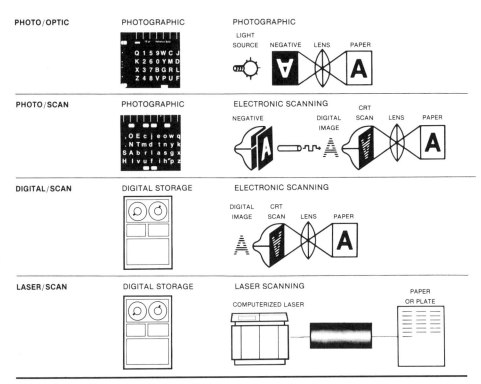

■ **FIGURE 7-2. Four ways to set phototype.**

Systems

Beyond direct entry, there are more output options. Basically, there are two types of "systems." The lower priced versions are standalones that have graduated to multiuser networks. Allowing an organization an extra two or three input stations is no small advantage, especially at prices of $5,000 or less for each terminal. When the photo unit (where the typesetting physically takes place) costs more than $20,000, it is easy to see that networks make sense if you need more than one input device.

In the early days of typesetting, the only way to set letters was with photo optics—light traveling through a negative letter exposed light-sensitive photo paper. Today, there are four ways (including photo optics) to set type photographically (see Figure 7-2). Photo scanning creates a master image on a scanning device that transfers the image into digital format. The digital image is then photographed onto paper. Digital-scanning typesetters have no master images. They hold patterns of letters in memory; when a letter is input, digital patterns are recalled and set as required. Even more remarkable are the laser typesetters. Laser type is a digital image that is usually burned, not photographed, on paper.

This new technology may be priced out of the range of in-house typesetters. But many type houses and newspapers have already bought laser typesetters. At speeds of up to 6,000 lines per minute, digital laser typesetters are far faster than any in-house operation would require.

■ Super Systems

The second type of system is the super network known as the *front-end system*. Often priced at more than $250,000, these phototype systems are affordable only to type houses and major type users. Bedford, Penta, Autologic, and CCI are some of the front-end manufacturers that supply hardware and software to newspapers and magazines (see Figure 7-3). Front ends autopaginate, meaning that pages are set *exactly* as they will appear in printed form, including headers, footers, page numbers, and headlines. Customers can be certain these systems are capable of moving your jobs over the phone.

The Machines

While shopping for a machine with which to interface, the names you will encounter at the low end of the market include AM, Compugraphic, Mergenthaler, and Itek. The more expensive multiuser systems offered by Alphatype, Berthold, and CCI are the beginnings of a trend that leads to the very expensive Bedford and Penta front ends. From 1982 through 1986, sales of the autopaginating front ends will exceed $1.1 billion on the U.S. market alone. If upgrading hasn't occurred already, your typesetter will be upgrading to a front-end system soon.

But that's not where most interfacers are. Except for the dumb stand-

■ **FIGURE 7-3. CCI 400 phototypesetting system. Photo courtesy Computer Composition International.**

alones, interfacing is everywhere. An overview of what's available is a synopsis of output possibilities.

■ Mergenthaler

After Gutenberg, Mergenthaler is the oldest name in typesetting. Founded in 1886 to market the linecasting typesetter invented by Ottmar Mergenthaler, this company is well known for selling the typographic right stuff. Printers and typesetters favor Mergenthaler equipment for its dependability, quality, and precision engineering. They tend to be expensive machines that are worth the price if you need a machine that's trustworthy under the rigors of heavy production loads.

But, like its competitors, Mergenthaler sells several machines for various markets, including relatively low-priced standalones. For years, the VIP was the standard throughout the industry. The Linotron series has also been a best-seller. Several new members of the Mergenthaler family may become the new standards.

CRTronic. A first for Mergenthaler, the CRTronic is a standalone unit that can also serve as the output hub of a minisystem. The least expensive version of this series is the CRTronic 100, priced at $20,000. With a Linotype Communications Interface (LCI) bringing the total bill up another $4,000, the CRTronic is aimed at the small printer and quick-print shop markets, not the type houses. A member of the new generation of inexpensive digital-scanning typesetters, the CRTronic may proliferate in the 1980s. Scanning priced at $20,000 was just a dream in 1982. By the end of the decade, prices may come down even further.

For interfacing, the CRTronic is equipped to understand both the standard ASCII and EBCDIC code sets. It can either read documents directly onto the terminal screen or send them directly onto disk for typesetting later. In other words, this is a typical standalone in today's market. But you won't find it at a type house. For $24,000, you can't buy a machine with the terrific speed required by professional typographers.

Linotron and Linoterm. The Linotron and the Linoterm are the descendants of the VIP. In the strict sense, these are the true output units. Type houses have a choice of buying several units like the CRTronic, or buying a Linotron or Linoterm photo unit and then interfacing typesetting terminals to that photo unit. For most typesetting companies, power and speed sway the balance in favor of the Linotron or Linoterm. If a type house is equipped with a front end, these photo units serve as the "back end," typesetting copy as commanded by the front-end computer.

Combined with MVP/2 terminals supplied by Mergenthaler, the Linotron and Linoterm units serve a variety of needs. The Linotron 101, for instance, is capable of speeds of about 30 to 125 lines per minute, depending on the quality of type expected. The Linotron 606 sets up to 3,000 newspaper lines per minute (see Figure 7-4).

Because the type is not photographed through negatives, these typesetters (and most competitive machines) are capable of setting a variety of type sizes. The Linotron 101 sets type from 4½ to 127 point in ½ point

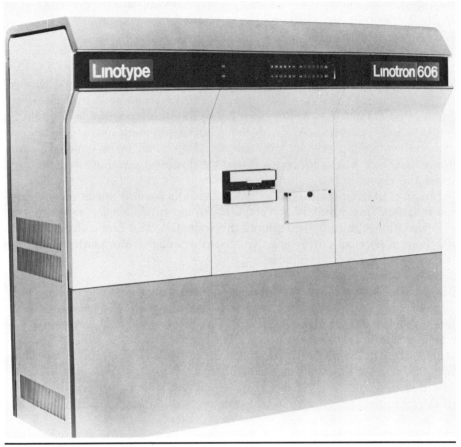

■ **FIGURE 7-4. Linotron 606 photo unit. Photo courtesy Mergenthaler Corporation.**

increments (see glossary). The components of these new digitals can lead to expert typography when used by professionals.

Omnitech 2000. The Omnitech 2000 signaled the beginning of the communications transition for Mergenthaler. Back in 1981, the Omnitech was outfitted with the WPI, a $4,950 package developed by George Smith of G. O. Graphics. G. O. Graphics created telecommunications boards for Mergenthaler, Compugraphic, and AM early on in the interfacing race and then later moved on to other typesetting companies. Nearly 70 percent of all telecommunicating typesetting machines are outfitted with G. O.-developed equipment (Shaftstall has another 25 percent, and the remaining 5 percent is divided among several smaller companies). G. O.'s fertility turned out to be a good thing for telecommunicators. Since the same "Silicon Alley" company created interfaces for the three largest direct input typesetting manufacturers, interfacing to those machines tends to be similar.

The Omnitech is capable of outputting to photo paper, dry-processed paper, film, or even paper printing plates. It sells for about $30,000. Billed as the first fifth-generation typesetter, it is aimed at the heavy production printer. Omnitechs won't be found in many in-house shops because of the higher price, but organizations with heavy and varying work loads will consider the Omnitech because of a long list of tempting features: inexpensive paper, 246 available sizes of type, vertical and horizontal ruling, slanted type versions, expanded and condensed variations, and reverse video (setting black on white or white type on black background). That may be a glimpse of what typesetters will be like by the late 1980s.

■ Compugraphic

Compugraphic (CG) is the workingman's typesetter. Usually less expensive than Mergenthaler, Compugraphic equipment populates the service type shops at small- to medium-sized printers, advertising agencies, in-house graphics facilities, and educational institutions. For those on a restricted budget, Compugraphic is often the choice. If you're outfitted with Compugraphics, you're in very good company.

In spite of the lower price tag, Compugraphic does produce quality equipment. The reason for Compugraphic's success lies in its ability to cut corners, enabling the company to sell its machines for less.

Early on, Compugraphic cut one corner by offering its own versions of popular typefaces. By executing its own but very similar designs and calling them Helios instead of Helvetica, Oracle instead of Optima, or English Times instead of Times Roman, CG saved the customer the cost of paying royalty fees to the type designer. With a royalty fee of $125 per typeface, a type house that bought 50 faces saved more than $6,000 by buying CG. Compugraphic, however, earned the enmity of many typographers, who bemoaned the butchering of their beautiful typefaces. Recently, Compugraphic began to offer typefaces in their original stylizations (complete with royalty fee), but there is still some lingering bad feelings among many typesetters.

But Compugraphic revolutionized typesetting and, more than any other company, created the impetus toward both in-house and interfacing. Compugraphic sells dependability at a good price.

EditWriter and ICI. In the 1970s, the EditWriters took the typesetting world by storm. In-house graphics shops were buying standalone typesetters when they should have kept paying for type. The 7500 and 7700 EditWriters were the classic standalone: A keyboard and CRT were directly connected to disk drives for storage and photo unit for output—a complete typesetting system in one package.

Two months into the 1980s, Compugraphic pulled off another coup by announcing a computer board called the Intelligent Communications Interface (ICI). The ICI was developed by G. O. Graphics for the EditWriters (Figure 7-5). Interfaces were established between the EditWriter and nearly 150 different computers within a year. In that first year, after the first ICI made its debut, more than 700 were sold, mostly as retrofits, for $5,000. That compares with the roughly 150 WordCom/CompuWriter interfaces sold from 1978 to 1981.

In the early years, Compugraphic was still able to keep track of what was going on with ICI interfacing. Two-thirds of the interfaces were with

■ FIGURE 7-5. EditWriter, perhaps the most popular standalone phototypesetter ever made. Photo courtesy Compugraphic Corporation.

word processors, one-third with computers. Wang topped the list of word processors, with nearly a quarter of all WP interfaces. But the most interesting result was the breakdown of computer interfaces: 73 percent minicomputers, 18 percent mainframes, and only 9 percent micros. Things have changed. The micros take the biggest share of the pie these days.

Computer Assistance Center (CAC). With every ICI computer board came an 800 number, a direct line to CAC. If users had a problem interfacing, they could get assistance by calling the Assistance Center. Using a telephone modem, a problem would be sent to the center over the phone. Experts on the receiving end looked at the problem as it was received.

The Computer Assistance Center (the name was later changed to Communications Assistance Center) equipped itself with Lanier, Xerox, IBM, Wang, Vydec, and several other word processors, all surrounded by an EditWriter. Each problem was handled individually, using the caller's specific word processor. The CAC offered solutions to tough problems, particularly for the first-time interfacer. Staffed with experienced veterans in computerization and word processing, the CAC went a long way toward establishing Compugraphic as a leader in interfacing support.

Modular Composition System (MCS). The EditWriter works best as it was designed, as a standalone with an independent terminal. Recognizing that the EditWriter could not reach the typesetting speeds necessary to support three or four terminals, Compugraphic has produced several photo unit/terminal combinations. From the ACM 9000 through the Trendsetter and Unisetter, CG has moved from a direct entry device reading paper tape to a second-generation typesetter.

The newest CG network is the Modular Composition System (MCS). Directly competitive with Mergenthaler's CRTronic, the MCS is built around a digital typesetter that sells for under $25,000.

Flexibility is the key to MCS. Its options include a computer printer for cheap proofs; a preview screen that allows you to view pages on screen before they are set on paper; and a 5-megabyte rigid disk drive. Pushing the modular concept to the limit, Compugraphic has created a system that begins at $20,000 but can go through the roof. The key is to buy what you need.

MCS also offers the Advanced Communications Interface (ACI) for those interested in "two-way links with the expanding world of office automation." The ACI Transmit option allows for talking both ways: sender to receiver and receiver to sender. At $5,000, the ACI is selling well. More than 40 percent of all MCS systems are being sold with the ACI included.

For type buyers, those sales figures mean that type houses will be full of ACI devices. For those going in-house, the MCS is an alternative; expandability is the key selling point. Because of the many options in photo units, number of keyboards, and additional disk drives, you can spend as much as you can afford. But your initial investment can be less than $30,000.

Personal Composition System (PCS). The latest CG system is the Personal Composition System. *The PCS is an interface.* An MCS photo unit is connected to an Apple Lisa microcomputer. PCS combines a futuristic input device (the Lisa) with a built-in interface to a state-of-the-art digital typesetter (Figure 7-6).

If the Lisa is as easy a device to use as its proponents say, input for typesetting becomes easier than ever before. The price for that simplicity is a $10,000 input station. But input isn't just galleys of bone dry paragraphs anymore. Charts, spreadsheets, and business graphics are all typeset as created on screen.

The PCS is built around the interface in a novel way. If PCS makes it, interfacing won't be an option; it will be built into typesetting. This may be a glimpse at postmodern typesetting, interfacing's second wave. At this time in the 1980s, typesetting in the 1990s looks like microcomputers for input, photo units as output. Dumb slave typesetting terminals may be universally scrapped for smart micros.

PCS is a package that may be ahead of its time. But it certainly is a peek at what typesetting may become.

■ Itek

In 1977, Itek made some news that not too many people were listening to—the DCI, Data Communications Interface, was introduced. This was a true pioneer, one of the first commercial interfaces available for *any* typesetter.

■ FIGURE 7-6. The PCS: Apple Lisa as word processing input to a Compugraphic photo unit. Photo courtesy Compugraphic Corporation.

Quadritek. The Quadritek typesetter manufactured by Itek could be upgraded with the Data Communications Interface. DCI filled a gap for hundreds of Itek users. In 1977, the ability to telecommunicate was revolutionary.

Changes in interfacing devices have followed pace with changes in microcomputers since 1977. The DCI offers translation tables limited to a maximum of 30 translations—a very small number for any complicated job. At a maximum speed of 50 lines per minute, the 1200, 1400, and 1600 series of typesetters aren't fast enough for professional type houses or even most newspapers. The CPS 100, Pagitek, Minitek, and Visitek are among the Itek products for those markets. The standalone Quadritek sells to that large pool of in-house organizations dedicated to self-reliance.

The first in line with a telecommunications package, Itek moved toward media conversion in the 1980s. At $11,500 and $800 per Translator Program, the Itek Converter isn't one of the cheapest media converters. The Converter was introduced in 1983, the same year as the Personal Composition System. Compugraphic and Itek are two companies going in different technological directions.

Mark IX and CPS 1000. These Itek machines are typical newspaper typesetting systems. At 600 lines per minute, the Mark IX photo unit is the heart of several systems specifically designed with newspaper production in mind. The telecommunications package allows for communication links between remote news bureaus and a central office. The CPS 1000 is capable of moving data back and forth to cable television networks and satellites; it will certainly accept information from a micro or word processor.

■ AM Varityper

AM Varityper has long been known as the most economical typesetting option. A Comp/Set 510-II, a basic beginner's machine with no frills, sells for less than $15,000. AM makes more direct entry options than any other manufacturer. Terminals include the 4800, the 5404, the 5414, the 5618, and the 5618 with Image Previewer. Standalone phototypesetters include the 500, the 510, the 510-II, the 3510, the 4510, the 5310, the 5410, the 5810, the 5900, the 6300, and the 6400. Most of the standalones can be used with several terminals to create systems.

AM sells in the same market as Compugraphic. Strategically marketed toward the publications and in-house markets, AM machines are not usually seen in major type production shops. But they are inexpensive and that suits them for mass consumption.

If you describe one AM machine, you more or less describe them all. An important fact unites the entire product line: They all communicate.

The AM interfacing option is called the Telecom. It's actually two different devices, one designed for the Comp/Edit series and a second for the Comp/Sets. If you are buying to fit your own in-house needs, the Comp/Set is probably the choice—they are less expensive and slower than the Comp/Edits. If you are about to interface to an outside vendor, the Comp/Edit will be the machine you are most likely to run into.

Telecom. AM's Comp/Edit Telecom boards sell for $1,995, half the price of the Mergenthaler or Compugraphic version. The Telecom was the first commercially available interface that allowed users to *send and receive* documents from a typesetter.

In 1981, this feature made for real communications. If a typesetter received copy that later required editing, changes could be made at the typesetting end on the VDT. Copy was then telecommunicated back to the customer for on-screen proofing. While idle as a typesetter, the terminal could be used for word processing input. If you had a minicomputer, the typesetter could also be made to emulate a typical programming terminal.

By 1984, AM had lost that advantage. Every major typesetting terminal can now be equipped with CP/M, meaning that typesetting terminals aren't dedicated terminals anymore. With appropriate software, they can be used for anything.

A major disadvantage of standard Telecom, for some type houses, is that the board as designed supports only *asynchronous* transmissions. IBM sends its data in *synchronous* mode (more on the differences between synch, often called *TTY*, and asynch later). Typesetters interested in interfacing with IBM word processors must purchase the Expander Box option for an extra $1,495. Even with the add-on, the price for the fully equipped Comp/Edit Telecom is under $3,500.

■ The Rest of the Field

By 1983, every typesetting manufacturer was offering interfacing; it had become a necessity. There are dozens of excellent typesetting packages available.

Alphatype produces an interface that permits Xerox 800 word processors to be used as satellite keyboards; you can also purchase the AlphaKey Systems Interface for telecommunications with translation tables. Autologic was the second manufacturer to market an ICI. Its version is more powerful that Compugraphic's and is used with the APS-5 and Micro 5 systems. Expensive autopagination systems for newspapers and publication offices are well worth the price if you need speed, especially at an overdrive of 4,000 lines per minute.

CCI's TypeLink uses hardwiring to create networks of word processing terminals for input to the CCI 400. EE Text and Electronic Information Technology, both hunting the newspaper market trails, offer telecommunications through the UPT and EIT translation table options. Quadex goes two ways. By selling a media converter specifically designed to convert 3M and Digital diskettes into Quadex media, Quadex is pushing hard in a small area of a very segmented market. But the shotgun approach is still being used with the Communications Option, an all-purpose telecommunications program.

There are more interfaces available from independent vendors, including Antares, Applied Data, Xitron, Telesystems Network, Burroughs, Graphic Products, Shaftstall, Kurzweil, and more. There's no telling what you'll be talking with these days.

The Choices: Which Should You Buy?

Whether you are looking for a type house with which to interface, are a typesetter upgrading to interface technology, or run an in-house shop, interfacing technology is mature and safe. Some options are more expensive, and some work better or more easily than others—but they all work.

How should customers decide which typesetter to use? First, make the in-house-or-out decision. The machines populating in-house graphics shops are not the industrial-strength typesetters you'll find at a professional type house. Once you've made this decision, you can move on to the output decision.

■ For In-House Only

First, determine how large your need is. A rule of thumb: Don't spend more than 40 percent of your annual typesetting budget on a typesetter. If you are spending $100,000 per year on typesetting, you might need the speed offered by a $40,000 typesetter. But you don't need a $75,000 type-setter to produce type valued at $75,000 a year. A machine that's priced in the $30,000 range will do nicely.

Most in-house shops should buy in the $15,000 to $30,000 price range, a market dominated by standalones. Do you need the quality of a Mergen-thaler? What sort of interfacing option will you require? Compugraphic and AM will fit the bill if you decide against Mergenthaler. The Bedford and Penta super systems should be considered only if you are spending hundreds of thousands of dollars on type—they are getting more inexpensive, but they are still best reserved to the sophisticated type house.

How good is the service from different manufacturers? Ask around before you buy. Service is handled by regional offices, and you may be in a particularly good or bad area for one of the major manufacturers.

If you have type professionals already on staff, ask them for suggestions. Ask your current typesetting vendor as well. If everyone around you has machines made by the same company, the professional pool in your area will be heavily influenced by that training. Learning a new typesetter can be like driving an automatic transmission after using manuals all your life. It works, but somehow you always prefer that old standard.

■ For Type House Customers Only

Answers for type house customers are simple. Look in the *Data Book* and find someone in your area who interfaces. Buying type locally can be important because telecommunications long-distance rates can add significant amounts to your total typesetting bill. Of course, if the typesetter is paying the bills (perhaps through a toll-free number), your geographic considerations are less restrictive. But it's still comforting to have good technological advice close by. Stick to the neighborhood if you're a new-comer to interfacing.

Any type house that can interface is technologically alive. Look for a type house with a Mergenthaler, Penta, Bedford, Autologic, Alphatype, or any other well-known system, and you won't have problems.

CHAPTER 8

In-House Typesetting

TYPESETTING AS OUTPUT IS THE GOAL of interfacing. There are two ways to achieve it. Type buyers can pay a type house or printer to produce galleys, or they can set the type in their own production department in-house. The latter alternative is becoming increasingly popular as lower prices make equipment purchases both more affordable and more attractive.

As well as assessing *what* typesetting machine to use, a look at *where* your type should be set is in order. Examining the ways of in-house typesetting is an education in the printing process. Understanding that process will be necessary whatever your output decision is.

Do You Want It, and Is It Worth It?

Before confronting any process, it is necessary to gauge your own intentions for an in-house shop. How far are you willing to take the shop? An internal discussion may quickly lead you to determine that in-house is not for you. Keep in mind that even when you decide to forego in-house, you can still save cash with the interface to outside vendors.

In-house is, quite simply, not an asset for the smaller organization. Refer to Figure 3-4, which gives a cost estimate for the first year. It is not inexpensive. If your annual type output is budgeted at less than $25,000, return on investment will take longer than two years, and the in-house shop may not make economic sense.

In deciding just how much of the printing work flow should be moved to the company graphics shop, the best advice is to start small. At most, only typesetting production and mechanical preparation should be transferred initially, although some organizations bite the bullet and actually begin printing their own material immediately.

Three Organizational Concerns

If you are to run a successful in-house shop, three organizational concerns must be addressed early on: the physical plant, personnel, and traffic control.

1. *Physical Plant.* The physical plant necessary for the in-house shop must be prepared and be available. The ideal location permits easy access for your editorial managers but is also removed from heavy traffic areas. If you anticipate possible growth of the shop, plan ahead for expansion. Reinstallation of phototypesetting equipment can be expensive.

   Your facility should be located no more than 125 feet from your word processor. Hardwiring is the easiest and cheapest method of interfacing. If that distance is impossible, you will have to use boosters or telecommunications, both of which are more cumbersome and more expensive than standard hardwiring.

   The site should be a well-lit room with windows and no carpeting, which can create static electricity that scrambles magnetic memory. There are sprays and antistatic rugs available, but prevention works best. Some form of ventilation is also necessary because phototypesetting papers are processed with photographic chemistry. Although the current generation of phototypesetters does *not* require special darkroom conditions, the chemicals can become a problem in a poorly ventilated area.

   When computing necessary space, allow for a large drafting table to produce mechanicals. A worktable and desk will also be necessary. An area of roughly 250 to 300 square feet is an environmental necessity.

2. *Personnel.* Your second concern is an issue that is tempting to avoid. Typesetting is a craft that is not picked up by operators in two or three casual training sessions. Union apprentices (not all typesetters are members of a union) serve three-year apprenticeships before becoming journeymen. Although it is conceivable that a bright keyboard specialist with no prior training in typesetting could master a phototypesetting machine after a few months, you don't have a few months to wait.

   Line length, fonts, leading, point size, em spaces, and bullets (see glossary) are just a few of the phrases that are second nature to a typesetter but totally foreign to a word processor. No matter what the phototype salesperson says, there are no quick and easy ways word processing personnel can learn how to mold pages, correctly determine type sizes, and use different typefaces properly. They can be trained to keyboard for effective transmission to the typesetter, but you will need at least one typesetting professional who understands phototypesetting and the art of typography.

   If you choose to do your own mechanicals, check with the art schools and community colleges in your area to find potential employees. A recent graduate with a degree from an accredited program in printing technology, advertising design, or graphic arts will be able to do crisp, clean paste-ups. You can save money doing your own paste-ups. Printer and ad agency paste-up charges range (depending largely on your geographic area) from $3 to $12 per page; a competent mechanical artist will do three to four simple pages per hour.

   Hiring additional personnel creates more expenses. Benefits such as medical plans, social security, unemployment taxes, retirement

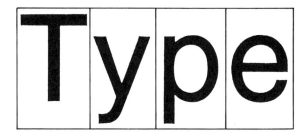

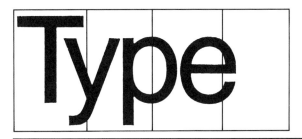

■ **FIGURE 8-1. Display type: phototypesetting output (top) vs. photo display output (bottom).**

benefits, and workers' compensation can add as much as a third to the total salary of your new employees. That's more overhead.

3. *Traffic Control.* The last important internal concern is trafficking production. The system you create can make this the worst of headaches or no problem at all. Decide which jobs will comprise a pilot program.

Be certain to appoint or hire an individual to be a traffic manager. For small operations, the typesetter can double as traffic manager. If you have a large-volume shop, setting several monthly periodicals, you will need one person *solely* for traffic.

Make this a muscle position. "Free" jobs, such as unimportant forms, signs, business cards, memos, and note pads, will all be marked "Rush!" once typesetting capability has been established. Unless the production manager has the clout to refuse or delay these jobs, you will have a deadline nightmare on your hands.

Dollar Costs

How much will it cost in real dollars? Your cash flow will be affected in three areas: equipment, personnel, and printing rates.

1. *Equipment.* Equipment is the biggest item. There are no cut rates for communicating phototypesetters. You should expect to pay at least $20,000 for a machine that can output through an interface from your word processor. If you are using quality display type, you also need a photo display machine. They are not as expensive as their intelligent cousins, but they are capable of producing the quality headlines that phototypesetters cannot create (see Figure 8-1). Photo display units cost between $3,500 and $5,000. A good supply of body and display type fonts (the negative master images through which light exposes the photo paper) will add another $2,000 to the bill.

Latent phototypeset material must be processed to create images. There are two grades of processors. "S" grade (stabilization) paper requires an $800 processor, but the type fades after about two months. "RC" (rapid contrast) processors cost approximately $3,500, and the paper lasts indefinitely. S and RC papers are usually purchased in 150-foot rolls; 8-inch wide paper costs about $45 per roll. Paper can also be purchased in 2-inch, 4-inch, 6-inch, and 12-inch wide rolls; costs are proportionate.

Light tables or drafting tables for mechanicals top out at about $750. Cheaper versions that are sturdy enough for short-term work can be purchased for $250. A serviceable waxer for applying wax that adheres type to mechanical boards costs about $250 (the cheaper hand waxers are slower, more difficult to use, and messier). Last, two very good chairs for your typesetter and mechanical artist add another $400. An artist's lamp, straightedge, paste-up accessories, phototypesetting chemistry, and lettering sheets are all necessary. The costs of phototypesetters, like all computerized equipment, are headed downward. Graphic arts supplies, on the other hand, are seldom inexpensive.

You may also be considering a darkroom. A graphics camera facility will require a fan, red lights, sink, processing trays, dryer, processor for diffusion transfer prints, film, paper, and chemistry. Prices start at $4,000 and climb to well over $15,000. You will also need trained personnel to operate the equipment.

2. *Personnel.* Salaries can vary by as much as 100 percent, depending on where you are. Typesetters in Dubuque, Iowa, don't make as much as their counterparts in New York City. Wherever you are, typesetting is a craft that cannot be bought cheaply.

Estimate a minimum of $14,000 per year (in 1984 dollars) for the professional typesetter who can double as traffic manager, *if* you are not in a large city. Check the "Help Wanted" section of your local newspaper under "Typesetter," "Graphic Arts," and "Printing." A person who is experienced in interfacing and is knowledgeable about computerization can cost much more than $14,000. A recent ad in a trade journal offered salaries of up to $40,000 for experts in typesetting research and development.

Doing mechanicals is almost invariably an entry-level position for most graphic artists, so allot $9,000 per year for a paste-up artist. Benefits and taxes will increase your employee costs by as much as one-third.

3. *Printing Rates.* Your decision to go the in-house route will definitely affect your printing bills.

In printing, bulk rates often apply. One customer will be charged more or less than another customer, for the same job, based on how much work is being done for the two clients. If you go in-house but wish to maintain ties with your printer, you will lose your favored position with the printer.

Job	Cost before In-House	Cost after In-House	Anticipated Savings	Actual Savings (or actual deficit)	Shortfall
Typesetting	$ 1,000	$ 0	$ 1,000	$ 1,000	$ 0
Mechanicals	300	0	300	300	0
Negatives	700	950	0	-250	250
Stripping	200	200	0		0
Platemaking	450	550	0	-100	100
Presswork	1,200	1,350	0	-150	150
Totals	$ 3,850	$3,050	$1,300	$ 800	$ 500

■ **FIGURE 8-2. An example of piecemeal estimating: estimated savings vs. actual savings.**

Because the printer receives only a piece of the job—negative making, stripping, platemaking, and presswork—instead of the whole job, your costs will be higher (see Figure 8-2). Those costs must be expected and included in your operating budgets.

Other Organizational Costs

So much for the out-of-pocket costs. But now there are other management concerns. You will have to purchase a machine. Research is necessary in order to make an intelligent decision. The time and energy required to look over the market is an unquantifiable—but nevertheless real—cost.

The in-house decision will cost a minimum of $50,000 the first year. It will also cause bureaucratic and personnel problems. The benefits you receive must certainly outweigh those concerns before you make the decision to go in-house.

Vendor Problems. Machines will break down. Equipment service agreement will have to be paid. *Downtime* becomes your worry and not the typesetter's. Vendors for film, paper, and other supplies will have to be contacted. Credit agreements with suppliers need to be established. Some vendors will not supply as quickly as needed. The combination of a new technology and new contacts can make for unpleasant days and nights.

Supervisory Problems. In addition to the monetary costs incurred when you hire employees, new problems will have to be solved. New interpersonal flare-ups are possible. You may have to deal with a typesetter's union for the first time. Keeping everyone happy during a period of technological change can be a challenge.

Four Benefits of In-House Graphics Shops

Excellent reasons for new technology are usually readily apparent or nonexistent. Here are four benefits of establishing your own graphics shop.

1. *Lower Production Costs.* As typesetting and production costs in general rise in the graphic arts, do-it-yourself options become more and more attractive. Type houses are being confronted with escalating labor, supplies, and borrowing costs. As they pass costs on to customers, prices rise. One way for any organization to combat that spiral is to become its own supplier of phototype. For a type user spending more than $100,000 per year on typesetting, it's possible to save $25,000 or more the first year, *after* paying for installation costs and salaries.

2. *Selling In-House Typesetting.* Another way to combat higher costs is to sell your in-house typesetting. Many in-house shops do contract work for other agencies. If you have leased a typesetting machine, you're paying for it 24 hours a day. During lull periods, you can utilize the equipment by producing type to be sold to your own customers. Getting into the typesetting business, of course, should not be done without due consideration.

3. *Control.* Organizations that are very concerned with fast turnaround and quality work have also joined the independent typesetting movement. Design control and perfect typography are important considerations. If you can't afford professional display type charges of a dollar or more per letter, in-house may be the answer. The quality of your current typesetting may not be good enough. It might also be too good. It makes little sense to pay type house prices for work that any competent in-house shop could do.

4. *Turnaround.* For many companies, a quick turnaround is crucial. If you have an in-house shop, you have the ability to rush important jobs through the shop in an emergency. Your printer is probably not geared to deal with your rush jobs; he has his own schedules to meet. In response to a customer's unreasonable deadlines, most printers implicitly accept the loss of your work by charging you very high prices.

   If you have your own production facility, *your* employees handle *your* rush jobs. It may cost you overtime, and some other jobs may be late, but the capability for quick turnaround is worth the price of in-house for some companies.

   This capacity can be abused. An in-house department that is flooded with "rush" jobs from six different departments will quickly become an organizational madhouse. Shoddy or late work will be done. Again, to avoid potential disasters, your production manager must have enough clout to enforce schedules and keep emergencies down to a minimum.

Checklist: Guidelines for a Smooth Transition

✔ Check to see that your current typesetting costs are reasonable. If you are simply being overcharged for type, another vendor (and not in-house) may be your answer.

✔ Make *absolutely certain* that your equipment and personnel can meet your present and anticipated needs. If you are doing six-level equations, a typesetting machine may cost as much as $50,000. You may be better off staying with a type house.

✔ You must have the cash flow necessary to carry off what you are planning.

✔ Remember to account for piecemeal estimating—higher printing rates when your printer receives only part of your job.

✔ If you don't know enough about graphics equipment to buy equipment intelligently, seek the expert guidance of either a consultant or employee. Your current printer may be willing to help you make a decision. If not, a consultant's fee can save you from making purchasing errors.

✔ Tell your current printer or typesetter what you are doing. Apprise the type house of your timetable for moving in-house so that it will know when to expect the loss of your work and will be able to substitute other customers. Keeping the relationship open and professional will help when you need advice.

✔ Carefully screen hardware manufacturers when you submit your Request for Proposals. To prevent after-purchase grief, you must get straight answers to questions about delivery date, service maintenance agreements, service and parts support, necessary peripheral equipment, machine features and capabilities, and installation requirements. The list of questions for equipment purchase and/or rental at the end of this chapter can be used as a fine-screen filter before purchasing equipment.

✔ Educate your current personnel. Be sure to reinforce the realization that the graphics shop is not for personal letterheads and Christmas cards. The facility must be used intelligently, especially in the first few weeks.

✔ Hire people who are demonstrably competent. Ask to see portfolios of completed work.

✔ Make a list of priority jobs. Give your traffic or production manager the corporate strength to enforce your decisions.

✔ Have your employees keep track of the time and supplies needed for each project. Bill back materials, equipment, time, and labor to the budgets of the appropriate departments. Periodically check the trail of billings to determine which departments are overusing or misusing graphics capabilities.

✔ Allow corporate department heads to use (or not use) your graphics shop for specific jobs. If the estimated billback is greater than the estimate of an outside vendor, don't use the in-house shop! This "competition" will serve as the best governor of in-house costs.

Strong organizations will do well to look at in-house as another source of organizational strength. Like all expansions, the in-house production shop will require careful management, a healthy cash flow, and resolute trafficking of the work flow.

In-house expansion is best done by a mature, well-organized staff that is goal-oriented and is willing to make tough decisions. Importing technology does not automatically make it easier for a weak organization to survive. If you are operating in the red now, in-house won't be the miracle that will push you immediately onto the plus side of the balance sheet. There are heavy start-up costs.

Questions for Equipment Purchase and/or Rental

If all things point to going in-house, and you are considering the purchase of equipment, here is a list of questions and requirements you'd do well to pose to every vendor whose equipment seems to fit your requirements (see the *Data Book* for a list of typesetting equipment vendors). The answers you receive may save a great deal of disappointment after purchase. The list was developed by Linda Strub Stazer, Graphic Design Department, Pfizer, Inc., in New York City.

1. List the equipment recommended to meet your specifications, including the FOB location, terms, and conditions. Please quote any options available that you think we may be interested in purchasing.

2. What is the approximate delivery date of all equipment relative to the receipt of a binding order?

3. List all lease and/or rental arrangements for the above equipment.

4. Enclose a copy of your service maintenance agreement, including the cost for an annual service maintenance contract on the recommended equipment.
   a. List the number of people within a 100-mile radius who are trained to repair the recommended equipment.
   b. Give the number of similar systems installed within the 100-mile area.
   c. List the location from which parts must be drawn to repair the recommended equipment.
   d. Give the approximate time required to draw such parts from repair location.
   e. Describe what is covered under the preventive maintenance visits and their frequency.
   f. Indicate the average response time to a service repair call.
   g. List the hours during which repair services are available.

5. Describe any additional items that may be required in order to make this system completely operational.

6. Describe the training provided by you for our personnel, including the length of initial training and a description of all training and application manuals. Please note any telephone hot-line training "advice" that may be available.

7. Describe any additional support you provide for this system.

8. List the names, addresses, and telephone numbers of all customers within a 100-mile area who have this equipment. Include a contact at these firms.

9. Give specifications (by piece of equipment), including the dimensions, weight, electrical requirements, Btu output, static sensitivity, any specialized plugs required, and whether the equipment requires a dedicated line.

10. Enclose a sample of material output on the unit recommended.

11. List the point sizes available on the output unit, including the method of achieving those point sizes.

12. How many faces remain on line at any given time?

13. Describe any reprogramming or mechanical operations required for font changes.

14. Describe the hyphenation and justification logic used by the recommended equipment.

15. List the rated speed of the output unit.

16. Describe the method of mixing sizes and styles of type, both inter- and intraline.

17. Describe the range of leading available, including the incremental values.

18. Describe reverse leading on the recommended equipment.

19. Indicate any backup systems to the one recommended that are available within a 100-mile area.

20. Give the number of lines of type visible on the screen at any one time.

21. Describe editing on the system. Describe the coding structures for specialized functions, such as point size, leading, and line length.

22. How many (maximum) input stations can be attached to the system?

23. How many (maximum) output units can be attached to the system? Name all capable of currently being attached.

24. State the minimum and maximum distances the input units may be from the output unit.

25. State any restrictions to this cabling (for example, cable must be always available to service personnel, cannot be buried in wall or ceiling, cannot be near electrical or telephone wires).

26. Describe the product of the photo unit. List the types of material available as output. Does it require special processing? Describe such processing and the equipment needed to produce it.

27. If a processor is to be purchased, will it require plumbing, and if it requires plumbing, will that plumbing require a temperature mixing valve and filtering system?

28. Describe all supplies and their prices that would be required for the operation of the recommended system.

CHAPTER 9

Establishing Telecommunications

YOUR WORD PROCESSOR IS WORKING smoothly; you are editing, revising, and moving text. Now to the important next step: How do you make that word processor cut your typesetting costs? Telecommunications now enters the picture. This is where your savings begin.

Protocols

If you've chosen telecommunications as your interfacing method, you first need to determine your word processor's *protocols*. The manufacturer will help out here by furnishing the correct answers for each implicit question in Figure 9-1, a checklist for the ten protocols discussed in the pages ahead.

Protocols are the accepted way to establish communication between computers. Protocols are conventions between computers. Both word processor and typesetter must be communicating on the same "wavelength," if they are to communicate. Protocols are dictated by the manufacturer of the hardware you are using.

Beyond data transmission protocols, the *modems* used must be coordinated. There are several types of modems and acoustic couplers. It is *not* necessary for both communicators to be equipped with the same type of modem, but it is necessary that the modems be calibrated similarly.

The elements of the protocol and modem equations are among the most obtuse and least understood factors in the interface dictionary. There's no reason to understand *all* the protocols, but if you understand what you're doing, it's more likely you will do it correctly.

There can be as many as a dozen protocols. Nine important factors have been selected for particular discussion here.

■ Code Sets

Basically, two code sets dominate typesetting data streams: ASCII and EBCDIC. They are the two standard sets used to convert letters, numbers,

Checklist: Establishing Protocols

Code set:	ASCII	☐
	EBCDIC	☐
	Other	☐

If other, what code set _____

Transmission:	Asynchronous	☐
	Synchronous	☐
Baud rate:	300	☐
	1200	☐
	2400	☐
	4800	☐
	Other	☐

If other, what transmission speed _____

ACK/NAK:	Yes	☐
	No	☐
Parity:	Odd	☐
	Even	☐
	None	☐
Number of stop bits per character:	1	☐
	2	☐
	0	☐
Number of data bits per character:	6	☐
	7	☐
	8	☐
Mode:	Transparent	☐
	Nontransparent	☐
Transmission:	Paced	☐
	Continuous	☐
X-On/X-Off:	Yes	☐
	No	☐
Line by line/X-On:	Yes	☐
	No	☐
Mode:	Attended	☐
	Unattended	☐

■ **FIGURE 9-1.**

and other keystrokes into bits. A New International ASCII was developed in 1978. There are new code sets, including 2741, DDCMP, and SDLC, but none of these is popular in communicating word processing documents to typesetters.

EBCDIC was created by IBM and is used in its computers. Almost every other mini and micro manufacturer uses ASCII, although some of the IBM-compatibles use EBCDIC. The primary difference between the two code sets is 7-bit versus 8-bit transmission. Both code sets translate keystrokes into bits (binary digits). As an example, the letter *d* on the keyboard is not understood in memory as a letter *d,* but as a binary combination of 0s and 1s. In this case, ASCII converts *d* into 1100100; EBCDIC converts *d* into 10000100. These binary digit codes can be expressed in terms of *hexadecimal code* when translating (see Appendix I for more thorough discussion of binary, hexadecimal, and the code sets). Hex, as it is called, is based on 16 characters, 0 through 9 and A through F. ASCII's *d* is 64 in hex; EBCDIC interprets *d* as hexadecimal 84 (see Figure 9-2).

Computers work in bits and understand bits in terms of *words.* In ASCII, each word is 7 bits long; in EBCDIC, words are 8 bits long.

ASCII, which has 7 bits to work with, can create 128 possible combinations of hex numbers and letters (2 to the seventh power is 128). This is exemplified in the ASCII chart shown in Figure 9-3. The right side of the chart is empty. Compare this to the EBCDIC chart in Figure 9-4, which has codes everywhere. An 8-bit code, EBCDIC, can convert 256 possible combinations (2 to the eighth power is 256). Thus, EBCDIC is a more powerful translation tool than ASCII.

ASCII, even though less powerful, is still more popular among IBM's competitors. Most keyboards don't have 128 keys, so why use a code set that provides unnecessary extra room?

ASCII and EBCDIC are not complementary even in the first 128 char-

Translating from ASCII to EBCDIC

Four types of translations: A—Alphanumerics to alphanumerics

H—Alpha to hexadecimal codes

R—Hex to alpha

V—Hex to hex

Alpha to Alpha	Alpha to Hex	Hex to Alpha	Hex to Hex
/Aa = a/	/Ha = 81/	/R61 = a/	/V61 = 81/
/Ab = b/	/Hb = 82/	/R62 = b/	/V62 = 82/
/Ac = c/	/Hc = 83/	/R63 = c/	/V63 = 83/
/Ad = d/	/Hd = 84/	/R64 = d/	/V64 = 84/
/Ae = e/	/He = 85/	/R65 = e/	/V65 = 85/

■ FIGURE 9-2.

FIRST HEX DIGIT

SECOND HEX DIGIT	0	1	2	3	4	5	6	7	8	9	A	B	C	D	E	F
0	NUL	DLE	space	0	@	P	`	p								
1	SOH	DC1	!	1	A	Q	a	q								
2	STX	DC2	"	2	B	R	b	r								
3	ETX	DC3	#	3	C	S	c	s								
4	EOT	DC4	$	4	D	T	d	t								
5	ENQ	NAK	%	5	E	U	e	u								
6	ACK	SYN	&	6	F	V	f	v								
7	BEL	ETB	'	7	G	W	g	w								
8	BS	CAN	(	8	H	X	h	x								
9	HT	EM	)	9	I	Y	i	y								
A	LF	SUB	*	:	J	Z	j	z								
B	VT	ESC	+	;	K	[	k	{								
C	FF	FS	,	<	L	\	l										
D	CR	GS	=	M	]	m	}									
E	SO	RS	.	>	N	^	n	~								
F	SI	US	/	?	O	_	o	DEL								

■ FIGURE 9-3. ASCII code chart.

FIRST HEX DIGIT

SECOND HEX DIGIT	0	1	2	3	4	5	6	7	8	9	A	B	C	D	E	F
0	NUL	DLE			SP	&	RHY						2	3	¼	0
1	SOH	DC1		RSP		/			a	j	°		A	J	NSP	1
2	STX	DC2	SYN						b	k	s		B	K	S	2
3	ETX	DC3	WUS	IRT					c	l	t		C	L	T	3
4									d	m	u		D	M	U	4
5	HT	NL	LF						e	n	v		E	N	V	5
6	RCR	BS	ETB	NRS					f	o	w		F	O	W	6
7	DEL		ESC	EOT					g	p	x		G	P	X	7
8			SBS						h	q	y		H	Q	Y	8
9	SPS		IT				±		i	r	z		I	R	Z	9
A	RPT	UBS	SW	EOP	[	]	½	:					SHY			
B			CU2		.	$	,	#								
C	FF			§	*	%	@									
D		IGS	ENQ	NAK	(	)	_	'								
E		IRS		+	;	¶	=									
F		ITB	BEL	!	¢	?	"									

■ FIGURE 9-4. EBCDIC code chart.

acters. They are, in fact, completely unintelligible to each other. If you have a word processor that uses EBCDIC, and your typesetter has an output unit understanding ASCII, you have interfacing problem number 1. The solution is to use translation tables to interpret EBCDIC for ASCII. (Of course, when you are first establishing an interface, you must know which protocol, ASCII or EBCDIC, you are using. Translations are otherwise impossible).

Interfacing problem number 2 is created by ASCII computers alone. One machine's version of ASCII is different from another computer's version of ASCII. There are many dialects of ASCII that are similar to each other but not quite identical. Therefore, even if both the input and output devices are supported by ASCII, it is still necessary to develop translations. How many translations will be needed can be ascertained only after you obtain a full copy of the ASCII codes used by your hardware manufacturer.

Interface problem number 3 is created by the hardware itself. A word processor keyboard has some keys, such as back slash and line feed, that a phototypesetter keyboard does not have. In order for the phototypesetter to understand those keys, however, they must mean *something* in the code set. Translation tables must be developed in concert by the type house and the typesetting customer.

■ Asynchronous and Synchronous Transmission

Transmission types are the ways in which bits are sent from one machine to another. There are two types: *asynchronous* and *synchronous*. Asynchronous is sometimes called *TTY* by experienced typesetters because asynch is a descendant of teletype transmission. Synchronous is sometimes referred to as "bisynchronous."

Asynch transmission is usually ASCII-based telecommunications. It requires 3 bits in addition to the 7 data bits of ASCII code to be sent (see Figure 9-5). The first shaded bit is known as a *start bit*. In asynch, the start bit is required to tell the machine receiving the information that a new character is about to begin. The start bit is followed by 7 data bits. The ninth bit is a *parity bit* (more on parity later; it's another protocol). The tenth and final bit is the *stop bit,* which signals the receiving machine that a word has been completed. So, in asynch, it's start, data, parity, stop; start, data, parity, stop; and so on until all the characters in the communications session are sent.

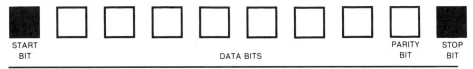

START BIT   DATA BITS   PARITY BIT   STOP BIT

■ **FIGURE 9-5. Line of asynchronous transmission: one character.**

Bisynchronous is a contracted form of the term binary synchronous. It is further condensed by most interfacers to synchronous. Binary synchronous was created by IBM for its series of 2770, 2780, 3270, 3770, and 3780 computers; some synchronous protocols have taken the names of their host computers.

In bisynch, there are no start and stop bits. The transmission of characters is synchronized. A relatively huge block of characters (typically 512) is sent at one time; a second block follows after a fixed amount of time;

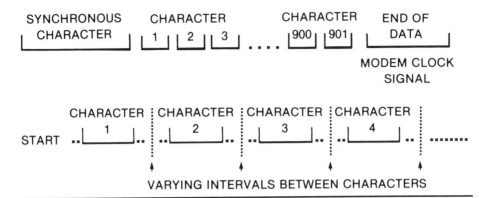

■ FIGURE 9-6. Asynchronous vs. bisynchronous transmission.

after waiting the same amount of time, a third block is sent, and so on. The receiving machine knows when a character has been received by *timing* the transmission. There's no need for stop and start bits for each character; the stops and starts are every 512 characters.

Bisynch allows for a steady stream of data transmission. Hence, bisynch transmission is faster than asynch, which is impeded by a series of sporadic stop and start bits.

To send a character by asynch transmission, *10* bits are required; start, 7 data bits, parity, stop. In ASCII asynch, there is 30 percent wastage. Three out of every 10 bits sent in a data transmission are not data. In EBCDIC bisynch, there's virtually no waste at all (see Figure 9-6 for a comparison).

Also contributing to asynch's slower transmission speed is the short wait between a stop bit and the next start bit. In a test conducted by Compugraphic in 1981, asynch transmitted a sample document (4,500 characters) in 1 minute, 23 seconds. The same document was moved by bisynch transmission 18 seconds faster—a 22 percent savings in time, phone costs, and labor.

There are no real advantages of asynch over bisynch. But, even though bisynch is better, asynch is *still very good*. We are judging grades of excellence here. The advantage of using bisynch for moving documents is really not enough of an advantage to sway you toward buying IBM equipment. It is a consideration, though, if you are moving extremely long documents at long-distance phone rates. As with the ASCII/EBCDIC decision, the synchronous/asynchronous protocol decision is dictated by your hardware.

■ Baud Rate

The *baud rate* is the number of bits per second that are understood by the typesetter's modem and then moved to memory. Baud rates range from 50 to 19,200; the most popular for typesetting WP documents are 300, 1,200, 2,400, and 4,800 baud.

To transfer bits per second (baud rate) into characters per minute, you simply divide by the number of bits necessary to move one character. For asynch, divide by 10: 1,200 baud is 1,200 divided by 10, or 120 characters per second. For bisynch, divide by 8: 1,200 baud is 1,200 divided by 8, or 150 characters per second.

Transmission rate is a protocol that is *always* determined jointly by sender and receiver. *The baud rate must be identical on both the sending and receiving modems.* In a hardwire, the baud rate is often expressed directly on a list of protocols on screen.

How fast should you go? The faster the transmission rate, the greater the possibility of transmitting errors. If you are transmitting extremely long documents, bisynch, with its faster baud rate, may be mandated. If moving information at the higher baud rates (above 4,800) is an absolute necessity, you *must* move to bisynch transmission.

ACK/NAK

Most word processing systems have *ACK/NAK* capability. *ACK* is an acronym for *a*ffirmative *ack*nowledgment; *NAK* means *n*egative *ack*nowledgment. When data are rejected because of an error in transmission, the receiving modem sends a signal, a NAK, to the sender. The sender then retransmits the offending character until the transmission is acceptable and an ACK is received. ACK/NAK, then, is a method used to signal and correct errors in transmission.

One of the less important protocols, ACK/NAK is an either/or alternative. Your transmission either has the protocol or it doesn't. Most telecommunications programs require a simple yes or no answer to the ACK/NAK question.

Parity

Parity discovers errors in transmission. The ninth bit in ASCII asynch is the parity bit. There are three possible types of parity: even, odd, and none. The typesetter and word processor must agree to use the same parity.

Data bits come through the stream in asynch ten at a time. If, as an example, an even parity is used, the start and stop bits of the letter *d* (shaded) and the 7 data bits are filled in with 1100100 (see Figure 9-7). The ninth bit is the parity bit.

START BIT | DATA BITS | PARITY BIT | STOP BIT

FIGURE 9-7. Parity bit.

The sending machine transmits the bits for letter *d*. Using the standard decimal system, if you add up the bits thus far, there are only 3. Since three is an odd number, the parity digit must be 1 in order to bring the total sum of digits to an even number—for even parity. Figure 9-8 shows the result.

On the receiving end, the typesetter is set up to receive even parity. Every character is checked for even parity by the typesetting machine.

■ **FIGURE 9-8. Even parity.**

Let's assume that a character with an odd number of 1s is received. A transmission error has occurred. A data bit that should be 0 is a 1, or vice versa.

After the error is detected by the typesetting machine, the offending character is flagged. At this point, type house personnel can then repair the damage or ask for retransmission (or your communications software will ask for retransmission automatically).

There is one problem with this strategy. If there are *two* errors in one character the two errors will counterbalance each other, and parity will still be achieved. Fortunately, this is a rare occurrence, but is another small strike against ASCII asynchronous.

Error checking is more complicated but more effective in EBCDIC bi-synch transmissions. Parity is not used, so a parity value of "none" is specified (in asynch, either odd or even, as agreed, can be used). For bi-synch, a programming formula in the software avoids the problem of double errors. After an error is detected, retransmission of the erring block is immediate; no flags to the operator are necessary.

■ Number of Stop Bits

This protocol is used to allow for ASCII transmissions containing only 6 data bits rather than the usual 7. In 6-bit data transmission, there is an extra, second stop bit (see Figure 9-9).

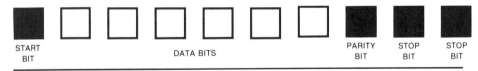

■ **FIGURE 9-9. Second stop bit.**

Six-bit transmission of data is used infrequently for typesetting. Its only practical value is for teletype communications. Six bits permit only 64 (2 to the sixth power) permutations for translations. With only 64 obtainable characters, the 52 letters of the alphabet (upper- and lowercase) and ten numbers, 0 through 9, leave only two spots for punctuation, returns, shift codes, etc. This, obviously, isn't going to work for word processing. But the number of stop bits is one of the protocols often required.

■ Number of Data Bits

In addition to specifying the number of stop bits, you may also have to specify the number of data bits. There are three possibilities: 6, 7, and 8. Seven data bits are used for ASCII asynchronous and 8 data bits are used for EBCDIC bisynchronous. Six bits are rarely used for word processing. Eight bits create 256 different translatable codes and are the most powerful. The 128 characters of 7-bit transmission are enough for most normal jobs. Hex codes and mnemonics can make 7-bit transmission more versatile. EBCDIC does not require as many hex code gymnastics.

■ Mode Transparent or Nontransparent

This protocol dictates whether the receiving machine reads what are known as *control codes,* the keyboard characters that initiate, stop, or modify a particular function. In transparent transmission, control codes are ignored (transparent here meaning that the machine does not see the codes). In nontransparent, the codes are "visible," and the receiver recognizes the instructions of the control codes and acts appropriately.

If the sending and receiving machines *are* the same type of machine, control codes can be helpful and the nontransparent mode should be selected. If the sending and receiving machines are *not* manufactured by the same company, chances are that they do not use the same control codes. To avoid control codes cluttering up a document with incomprehensible commands, use the transparent mode.

■ Paced or Continuous Transmission

Movement of data can be controlled by the receiving machine. At high speeds (like 4,800 baud), it is often possible for the transmitting machine to move information faster than the typesetter can accept it. The typesetter must control the rate of transmission or information may be lost. This is called *paced transmission.*

At slow speeds like 300 baud, *continuous transmission* is recommended. Neither the sender nor the receiver controls the pace, since information is continuously moving through the interface. Because of the relatively slow rate of transmission, there are few problems in accepting information.

X-On/X-Off. There are two ways to pace the information flow. The most common is *X-On/X-Off.* When this protocol is in effect, it can send a special message to the sender. X-Off is decipherable as "transmitter off." The X-Off code stops the stream of data for a moment. When the receiver has accepted and understood all of the data previously sent, it transmits an X-On signal to reconvene transmission.

There are standard codes for both X-On and X-Off, shared by ASCII and EBCDIC. X-On is hex code 11 (binary 00010001); X-Off is hex code 13 (binary 000010011). These binary numbers are *universally* accessed by control codes. X-On is always Device Control Code 1 (DC1). X-Off is always Device Control Code 3 (DC3). X-On/X-Off is often called *DC1/DC3.*

Line by Line/X-On. The second way to pace transmission is with *Line by line/X-On.* The receiving device sends an X-On code after *every* line has been received and understood. The process, then, is: send, wait for an X-On message, send, wait for an X-On message, and so on. If the receiver is in danger of falling behind in processing information, it simply paces trans-

Checklist: Asynchronous Transmission

Code set to be used: ASCII ☐
EBCDIC ☐
Other ☐

If other, what code set _____

Number of data bits per character: 6 ☐
7 ☐
8 ☐

Number of stop bits per character: 1 ☐
2 ☐

Parity: Odd ☐
Even ☐
None ☐

Protocol: X-On/X-Off ☐
None ☐

If X-On/X-Off, X-On code to be used (usually DC3) _____
If X-On/X-Off, X-Off code to be used (usually DC1) _____

Transmission speed (baud): 300 ☐
1200 ☐
Other ☐

If other, what transmission speed _____

Sign-on code: _____

Modem

Set for asynchronous transmission: ☐

Set for duplex pattern: Full ☐
Half ☐

Transmission speed: 300 ☐
1200 ☐
Other ☐

If other, what transmission speed _____

Set optional features (autodial, etc.) as necessary.

■ **FIGURE 9-10. Sign-on for ASCII.**

Checklist: Synchronous Transmission

Synchronous protocol to be used: 2780 □
           3270 □
           3770 □
           3780 □
           Other □

If other, what protocol _____

Synchronization character: Standard □
    Other □

If other, what character _____

End of data character: Standard □
    Other □

If other, what character _____

Number of data bits per character _____

Transmission speed (baud):   1200 □
    2400 □
    4800 □
    Other □

If other, what transmission speed _____

Sign-on code _____

Modem

Set for synchronous transmission: □

Set for half-duplex transmission: □

Transmission speed: 1200 □
    2400 □
    4800 □
    Other □

If other, what transmission speed _____

Set optional features (autodial, etc.) as necessary.

■ FIGURE 9-11. Sign-on for EBCDIC.

mission by not sending an X-On message. Thus it's unlikely that data will overflow and be lost. The X-On code is usually the same DC3 code used in X-On/X-Off pacing. Line by line/X-On makes for extremely slow-paced communications.

■ The Remaining Protocols

There are as many as a dozen other protocol options to consider before you interface. The *send/receive* option allows for bilateral communications. This means that the typesetter can either send information to the word processing computer or receive it.

Unattended/attended mode is a handy option to have. In the attended mode, typesetting personnel must watch the screen as information is communicated. When an error is made, a corrective action must be taken before transmission resumes. This mode makes for long, labor-intensive sessions watching terminal screens. Using the unattended mode, personnel can set up the interface and turn to other activities for as long as it takes to fill a diskette. Transmission errors are simply flagged and corrected at the end of the interface session.

If you're using EBCDIC, you will have to assign the correct version of the EBCDIC code set as a protocol. Alternatives here include 2780, 3270, 3770, and 3780.

There are other protocols that may be needed. The best advice is to depend on two sources of information: technical documentation from the manufacturer of your hardware *and* support afforded by the manufacturer's system engineers. The most common annoyance affecting nearly every interface is the unavailability of technical information. What port should you use if the ports are not marked? What software diagnostics should be performed? Don't be reluctant to ask the manufacturer questions. That's the best source for this arcane, but very necessary, protocol information.

Sign-On Document

Once you have determined the protocols necessary for your interface, they must be put into one document. That document, called the *sign-on,* is the first transmission of any interface session.

The sign-on is sent from the word processing hardware, notifying the typesetting machine that the telecommunications session is about to begin. This notification reserves space (in the typesetting work flow) for telecommunications.

The sign-on also records the various protocols that govern each transmission. Once the sign-on is accomplished, the two machines will compare notes and verify the possibility of communications.

The ASCII and EBCDIC sign-on documents look very different (compare Figures 9-10 and 9-11). The ASCII version is longer because there are more protocols to consider. The on-screen document often looks like a fill-in-the-blank quiz. Once the typesetter and the type buyer (or the in-house graphics shop and word processing departments) have agreed on protocols, the sign-on document is used to establish the expected format.

Modems

There are five considerations when deciding which modem to buy: connections, type of transmission, baud rate, modulation, and line types. Depending on the equipment, these five traits may or may not be modified. The more expensive modems allow various combinations; cheaper versions are preset at one formula. Prices range from as low as $100 to well over $1,000 (see the *Data Book* for specific prices).

■ Connections

There are two types of connectors from the computer, phototypesetting machine, or word processor to the telephone wires. The *acoustic couplers* are the least expensive alternative. They are connected to the computer through a hardwire from the RS-232 port. At the coupler end, a standard telephone fits into two cradles (see Figure 2-8). A *direct connect modem* does not require a telephone. The modem is connected to the RS-232 port on one end and directly to a modular telephone jack on the other.

Acoustic couplers operate at slower baud rates than modems. If cheap models are purchased, the couplers tend to be less reliable than modem devices. They are adequate for small telecommunications tasks.

If you own (or wish to communicate with) an IBM computer transmitting bisynchronous, you must use a modem because acoustic couplers will move data only through asynch transmission.

■ Type of Transmission

Some communication devices allow for asynchronous transmission; others allow only for bisynch. The best modems permit both types of transmission. See Figure 9-12 for a comparison of the acoustic coupler and five types of modems available. The Bell 212A and its clones are the most

Types of Modems: A Bell Compatibility Check

Type of Modem	Duplex Pattern	Synch/ Asynch	Baud Rate	Frequency/ Phase
Acoustic coupler	Full	Asynch	0-300	Frequency
103	Full	Asynch	0-300	Frequency
201	Half	Synch	2400	Phase
202	Half	Asynch	0-1200	Frequency
208	Half	Synch	4800	Phase
212A	Full	Both	0-300, 1200	Phase

■ FIGURE 9-12. Characteristics of acoustic coupler and various types of modems.

popular modems, partly because of their adaptability. If you are not word processing with an IBM, you don't necessarily need a modem capable of bi-synch transmission. If you are buying a modem for a phototypesetting shop, at least one of your modems should be capable of bisynch communications in order to interface with IBM users.

■ Baud Rate

Some modems are capable of only one transmission speed. Others, like the Bell 212A, offer several baud rate options. Normal telephone lines can move data at rates of up to 4,800 baud. For faster speeds, you will need to install special lines to move your information through in-house hardwires.

The most popular dividing lines for modem speed are 300, 1,200, and 2,400 baud. The faster models may be capable of both the faster speeds and the slower speeds as well. A modem that works only at 1,200 cannot communicate with another that's limited to 300.

■ Modulation

There are two ways the modem can convert your binary signals into the audible tones known as *analog* signals (the tones that the telephone modem can understand and then convert—demodulate—back into binary). Devices that convert through *frequency modulation* turn digital binary signals into analog signals of varying cycles per second. Instead of using cycles per second, *phase modulation* modems convert digital into analog of varying wavelengths. Thus analog is varied either by time (frequency) or by wavelength (phase).

The primary significance here is that to make the interface work you must be certain that both the receiver and the sender are using identical modulations. Using the checklists provided will ensure that all elements of the interface link coincide (see Figure 9-13).

■ Line Types

There are three types of communication: *simplex, half-duplex,* and *full duplex.* In simplex, the data are sent by one machine and understood by another. Simplex modems are not capable of two-way conversations. Because it cannot send error messages to the sender, a receiving simplex modem cannot distinguish between information and unintelligible garbage.

Half-duplex modems are capable of both sending and receiving. Receiving modems send messages only when there is a lull in conversation; they do not interrupt the flow of information.

Full-duplex devices talk any time, even when they are listening to another modem. This may sound like the best alternative, but half-duplex is actually a more intelligent way of communicating. Do you want to talk to someone who's always talking? Good listeners wait their turn.

If you're moving data with bisynchronous transmission, the half-duplex modem is necessary.

Checklist: Synchronizing Modems

Type: Acoustic coupler ☐
                                                      103 ☐
                                                      201 ☐
                                                      202 ☐
                                                      208 ☐
                                                     212A ☐

Transmission type: Synchronous ☐
                                            Asynchronous ☐

Baud rate: 300 ☐
                                                     1200 ☐
                                                     2400 ☐
                                                     4800 ☐
                                                   Other ☐

If other, what speed _____

Modulation: Frequency ☐
                                                   Phase ☐

Line type: Simplex ☐
                                               Half-Duplex ☐
                                               Full-Duplex ☐

Options: Automatic send ☐
                                         Automatic answer ☐
                                           Monitor lights ☐

Other options desired _____

■ FIGURE 9-13.

Buying Modems

The modem purchase decision can be quite simple: If you are a type customer who telecommunicates with only one typesetter, find out what modem that typesetter uses and buy it. When two identical modems are communicating, the movement of data is usually perfect.

For the typesetter, the most important factor in selecting the right communications device is that your modem or coupler allows compatibility with the greatest number of computer users. The Bell 212A modem, the Hayes SmartModem, and several other programmable modems are popular for this reason. You can adjust protocols and modem specifications so that the only limitations are those created by the computer with which you're communicating.

Beyond compatibility, there are several options to consider when purchasing a modem. *Automatic dialing* allows the customer or typesetter to dial numbers on the terminal screen while the modem is connected. *Automatic answering* is particularly useful for both in-house departments and heavy production type houses. In the in-house graphics shop, you may not have the staff necessary to both dial and answer. The modem that automatically answers the phone is your solution. In the type house, why spend employee time answering the phone? If you wish, you can set up an interface to accept information at any time—even when your employees are not available to operate the machines.

Rounding out the possibilities are *monitoring lights* and *self-diagnostic tests*. Monitoring lights signal that an aspect of the interface is in progress with a series of lights that say "communicating," "sending," "received data," or "modem ready." By letting you know exactly where things stand, it's impossible to waste time. If a session goes wrong, you know it.

The self-diagnostic tests tell you when something is wrong before you communicate. After discovering possible problems, some modems will also specifically point out the source of error.

Once you have decided what you want, there are several ways to get it. Bell offers both purchase and lease programs. Scores of other manufacturers are listed in the *Data Book*. It is possible to lease modems. This might be valuable for an organization that telecommunicates one large job every year. If all you move over the wires is an annual membership directory, leasing makes sense.

Testing Modems

Telephone technology is very durable, so the modem will usually outlast your computer's usefulness. You shouldn't have to worry about service on any modem bought from a reputable source.

In order to test the modem, use a test document you created. Find a simple job with plain paragraphs and few control codes—remember, this is not the place to rush matters.

Simplicity will ensure success so long as you have established a series of homogenous protocols and modem patterns. You want the modem to run smoothly the first try in order to dispel the fears surrounding the new technological process. After demonstrating it, prepare a manual for your employees. Include a keystroke-by-keystroke sequence of the correct protocols. It is important to hold onto that successful formula.

The next step is the final task in preparing the interface: building the translation tables.

CHAPTER 10

Building
Translation
Tables

TRANSLATIONS ARE THE CRUX of any interface. For the typesetting customer, understanding translations and creating the correct tables are the single most important step *in any interface*. Assuming your typesetter is equipped with communications software, its software allows you to translate a string of word processing codes into a parallel string of typesetting codes.

It's possible to make *any string of letters mean anything you wish*. Because of that liberal translation power, many interfaces are begun incorrectly. Perhaps the most common error made in establishing communications is spending too little time developing the *right* translation tables.

Mnemonics: How Do They Work?

A *mnemonic* is an alphanumeric code used to express complicated commands in shorthand statements. A typical example of a simple mnemonic is TS12, meaning a type size of 12 points. Mnemonics are used for two reasons: to save keystrokes and to embed typesetting commands (such as type size and line space) into word processing documents.

■ Saving Keystrokes

Mnemonics save keystrokes by allowing operators to profit from individualized typing patterns. For example, if the phrase "office automation" is often used in a document, a word processing operator can use the mnemonic "oa" each time the phrase is required. After a job is completed, the mnemonic will be automatically translated into the words "office automation." These translations are universal. *Every instance* of oa will be translated. Thus, the word "load" will become "loffice automationd." The creator of mnemonic coding must make certain that the mnemonic will never be mistakenly translated.

One way to avoid such mistranslations is to forego simple mnemonics such as oa. A special symbol can be used before every mnemonic code: a dollar sign, for example. A mnemonic that reads $oa is never translated incorrectly. The translation of $oa is "office automation"; since the word "load" does not contain the string $oa, the incorrect translation is avoided.

■ Keying Typesetting Codes

The most important function of mnemonics is to encode typesetting parameters into word processing documents.

A word processing keyboard is not a typesetting keyboard, but it is being used as one. The keyboard does not have all the necessary keys for font selection, line space, em space, flush left, and dozens of other functions necessary to typesetting.

Mnemonics are the answer. They allow the word processor to substitute existing keys (or combinations of keys) for necessary typesetting keys. For example, $LL22 might be used to mean a line length of 22 picas.

■ Four Steps in the Translation Process

How does the typesetter understand the mnemonic coding you have created? The first step in moving information from a word processor to a typesetter is writing the translations into one document—the *translation table.*

The second step is to determine, from the hardware manufacturer's specifications, several special codes. These one-line codes are understood by the interfacing device as beginning and ending statements of a translation table.

After being careful not to make any keyboarding mistakes when typing the translation table, the third step is to send the translation table to the typesetting machine. This establishes a common ground for translations. Using the previous examples, $oa will be understood as office automation and $LL22 as line length 22 picas.

The final step is to send word processing documents to the typesetter. If the tables are input correctly, translations are made automatically. If the translation does not work, you must begin to debug the translation tables. Errors in translations are frequently due to keyboarding mistakes in typing the original tables. After debugging is completed and the typesetter has received and translated a document, the job is ready for phototypesetting output.

Word Processing Input: A Troubleshooting Guide

There are two major difficulties to resolve on the word processing end of the interface: the deletion of unnecessary coding and word processing conventions.

■ Coding Deletions

Word processing input contains many codes that are unnecessary to typesetting. Page breaks, format lines at the top of screens, tab setups, double spacing, and a dozen other screen features must be eliminated. Printer commands, job names, and menus should also be disregarded.

Why doesn't the typesetter simply ignore what it does not need? The problem is that *typesetters are incapable of ignoring anything.* When an unneeded, untranslated code is introduced to the communications interface, the software attempts to translate that code. When a translation is impossible, the transmission of the data is completely halted or the data received become jibberish.

These problems mean the translation table must be refined. All word processing codes not needed by the typesetting machine must be translated *to mean nothing.* The interfacing software strips out all these codes before they reach the typesetting machine, which doesn't get confused by codes it cannot understand.

■ Word Processing Conventions

Personnel are trained to use word processing input copy as though the material were being typed. But typed input is very different from typesetting. These differences can cause major problems if they are not resolved by a working translation table. The following suggestions will make your debugging process move along a bit faster.

1. *Double Spacing.* After periods, a typesetter does not set a double space. Single spacing is used so that when lines of typesetting are set justified (even on both margins), the typesetter's software automatically strips one space away at the end of each line. There's no reason to have a space because the last letter of each line is the last character in that line.

   Word processing personnel, like typists, double-space after periods. If double spaces are transmitted to the typesetter, justification problems may result. To eliminate this problem, it is necessary to prepare a translation in the table that requires all double spaces to be translated into a single space.

2. *Hyphens and Dashes.* Most word processing hardware does not allow for dashes. The conventional method for signifying a dash is to combine two hyphens. But typesetters do distinguish among several kinds of dashes—and they are all called for by different keystrokes.

   Two hyphens for a dash is not professional typesetting. The solution here is to create a translation that converts two hyphens in a word processing document into a typeset em dash.

   En dashes are shorter than the em dash. They are often used to separate numbers, as in 1954–55 or Paragraph 23–4. The easiest way to input the en dash is simply to use a dollar mnemonic. For instance, $- or $ND are two possible strings that can be used by word processors. An appropriate translation will convert $- into a typeset en dash.

3. *Mathematic Symbols*. Some mathematic and scientific symbols, such as $\sqrt{}$, $\varnothing$, Δ, and $\mp$ are not available on word processing keyboards. For fractions, the typical word processing convention is to build the fraction, such as in 1/2 (1, slash, 2). Such construction of fractions is considered substandard typesetting. Individual translations for each string of characters available on the typesetting fonts (but not on the word processing keyboard) will have to be written.

If you are doing technical or scientific keyboarding, the best answer to the symbols dilemma is to create a chart (see Figure 5-2). The symbols chart is best prepared by typesetting personnel who are most familiar with the location of each mathematic or scientific symbol on the typesetting fonts.

If you need only a few fractions, a few simple translations added to the tables will be adequate.

4. *Indents*. Word processors invariably use tabs for paragraph indents. As in the standard indent used in typewriting, the first tab is five spaces. This cannot work for typesetting.

Typesetting spaces are not fixed. For every line of type the actual amount of territory a space occupies will vary. This variance in spacing allows for justification. Through *h&j programs* (hyphenation and justification), typesetting software keeps a count of the accumulated widths of the characters in each line. As a line nears the pica limit set by the typesetting operator, the software automatically commands a return.

Before the return, the program computes the amount of unoccupied horizontal space that must be distributed throughout the line in order for the line to be justified—even on both margins. The program then divides up all the available space and distributes it evenly between each word in the line. The spaces in every line of type, then, are not the same.

If you want all paragraph indents to be exactly the same for every paragraph, you must use the em and en spaces specifically created to allow for standard indents.

Paragraph indents, then, require a special translation. Word processing operators cannot simply use a standard tab or type five spaces for an indent. If the tab is translated as a two-em typesetting indent, then all tabs will be two ems—thus creating problems if you wish to use tabbing to create a chart. If five spaces are translated as a two-em indent, word processing operators must carefully type out five spaces before each paragraph.

Typing five spaces slows down keyboarding speed. The solution to the indent problem is found in the returns.

5. *Returns*. There are two types of returns in word processing: *soft returns* and *hard returns*. Soft returns are created as words are wrapped in keyboarding; these returns are not the result of striking the return key on the terminal. Hard returns are purposely typed by the keyboard operator. How does the translation software distinguish between the two returns?

The solution is actually quite easy. First, obtain a copy of the

```
Mary said, "I know a man named 'Ralph' who's 5' 3¼" tall."
```

Mary said, "I know a man named 'Ralph' who's 5' 3 1/4" tall."

Mary said, "I know a man named 'Ralph' who's 5' 3¼ " tall."

■ **FIGURE 10-1. The problem: quotations, apostrophes, and symbols.**

ASCII or EBCDIC code charts from the manufacturers of the word processing and typesetting hardware. (Several translation tables and code set charts are displayed in the *Data Book*.) Every code set will give you the information you need in order to translate the returns correctly.

Soft returns and hard returns have different hex codes. Soft returns are of no value to the typesetting machine, which will insert its own soft returns after receiving the document. The soft returns, then, must be translated as nothing.

Hard returns must be translated. In the majority of cases, a hard return signifies the end of a paragraph.

For typesetting, the end of a paragraph requires a flush left code (which tells the photo unit to set the copy pushed to the left, rather than justified), a return, and then an indent to start the next paragraph. This is how hard returns are translated: flush left, return, em space, em space (if two ems are your indent).

This solves two problems. Hard returns become flush left, return, and you have a way out of the five-space indent difficulty. What happens when you want to interface copy that requires hard returns that aren't followed by the beginnings of paragraphs? Create another translation table in which a WP hard return simply means flush left, return. That translation table can be used for specific cases.

6. *Quotation Marks.* This is the classic conundrum for interfaces. Figure 10-1 gives an extraordinary visual statement of the problem.

A word processor does not have different keys for beginning and ending quotation marks (typesetters call them "open" and "close" quotes). In fact, some word processors only have one key for quotations, apostrophes, inch marks, and foot marks. If you want a quotation mark or inch mark, you must type the apostrophe twice.

The problem is that typesetting requires beginning quotation marks (") to be open—curving open into the quote. Ending quotes (") curve the other way, again toward the quotation. An apostrophe (') always curves back toward the beginning of the word in a contraction. Inch and foot marks (",') don't curve at all.

How can you possibly translate that one key correctly all the time? Quotes and apostrophes are usually translated using long programs resident in the interfacing software. Typically, this software operates by translating the first two paired quote marks as an open quote. The next pair is translated as a close quote. If the quote mark does not occur in pairs, the software translates as an apostrophe. If the word processor uses quote marks for quotations, the first such mark is an open quote; the second is a close quote.

If you attempt to correct an occasional error, you may override the quote translation program and be left much worse off than when you started. Massaging that error manually at the typesetting keyboard may be the better solution.

Typesetting Problems: The Troubleshooting Continues

Problems on the typesetting end of the translation table break down into three areas: code insertions, technical typesetting parameters, and technical type versus straight matter.

■ Code Insertions: The Critical Decision

Somewhere in the process of transferring information from a word processing unit to a phototypesetting machine, typesetting codes will have to be inserted into the documents to be typeset. Where should these codes be input? Should you train your WP personnel to key in codes correctly, or should the typesetting professionals massage the document after the keystrokes have been received?

This is a critical decision. Whatever you decide at this point will not only affect the ease of the interface but will also largely determine how much money the type customer will save by interfacing. What are the pros and cons of word processing operator versus professional typesetter?

■ Using Your Word Processing Operator: Pros

1. The least expensive way to interface is to have word processing operators insert typesetting codes. Phototypesetting personnel are paid more than word processing personnel. Typesetting costs more than word processing; every code inserted by word processors and translated by an interface saves you money.

2. Typesetting is clean and quick. If documents are thoroughly checked for errors at the word processing stage, you can be certain that typeset pages will be error-free. The typesetter's personnel cannot create errors if they don't touch your documents.

3. If a document is sent to the typesetter ready to be typeset, turnaround can be much faster. The typesetter need only send the job to the photo unit for quick output. No time-consuming input steps are necessary.

4. If a job is constructed by your personnel on your office word processing system, you have total control over the way the job will eventually be typeset. Document integrity is ensured. The job will not be set the way the typesetter *thought* you wanted it.

■ Using Your Word Processing Operator: Cons

1. If you don't use a phototypesetting professional's skills, the type will *not* look as good. Regardless of the claims of typesetting sales reps,

typesetting is not as simple as inserting a few codes in a document. Correct typographic decisions have been made for you in the past by professionals, whether or not you were aware of it. Those decisions will no longer be available to you if you don't use the professionals.

2. It will cost you to educate word processing personnel. Word processing for typesetting is not easy; you may or may not be able to train your operators to be effective typesetting keyboarders. The education process takes time and can be frustrating, both to management and personnel.

3. As you move to in-house input for typesetting, errors in keyboarding will be made. Correcting errors is more difficult and more time consuming than input. Typesetting companies *must* charge premium rates for massaging documents that have been communicated with errors. If you transmit jobs that have too many errors, the typesetter may simply have to reset the job entirely. In this case, you will be charged for the communications session and for the typesetting, as well as having to pay your word processing personnel for their incorrect input.

■ Using the Typesetter: Pros

1. The typesetter is an intelligent, competent professional who knows how to use the hardware. The type will be produced correctly and efficiently. It will also be more aesthetically pleasing.

2. If your word processing operators supply keystrokes, keyboarding is cheaper. Documents can then be massaged by the type craftsperson. You are paying typesetters only for their superior typographic knowledge. The costs of expensive keyboarding are eliminated without losing excellent typography.

3. The translation tables are relatively simple. You must supply translations of word processing conventions and peculiarities, but typesetting parameters are input at the typesetting end. Those codes need not be included in the translation tables.

■ Using the Typesetter: Cons

1. Having the typesetter massage documents to insert typesetting codes will slash possible savings to only about 10 percent. You can save upwards of 50 percent on your current typesetting by doing it yourself.

2. If the typesetting personnel are used, the speed of communications is somewhat sacrificed. Each document must wait for typesetting input by typesetters.

3. Because the typesetter is typing codes not controlled by the customer, it's possible that errors will be made. Thus, the job flow is back to the traditional circuit of output, proof, check for errors, new output, new proof. That slow process can be eliminated if errors are corrected before communications and there is no chance for errors to be made by the typesetter.

■ Who Should Code?

By now, you will have surmised that there are three possible translation alternatives open to any prospective interfacer. Each will obviously affect the translation tables that you see. Each option will create opportunities to save time and money in typesetting. The more difficult options offer greater savings, but even the easiest of the three will result in significant cuts in type costs.

Alternative 1: Coding by Word Processing Personnel. This strategy will require hard work at fine-tuning a translation table that will eventually work perfectly. If you are willing to invest the time necessary to determine fully what your translation tables need to accomplish, and if you are resilient enough not to surrender to frustrations, this is the best way to go. Writing and debugging translation tables take time, but this area is where the most money can be saved.

The major problem with this method is your word processing operators' lack of typesetting knowledge. If you go with alternative 1, word processors, in fact, become typesetters. This step will require training and educating personnel. Attitude and effort are the significant keys to success here.

Alternative 2: Coding by Typesetters. If you are not particularly concerned with the monetary advantages offered by interfacing, coding by typesetters requires only a transition from paper to electronic manuscript. That is not a radical change in the production flow and will cause very little organizational trauma.

This is an intelligent first step for most new interfacers. By first establishing that communications work, and then moving on to more complicated approaches, you are not saving large amounts of money but your employees will know it works. The confidence gained will be essential as you slowly move toward more difficult strategies. Type quality is maintained and there is very little chance of disastrous failures affecting production deadlines.

Alternative 3: Coding by Format. Inputting complete typesetting codes is not the only way to supply typesetters with typographic information. A typeset job must contain information that gives the typeface name, the line length, the line space, the size of type, the minimum and maximum letter-space values, and the word-space values. It is not necessary to train word processing operators to input that information—and a hundred other typesetting codes.

You can use the power of translation tables to create *formats*. There are two ways to format copy at the word processor. First, word processing personnel must know the basics of typography (Appendix II is a short primer on typography). When a document is being typed on the word processor, the keyboarder merely types "MH" prior to a main headline, "TX" before text, "FT" before footnotes, and so on. No typesetting parameters are used.

Meanwhile, the typesetter has installed in your translation table the appropriate translations to convert those alphanumeric codes into the correct typesetting codes. The formats are easy to use, especially because the formats never change. Only the background translations are different for each job; word processing coding is always the same.

The second type of format coding eliminates the translation table altogether. The word processing personnel use the formats and send the job intact to the typesetter. The typesetter then uses the powerful typesetting software to globally search and replace the formats for the correct typesetting parameters. This requires massaging on the part of the typesetter, but much less than if they coded the job entirely.

This second method is used most often in the word processing industry. If you're unsure about typography and typesetting, the compromise format coding approach saves a bit less than WP coding of type specs, but it is safe.

Which is the right method for you? The answer to that question depends on your organization's resources and talents. The easiest implementation is to begin with the simplest method and then move slowly to more complicated coding at the word processor level.

The move to interfacing, then, can be accomplished through a three-level transition; first, traditional coding by typesetters of electronic manuscripts; second, format coding by your word processors; and, finally, complicated coding input by word processors confident in their abilities.

■ Technical Parameters in Typesetting

No matter how good your word processing personnel become, or how much you refine your translation tables, the typesetting craftsperson will always be a necessary part of the equation. Some typographic esoterica will probably never be learned by your word processing operators.

Those talents are the reason we'll always need typesetters for good typography. If word processing personnel do learn those special skills, they have become typographers and won't stay in front of word processing screens much longer. The pay for typesetters is much better than for keyboarders.

Type massaging cannot be eliminated if you expect your pages to be well set. Display typesetting, to cite one case, is the setting of headlines. It is not now possible to interface to those typesetting machines that are manufactured specifically for the production of high-quality display type. You should not sacrifice display typesetting for poorer type that's interfaced.

■ Technical Type versus Straight Matter

If you are not now interfacing, it is not worth the time or effort to learn how to interface multilevel equations or 12-column tabular material. It takes years to learn how to set complicated equations.

It is possible, though, to set simple equations or charts containing multiple tabs. That possibility must be tempered by the realization that difficult typesetting could create real budget problems. Assume that your word processing keyboarders create an equation that is transmitted. After communications, the typesetter sets the equation and finds that it's incorrect. After some time is consumed (and charged to you), the typesetter finally concludes that your equation is too difficult to repair and the material is reset. Your costs? The original keyboarding at the word processor, the time spent in massaging that version, *and* the keyboarding for the correct version. The interface has actually cost more than traditional methods!

The moral, of course, is to leave complicated typesetting to the professionals. Especially when first beginning to communicate, straight matter must be the core of any financially advantageous interface.

Writing the Translation Tables

Using simple letter combinations for your mnemonics, you will recall, creates some problems. An alphanumeric code for line length, LL, creates a translation for the word "tall" of "taline length." Dollar sign mnemonics are one way to avoid these errors in simple conversions. But beyond dollar mnemonics, what will the set of mnemonic codes look like? How many codes does an interface require? Which codes will you use?

■ What Codes Should Be Used?

Several industry groups, including both typesetting and book publishing organizations, have promised an industry-standard set of guidelines. Gen-Code, a generic coding system offered by the Graphics Communications Association, was adopted by the Department of Defense in late 1983. Gen-Code was still in draft form a year later.

If, and when, standard mnemonic codes are used throughout the typesetting industry, it will mean easy translations for both word processors and typesetters. Typesetting personnel will not have to learn new codes for every new customer. Word processors can move from one typesetter to another without learning new translation tables. Prefabricated tables need not be tested by the user.

Unfortunately, while interfacing grows, standardization continues to elude both typesetters and word processors. Disks, operating systems, code sets, and even modems have not followed the lead of the RS-232 plug—the one existing standard that has facilitated telecommunications. Standard mnemonic coding will eventually do the same for interfacing.

Dozens of new interfaces are established every week. Rather than waiting for a standard, some sort of mnemonics must be used until an accepted, universal set of translations has been created. The proposal that follows represents a translation table that has been used by colleges, in-house graphics shops, and typesetters with equal facility. This is not a suggestion for a competitive standard. It's simply a set of mnemonics that works.

■ The Proposal

Coding separates itself into several neat categories for typesetting composition: typesetting parameters, typographic patterns, spacing, tabs, typesetter commands, and leaders and special characters. These groupings will be kept intact through the use of coherent, two-letter mnemonic codes.

Typesetting Parameters. When deciding on mnemonic codes, typesetters often make the mistake of creating codes that reflect, naturally enough, the terminology of the typesetter. But the typesetter will not be using the codes. The word processing operator should not be forced to learn the arcane terminology of typesetting. Simple words can and should be substituted for technical terms to make things easier for the word processor.

For instance, $LL should be translated to mean "line length," rather than the typographic term "measure." $LS can mean "line space," rather than "leading" or "lead." $SZ can refer to "type size," a more graphic description than the preferred typographic term "point size."

How will these codes work together? A string such as $LL20$SZ10$LS12 means the type will be set 20 picas wide, in 10 point type with a 12 point line space. If you supply word processing personnel with a clear code chart *and* correctly translate the codes, they will be able to handle the typeset coding.

Typographic Patterns. There are two types of patterns on typeset pages: *standing patterns,* which affect large sections of copy, and *single line codes,* affecting only one line of copy.

For standing patterns, continue the strategy of eliminating technical typesetting terms by ignoring technical terms, such as quad left. Use $RR to mean ragged right copy, $RL for ragged left, and $CC for centered composition. When several lines are set ragged or centered and you wish to return to justified composition, use $RX (ragged off).

The single line code most often used is $FL, meaning flush left. The appropriate code for flush right is $FR.

Spacing. The ems and ens proposed for standard word processing paragraph indents are $EM and $EN. Any code beginning with $I will be reserved for other indents. To indent from the right margin, use $IR. $IL is indent left, and $IC indents equally from both the right and left margins. To set the number of picas to be indented, follow the $I codes with a two-digit number. Thus, $IL04 means a left indent of four picas.

To turn an existing indent on and off, use $IO for indent on and $IX for indent off.

As discussed earlier, letter spacing and word spacing are best left to typesetting professionals. But it is possible for word processing personnel to adjust line-spacing values: use $PP and $MP for plus or minus one point of line spacing ($+P or $−P are also possibilities).

Tabs. Tabs are among the more difficult problems for word processors to solve. Reserving $T for tabbing will help clear up coding problems.

$TX clears all existing tabs. $TS_____(for tab set) establishes a tab number and tab length. For example, $TS0113 means that tab 1 (01) is 13 picas (13) long. $TB will move the copy forward one tab, replicating the way tabs work in word processing. Finally, $TR is used as a tab return (returning while staying within the tab length specified).

Typesetter Commands. Typesetting commands are usually machine-specific, but $EX and $CO are obvious codes for "Execute" and "Command," if needed. Some typesetters are capable of receiving interfaced copy and storing it on diskettes. Others set the type immediately upon receiving a communication. If the latter is the case, you may need $PO (photo unit on) and $PX (photo unit off) codes.

The $PX mnemonic will be useful when sending long documents. It's quite possible to move information faster than the photo unit is capable of handling it. In this case, turning the photo unit off will allow typesetters to store the information for output after the communications session is complete.

Leaders, Hyphenation, and Special Characters. $L codes should be limited to line-space and line-length mnemonics. To create a dot leader (a row of dots through an entire line), use $DL. $SL means a solid line. Typesetters call a straight typeset line a baseline rule, but $RL has already been used to mean ragged left. $SL (straight line) will have to suffice.

To store an alternative leader character, use $SC— (stored character, followed by the character). If you wish a series of asterisks, use $SC*. To access the alternative leader code in a line, use $UL (use leader).

There are at least two types of hyphens required in typesetting, as well as several types of dashes. The standard word processing hyphen will work for normal hyphenation in words such as *on-line*. Typesetting software usually includes a *hyphenation logic* that controls when and where hyphens are placed to allow for justification. There are problems with any hyphenation logic; most will hyphenate before *any* "ing" syllable. That's fine for words like "morning" and "during," but "sing" can be hyphenated as "s- ing."

To eliminate those errors, an overriding hyphen code is needed. The discretionary hyphen ($DH) correctly points to those syllables that should be hyphenated. This hyphen is discretionary because the typesetting machine will use it *only if needed*.

Finally, you will also need to determine what special characters you wish to define. There will be several sorts of translations necessary. Scientific and mathematic symbols may be the first set of mnemonics that are needed. You can also save keystrokes by using shorthand translations: $wp for word processing, $oa for office automation, and $tc for telecommunications may come in handy.

You must be certain when creating shorthand that you do not make definition errors. If you define the same code to mean two different things in one translation table, the interface usually doesn't stop working at the mistranslation; it never begins to work. This error can be among the hardest to discover and repair.

Figure 10-2 shows the suggested mnemonics. Any of these codings can, of course, be adjusted, but care should be taken. These mnemonics have proven themselves. Figures 10-3 and 10-4 show word processing input and typesetting output using the translations.

Command	Mnemonic	Function	Comments
TYPESETTING PARAMETERS			
Line length	$LLxxxx	Width of typeset copy	First two digits picas, second pair points
Style	$STxx	Typeface or font	One letter (type disk), one number (variation)
Size	$SZxx	Type size	Two digits in points
Linespace	$PLxx	Baseline to baseline distance	Two digits in points
TYPOGRAPHIC PATTERNS			
Ragged right	$RR	Even left margin, ragged right	Remains in effect until cancelled
Ragged left	$RL	Even right margin, ragged left	Remains in effect until cancelled
Ragged cancel	$RX	Returns to justified copy	Cancels any ragged command
Flush left	$FL	Even left (one line)	Use at end of paragraph
Flush right	$FR	Even right (one line)	Use at end of paragraph
Center copy	$CC	Centers composition	Use as required
SPACING			
Em space	$EM	Blank space width of M	Use for indents
En space	$EN	Blank space width of N	Width of numerics
Indent left	$ILxxxx		Digits in points and picas (see line length)
			Remains in effect until cancelled
Indent right	$IRxxxx	Move right margin	Digits in picas and points, remains in effect
Indent both	$IB	Moves both margins in	Specify length, moves both this length
Indent on	$IO	Turns indent on	Digits in picas and points, remains in effect
Indent off	$IX	Returns to normal margins	Cancels indent left, right, and both
Hanging indent	$HI	With indent in effect uses hanging style (first line of paragraph not indented)	To cancel send another $HI command
Insert space	$IS	Inserts maximum available space	Evenly divides space between multiple entries on one line
Minus one point	$MP	Deletes one point of linespace	
Plus one point	$PP	Adds one point of linespace	
Zero linespace	$ZL	Returns carriage without linespace	
TABS			
Tab clear	$TX	Clears all existing tabs	Use before setting new tab lengths
Tab set	$TSxxxx	Sets tab lengths	Use to create new tabs
Use tab	$TB	Moves carriage to next tab	Insert in copy when tabbing
Tab return	$TR	At end of line, returns to left margin	Use after last tab before returning (Normal return returns to start of last tab)
Margin set	$MSxxxx	Overrides default left margin	
SPECIAL CHARACTERS			
Cent sign	$CN		
Open apostrophe	$OQ		Use two for open quotes
Closed apostrophe	$CQ		Use two for closed quotes
Em dash	$MD	Dash 1 em wide	Use in sentences
En dash	$ND	Dash 1 en wide	Use in dates (1966–67)
LEADERS			
Leaders=dots	$DL	Restores leaders to dots	Be sure to change style back to previous setting
Leader=line	$SL	Changes leader to solid line (rule)	Be sure to change style back to previous setting
Leader=character	$SCx	Changes leader to specified character	Leader character remains until changed
Use leader	$UL	Fills available space with leader in effect	
HYPHENATION			
Nonline breaking	$NL	Causes hyphenated word to be on one line, never ending a line at this hyphen	Use in phone numbers, etc.
Discretionary	$DH	Hyphen will be used by justification program only if needed	Insert code to override bad hyphenation logic
TYPESETTER COMMANDS			
Command	$CO	Sends command character	Precedes special instruction code sequences
Photo unit off	$PX	Allows file write without activating phototypesetting	
Photo unit on	$PO	Turns on photo unit	Cancels Typesetter Off command
Baseline position	$BP	Indicates top left of page	Use for multiple columns set by typesetter
Baseline return	$BR	Returns to baseline position	Use to return to begin second column
New margin set	$MSxxxx	Sets margin at start of second column; automatically indents	Length from left margin of page, picas and points
Lead maximum	$LM	Moves to lowest typeset point	Use at end of copy in multiple column work

■ **FIGURE 10-2. Table of mnemonics.**

```
$SZ21$STa2$LL3000$PL140$SL170$FL
AM TYPESETTER GUIDELINES$CC$SL
$FL$SL
$SZ12$STa1$EM$EMThe AM Varityper Comp/Edit is a composition
system that produces camera-ready phototype for mechanical
reproduction. Because of the telecommunication capabilities
of the ACS Comp/Edit, users may input copy on a variety of
terminals on campus. The copy is stored and may be retrieved
at any time for transmission to the typesetter. Refer to
$OQ$OQInstructions for Transferring Files from the VAX using
the AM Terminal$CQ$CQ and $OQ$OQTable of Typesetting
Mnemonics$CQ$CQ if help is needed when communicating your
job to the typesetter.$US$FL
```

■ **FIGURE 10-3. Word processing input.**

AM Typesetter Guidelines

The AM Varityper Comp/Edit is a composition system that produces camera-ready phototype for mechanical reproduction. Because of the telecommunication capabilities of the ACS Comp/Edit, users may input copy on a variety of terminals on campus. The copy is stored and may be retrieved at any time for transmission to the typesetter. Refer to "Instructions for Transferring Files from the VAX using the AM Terminal" and "Table of Typesetting Mnemonics" if help is needed with communicating your job to the typesetter.

■ **FIGURE 10-4. Phototypesetting output.**

Writing the Tables

The physical writing of the tables is neither creative nor interesting. The tables should be input by the person in your organization who best understands them.

The rationale here is that translation tables are not easily understood. A word processing document containing mnemonics is difficult enough, but a table consisting entirely of mnemonic codes and alphanumeric equations can be extremely obtuse. The keyboarder should understand the codes because he or she will tend to make fewer typing errors.

The first step when writing translations is to obtain a copy of the typesetter manufacturer's suggested translation tables. There are several sample tables in the *Data Book*. After receiving a copy of the suggested tables, the type house should prepare its own tables. In some cases, a specific table should be created for each major customer.

The customer telecommunicates the translation table to the typesetting machine at the beginning of each interface session. Both type house and customer have specific responsibilities. *The type house should create the tables. The customer must keyboard and telecommunicate them.*

When the translation is actually written, there are four possible choices of translating: from alphanumerics to alphanumerics, alphanumerics to hex codes, hex codes to alphanumerics, or hex to hex. The typesetting hardware (or interface hardware) manufacturer determines the format of the mnemonic equations. Every interface will, however, follow a similar pattern.

■ The Equations

In Compugraphic's tables for the ICI, a typical strategy is used. The first line of the translation document is a signal code: */=//==//*. Without that line beginning the document, all translations are impossible.

The translation itself begins with a mark called a *delimiter*. The delimiter is a mark that sets the limits of an equation—the mark appears at both the beginning and ending of the translation. In this case, the slash is used. The next character identifies which type of translation will follow: A means alpha to alpha, H means alpha to hex, R means hex to alpha, and V means hex to hex.

The reason there are four possibilities is that some translations can be as simple as $oa = office automation. Others, however, must involve hex codes. To translate a return code, for instance, you cannot use an actual return (a return signifies the end of a translation). The hex code for the return must be used.

Continuing the translation, a dollar sign notifies the interface software that a mnemonic is about to be created. The string will read, so far, /H$. Here the translation begins.

The translation can take many forms. Since H is an alpha to hex translation, a word processing alphanumeric is to be translated to a typesetting hex code. For our example, make the equation read FR=3F. The last step is to mark the end of the translation with another delimiting /. The complete translation reads /H$FR=3F/

This particular translation enables the word processor to type $FR when a flush right command is required. The assigned hex code for the flush right key on the Compugraphic typesetting terminal is 3F. When the $FR is sent through the interface, the interfacing software translates $FR as hex code 3F and the typesetting machine "understands" 3F as flush right. The translation is complete.

If you wish, a comment can be added to the word processing translation table. This comment will simply tell users *what* the translation does. Several lines of codes will then read:

/H$FR=3F/ . . . . $FR is translated to flush right

/A$MV=Mohawk Valley Community College/ . . . mnemonic code

/V0000010000000100=00000010/ . . . . translates two spaces to one space

The process continues until all the translations you need are written. It is not necessary to write *all translations* the first time you create a translation table. One of the great advantages of word processing tables is that editing and revisions are easy and fast.

149

Checklist: Successful Translation Guidelines

- ✔ Don't be the first! Before you move toward interfacing, make certain there are several organizations that have already implemented what you have in mind. Those people will certainly be able to answer questions. More important, you will be certain that answers will be available.

- ✔ If you have an in-house typesetter, use the trained personnel in your graphics shop to create translation tables. Your word processing operators may be dazzled by the series of seemingly unfathomable codes; it is less likely that typesetting professionals will make input mistakes.

- ✔ Do not attempt to teach your customers (if you are a typesetter) or word processing personnel how to be typesetters immediately. Keyboarding is not typesetting. Because they are different crafts, use simple, nontechnical terminology when creating mnemonics.

- ✔ Use the translation table suggested here or another standard table. A standard set of translations has been debugged and has been proven to work. Your own creative version of a table may work better for you eventually, but move away from a standard slowly.

- ✔ Assign only one person to create and update tables. An illogical table created by more than one person won't work.

- ✔ Once the interface is working, leave the translations alone for at least several months so that word processing operators can become familiar with typesetting input.

- ✔ If you do make changes in a translation table, *always keep a backup copy of your last working table.* Don't risk losing an entire working table to a power outage.

- ✔ Don't revise unnecessarily. You will not only risk making changes that do not work, you'll confuse your operators. Every time you make a change, every person who uses the tables must be notified and then has to relearn basic working techniques. Constant changes are annoying and unproductive. If you are a typesetter, frequent bothersome changes are not the way to keep customers.

- ✔ Document your translation tables. Create large charts of your translations in easy-to-read, easy-to-learn formats. Mass distribution of the documentation will create familiarity and then acceptance.

- ✔ Be patient. The interface will probably not work immediately—but it will work.

CHAPTER 11

For Type Buyers Only

COMPUTERS ARE INANIMATE, but interfaces are not. The most important factor in any interface is the people who implement it. How do you find the right typesetting company to handle your interface?

How to Select a Typesetter

Let's assume that you want to change typesetters. There are several steps to follow to find and then select a typesetter that offers both interfacing capability and quality typesetting output. The suggestions offered here relate only to the interface. Price bids and quality checks will be necessary as well.

■ Which Type Houses Interface?

Your first step is to find out what's available. The *Data Book* gives an up-to-date listing of typesetters with interfacing capabilities. Another source is *TypeWorld*'s annual directory of telecommunications facilities. No list can be complete; every week new interfacers appear.

Hardware manufacturers are a good source of information. Ask Compugraphic, Mergenthaler, and the other large typesetting manufacturers for a survey of typesetters in your area that are capable of interfacing. Shaftstall, Applied Data, Kurzweil, and other interfacing hardware suppliers will be able to add to the list.

Armed with your lists, keep hunting. Ask other type users in your area for advice. The suggestions you garner here will be particularly valuable. You will not only learn names but you will also be able to secure recommendations, pro and con.

Narrowing the Field. When you have several potential typesetters in mind, invite them to visit your organization. Ask these questions: What sorts of modems do you have? What is the disk capacity of your typesetter (how much can your disks hold before you have to change disks)? Do you have a dedicated telephone number that is used strictly for telecommunications? How do your sign-on procedures work? Can you make suggestions as to how we should code our documents? Do you have manuals we can use?

There are no right answers to most of the questions. You are looking for intelligent answers. If the typesetter is completely new to interfacing, it's possible that you will be a source of information rather than the other way around.

How do you judge the typesetter? If the typesetter offers telecommunications but does not have a dedicated telecommunications number, it may not be a serious user. If you find yourself explaining questions or even basic terminology, take heed. The answers to your questions should narrow the field.

■ Costs

As in any business decision, the costs involved will influence your decision. Price quotations are a major consideration.

There are some hidden costs involved in this decision. Check long-distance telephone rates. If you are in Evansville, Indiana, telecommunicating to Chicago will be cheaper than to Houston. The differences in telephone rates can influence your decision, especially when you are moving hundreds of pages that require hours of telephone time.

A local typesetter can be a good choice. Not only do you eliminate long-distance rates but you also have the advantage of professional advice close at hand. But if you are not located in a large city, your options may be limited. Long-distance interfaces are more expensive, but they are certainly not prohibitive.

■ Interfacing Quality

When you have identified potential type houses, ask each typesetter questions about current customers. With whom are they currently interfacing? How many interfaces have they established? Most important, have you ever interfaced to my word processor before? It is *very helpful* to you if there is already a working interface established with your hardware. You are then able to lean on the experience of others instead of blazing new paths. Other criteria being equal, go with the typesetter that has experience with your machine.

If you are considering an interface with a printer, make certain that typesetting isn't a sideline. An interface requires dedication, and a printer may not want to invest the necessary time to make communications work as well as you wish.

After getting this information from potential type houses, ask their current customers questions: How good was the advice they received from the type house? Do the translation tables work well? Do they encode typographic information in their documents, or are jobs simply sent ASCII to ASCII? What percentage of their type costs have they saved?

■ The Contract

Don't sign any long-term contracts early on in the negotiations for typesetting. Even a one-year contract should not be signed until the following steps have been accomplished.

First, you should write a sample document on your word processor and be pleased with the telecommunicated result. Go to the typesetter's office and have your employees send a document while you are there. What is the result on screen? Does it work?

Second, continue the test with a more complicated document. If you are using mnemonic coding, each code should be translated correctly. You will be charged for any coding errors, so make certain now that there aren't any, or, if there are, that they are corrected immediately.

Third, do your homework in contacting other clients of the typesetting vendor. A sales pitch is the best of circumstances for the typesetter. Only the customers can give you accurate appraisals of the typesetter's resiliency, technological proficiency, and overall manner. Will the relationship be as friendly over a period of time as it is during the sale?

If you are satisfied, work out a three-month trial before committing to a long-term relationship. If the interface works, you can sign an agreement for a longer period later.

The In-House Shop

The in-house shop was discussed in Chapter 8. Now you know what is involved in interfacing. If you are word processing, it's clear that there are several technologies to be developed in your organization. Interfacing and phototypesetting may be too much to handle at one time. Here is a sequence of events that might work for an in-house shop.

1. After researching interface devices, buy the equipment and software you believe are right for your organization.

2. Find a typesetter with interfacing capability.

3. Establish a commercial interface with the typesetter—you are now communicating with an outside agency.

4. Make this interface work for a minimum of six months. Establish a work flow and a set way of doing things. Allow your employees to become comfortable with the interface.

5. Compare current type costs with your type bills before interfacing. How much have you saved?

6. Armed with the knowledge that you are already saving a certain percentage of your former costs, is in-house interfacing now worth it? Assume you have saved 35 percent by moving your keyboarding in-house. It does not make sense to continue toward the in-house type shop if it will save you only an additional 7 percent. So how much more will you save?

7. If the numbers add up, go ahead with the in-house graphics facility. But think small. Start with simple jobs and do not attempt to make a

quick, overnight transition from the commercial interface to in-house typesetting. Because you have already established an interface, consider purchasing the same equipment used by the typesetter with which you are interfacing. If you do, the interface is simply a matter of dialing a different telephone number—a calm introduction to in-house typesetting.

If you are not now setting type yourself, the possibilities are excellent that once you've saved money with the commercial interface, you will not go to in-house. Your graphics budget will be significantly decreased. When you are already saving half of what you had formerly spent, saving an additional small percentage is clearly less attractive.

In-house is certainly still valuable, but you may decide to implement that change well after the first change of interfacing. There have been instances of in-house and telecommunications being accomplished simultaneously with great success. One organization saved $50,000 the first year—that's *after* the expenses of new employees, new equipment, and a new production flow. The second year, the previous annual budget of $250,000 for typesetting was reduced to just over $100,000—a 60 percent cut in costs. This cannot be accomplished without in-house typesetting.

Alternative Applications of In-House

If you have a graphics shop and are considering an interface, you are not alone. The in-house shop works and it pays for itself in cut costs. Adding interfaces to your in-house shop could save you even more.

In its infancy, the in-house shop may be working two shifts, keyboarding simple jobs like annual reports and brochures. But most of the work is input on a word processor. There is no interface at this point, so your typesetting personnel must spend a lot of time retyping computer-stored documents. That's a lot of work.

Then your research on telecommunications and hardwiring leads to a proposal to purchase interfacing hardware. The interface is established; you are moving documents from the word processor directly to the typesetter, without retyping. Electronic manuscripts have replaced paper for the bulk of the typesetting load.

Because retyping is now unnecessary, your employees work much faster, and a 16-hour day is no longer necessary. The employees, and your typesetting machine, are not being utilized constantly. Your lease on the typesetting machine is for 24 hours a day. You have employees who need work to do because technology has streamlined production. But you don't *have* the work.

The solution? Go out and get the work from customers: Sell your typesetting capabilities. In-house typesetting companies are a growing trend in the industry. Selling type is not easy. You will have to wear a new hat and become a typesetting vendor. But selling typesetting does pay the lease on the machines.

Implications of Universal Interfacing

Telecommunications and interfacing have been widely available since the early 1980s. It is projected that 80 percent of typesetting will be interfaced by the 1990s. Why not sooner?

The typesetting companies are the reason. These are the implications of universal interfacing for the typesetters:

1. Easy switching of vendors for customers. Moving typesetting accounts from one typesetter to another will be as simple as dialing a new telephone number.

2. If typesetting is sold by in-house graphics shops, many former customers of type houses will become competitors.

3. It will no longer be possible for typesetters to establish a monopoly on typesetting in a geographic area. Customers will have access to many more typesetters. Telephones can send manuscripts anywhere in the country.

4. Customers must purchase equipment that costs less than $2,000; the costs to the typesetter, depending on the type of interface chosen, can exceed $50,000.

5. Typesetters must establish guidelines and manuals to be used by the customers.

6. Typesetting companies must learn new techniques and create new pricing structures.

As you can see, typesetting companies get very little in return for establishing interface capabilities. They must pay the bulk of the out-of-pocket costs for both software and hardware. They also must make the interface an easy road for the customer, or the customer will find another typesetter.

These are the reasons why interfacing has not moved more quickly. Typesetters might view interfacing a bit like offering a manufacturer's rebate: As long as no one makes an offer, the sellers win. When one seller offers a rebate (interfacing), everyone must.

Interfacing is here, and the race is now on. In the early 1980s, typesetters that interfaced were the first to offer the capability to customers in their area. To survive today, typesetters are being forced to buy the technology because the industry has demanded interfacing. That means that *better interfacing* and *better documentation* will be the selling points of the next few years. And within a few years, finding a typesetter that interfaces will be as easy as is finding a typesetter today. The customers will again be the winners.

CHAPTER 12

For Typesetters Only

TYPE HOUSES ARE FACING A DILEMMA. Interfacing costs you money, time, and effort. In the interfacing marketplace, typesetting companies will make less money because they are charging less. Customers are the ones saving money.

But if every typesetter around you is offering interfacing services, you must also or your marketing position will be severely threatened. For those who have not yet interfaced, telecommunications and the other interfacing options are quickly moving from the status of flashy selling points to the position of economic necessity. In other words, you're being *forced* into interfacing, whether or not you wish to.

There are two ways to react: You can devoutly refuse to buy the new technology and let your business suffer the inevitable losses, or you can gracefully accept the fact that you're in a profession that will drastically change its methods every few years. Interfaced output is just another revolution in an industry that has moved from hot metal to phototype and then from phototype through scanning to laser in 30 years.

Most type houses have or will opt for interfacing. If you are reading this book, that's good evidence that you are concerned about the technology.

Using the Technology: New Opportunities

The increases in equipment costs and decreases in typesetting billings are only part of the picture. Interfacing does create new opportunities to sell type. Faster typesetting means more typesetting. What can you do with the new technology?

First, there are new customers. Typesetting is no longer a regional product. Telephone lines can be utilized to expand your marketing area.

Second, there is more typesetting from old customers. Type is more attractive than typewriting, and it's cheaper to produce directories, manuals, and sales lists through typesetting. Typesetting requires 40 percent less paper than typewriting, resulting in cheaper printing bills. Because typesetting has become more economical, customers will use typesetting more often.

Third, there are more customers. Word processor buyers will be looking for typesetters with interfaces. The computer printout is no longer an acceptable form of communication. Businesses that in the past were content with typewriting will move toward typesetting. Type can be cheaper, and it is certainly more aesthetically pleasing.

Overall, then, your business will change, but it need not suffer. If you use good marketing sense, interfacing can be positioned with new customers to work for you. Because you will not be inputting copy, typesetting turnaround will be faster. Your total profit and loss picture can actually be improved.

Marketing the Technology

If you do not have an interfacing capability now, a terminal with telecommunications option can be had for as little as $5,000. A media converter or OCR device will cost much more. But once you have the equipment, how do you sell the service?

■ Debugging Your Interface

There are two good ways to perfect your interface capability. One way is to do it with an established customer who is willing to work with you on the debugging. Be certain, though, that the customer is fully aware of the possible frustrations.

A better alternative is to buy a microcomputer and establish an in-plant interface. Once you have debugged internally, then you are ready to move into commercial interfacing. After the micro has served its experimental purpose, you can use it either as a computer for accounting or inventory or as an input terminal for typesetting.

■ Announcing the Services

Before you are ready for full-scale implementation of the service, let your current customers know that you will be offering an interface soon. Don't promise an interface by a given date: If you don't meet your deadline, you could aggravate customers eagerly anticipating the new option. Informing your current customers will ensure that they do not look for other interfacing avenues at the same time you are about to install communications.

Be prepared to announce the interface after it's debugged. Use brochures, newsletters, and industry publications like *TypeWorld* and *The Typographer*. Include the information in any periodical mailing you distribute. The format of your announcement should be determined in part by your market area. Look over the competition in your area and decide on your advertising approach based on what competitive type houses are offering.

■ Finding the Market

Your interface has three potential markets. Make certain that your announcements reach each market.

Current customers are obvious choices. Be very sure to include *every* customer with whom you are doing business. Those small accounts whom you don't inform because they are "too small" or "not interested" might well be interested in microcomputer interfacing. Remember, micros are now a commodity that nearly every company can afford.

Past customers are ideal candidates for a second mailing list. Interfacing is a good way to reapproach old customers who have moved to other typesetters. "We're better than we were" is the right sales strategy in this case.

New customers will be the major thrust of your marketing research. To find them, buy the mailing lists of the American Word Processing Society and the Data Processing Management Association. Find the members in your area. Remember that with interfacing, your area has grown to include a larger geographic space. Talk to word processing sales reps and find out if there is a local users' group. Sales reps are also good sources of information on who is in the market for word processing hardware. These people are potential interfacers.

Once you have established an interface, announce it to any organization you can find with the same word processing equipment. Interfacing with these organizations will be much simpler to establish, both for you and for the user.

■ Marketing Strategies

Two marketing strategies work well. If you are the first type house in town to offer interfacing, let your customers know. If you are not the first, be better.

When everyone is interfacing, the successful interfacers will not be those who interfaced first. The major selling points will not be price or availability. Your sales thrust should be *customer service*. Here are some tips on being better.

Documentation. Offer your customers a manual of protocols and policies (see Figure 12-1). As a mailer, this manual immediately makes a large number of customers aware of your capabilities. It will also be invaluable to your own employees (and to your customers') when they are creating a working environment. The manual should include baud rates, a sample translation table, the ASCII code set used by your typesetting manufacturer, and a discussion of necessary protocols.

A second document should be a table of suggested mnemonics. This table will probably be used by a minority of your interfacing customers. Do not include the table in the interfacing manual because it may confuse matters—customers might mistakenly think that mnemonics is the *only way* to interface.

When writing the mnemonics table, consider using the system discussed in Chapter 10. These suggested mnemonics work, are easy to use, and easy to understand. If you wish to create your own system of mnemonics, don't

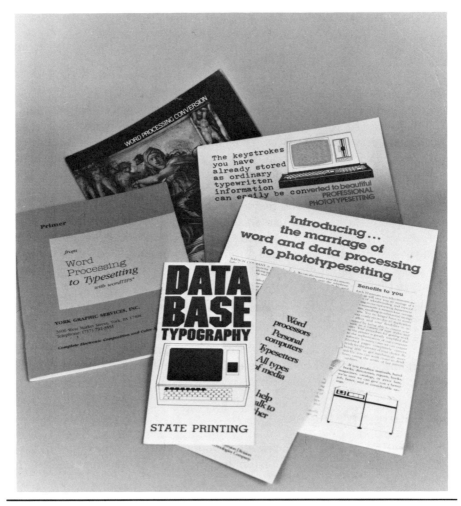

■ **FIGURE 12-1. Create a brochure to sell your interfacing services. Photo: Thomas D. Maneen.**

experiment with your customers. Test the system in-plant. If it works well, then move on to commercial use. Writing mnemonics is time consuming and difficult; that's one of the reasons a standard mnemonic code will be valuable.

Testing Documents. Many customers wonder whether an interface will work. Offer to conduct a one-document trial, free of charge. That offer will convince most potential customers to attempt the interface.

Assuming your technology works, a simple document can be keyboarded by your personnel on the customer's word processor. Keyboarding by sales reps can be especially impressive since they are not accomplished word processors. If they can make the interface work, it's almost certain that a customer's employees can also.

If you intend to market telecommunications, your sales staff must be equipped with a modem to permit communications from the word processor. Once the interface works, selling a system that will cut the customer's costs by 30 percent will be easier.

Seminars. Free seminars are one of the best ways to both attract promising customers and to advertise your services. They are an ideal way to establish your reputation as an interface leader and to share information. Your employees can spend a day with a dozen or so employees of potential customers. A preliminary talk about type terminology and how typesetters work can be followed by an in-depth discussion of what will happen when a document is translated. This is training at its best. The more operators know, the better they'll be able to do their jobs. The seminar should also offer training on how to use mnemonics and translation tables. A discussion between your personnel and the operators should result in an explanation of why your way is the best way. Finally, you should explain what physically happens during interfacing. For telecommunications, who calls whom? What numbers are used? How long does it take?

Controlling the Tools. Offer your customers the services of your personnel for the input of translation mnemonics. The keyboarders will need to know *what* codes to use, but your personnel should input them. At first glance, translation tables appear confusing and can be input incorrectly. Since your employees know what they are typing when they type translation tables, they are the best people for the job. This is not only good marketing, it is also good technology. Input by your personnel will save hours of debugging time. Your unselfishness is also an obvious point your sales force can emphasize.

Language. In both your documentation and your speech, use simple English. Most customers are simply not interested in terms like RS-232, binary, machine code, and analog; they just want to save money. Impressive technological talk won't impress potential customers.

Sharing Information. Prepare lists of customers with whom you are already interfacing. After securing permission from the customers, distribute the lists to both potential new customers and existing interfacers. Consider the creation of an interface users' group. This will allow you to share information with your customers and also allow them to share ideas among themselves. If one user constructs a better mnemonic code, everyone will benefit. Problems and changes in procedure can be resolved in groups; individualized attention will not be necessary. The users' group can be especially attractive to the first-time interfacer.

Employee Sharing. If you are moving into heavy interfacing, and obtaining a major account is important, offer to have your personnel available to your customers for the first two or three days of the interface. Appoint a person to be a hands-on teacher. The best person for this job is the employee responsible for creating your translation table mnemonics. By first demonstrating how mnemonics coding works, and then through step-by-step instruction, your teacher can make interfacing easy and fun. Do not send a sales rep as a teacher. A working, hands-on person who knows typesetting at its most basic level is what is needed. Cooperation between your employees and your customers begins here.

Pricing. As with most typesetting, it is hazardous to talk price in general. Every job is different, but every customer wants the promised 57 percent savings. You know that 20 to 30 percent is a more reasonable expectation. How do you resolve this issue?

Give potential customers general indications of the savings to be expected. Customers should be told exactly what mnemonic coding and format coding are worth to you. If ASCII to ASCII straight matter without typesetting codes is worth 20 percent in savings to the potential interfacer, say so. How much is copy completely encoded, requiring no massaging by your employees?

Typesetting prices are based upon difficulty. Interfaced type prices will vary the same way. It is impossible to know how difficult a job is until it's been transmitted. How good are the codes input by the operators? How thorough are they? Do your employees have to massage every paragraph because of input errors? You need the answers to those questions before you can quote actual dollars and cents.

Skirt the issue of actual dollar prices until these questions have been answered. But be prepared to give your customers a solid indication of the *percentage of savings* possible.

Pricing the Type

Technical type is difficult to interface, whereas straight matter is usually easy. Your pricing structure must reflect these differences. Offer large discounts—up to 50 percent—on straight matter that is completely encoded at the word processor level. If your employees simply output the material, with no massaging whatsoever, 50 percent is warranted.

If you are involved in technical typesetting, it may take months for interface development. That time is your investment. The percentage of savings received by your interfacing customers should be lower than with straight text. A 30 percent reduction in price should allow you to recoup your investment costs fairly. You will also, of course, be able to produce more type because you need not keyboard the copy you are typesetting.

If you have already developed an interface with one customer and a second customer has precisely the same equipment as the first customer, there are no new development costs. What should you charge? A cheaper rate could be charged because the interface has already been established.

You should recover your own development costs. Remember that it isn't necessary to undercut yourself; your *higher priced interfaced type is still less expensive than conventional typesetting*. You took the risk to develop the interface. Like hardware manufacturers, your pricing structure should not be altered. You do, however, now have that option.

The interface, then, has become a pricing/profit tool. After the expense of the interface has been paid, you have some latitude in estimating prices on an individual basis. If you want to cut your base price of 30 percent savings to bid a job that you do want, you have that marketing strength.

■ Professional Pricing Guidelines

1. Develop a pricing policy that combats illogical pricing. A possible strategy is to differentiate among straight matter, difficult type, and technical type and then develop prices based on whether the type was coded in-plant or by the customer.

2. Don't be tempted to charge traditional rates for interfaced typesetting. This may work for a very short time, but your customers will soon discover that interfaced type is not as expensive per page. Develop fair pricing policies that will benefit both your company and the customer.

3. Be creative. Most type houses will have to abandon the traditional hourly rates for typesetting. If a job is interfaced and then output in 1 minute and 32 seconds, does that mean you charge the customer for a minute-and-a-half at $55 per hour? Of course not. New pricing structures will have to be developed for interfaced typesetting. Most documents are stored on disk. How many characters are contained on each file of the disk? The type house may have to develop prices based on the number of files or number of bits transmitted and outputted.

4. Be fair. Your customers will be aware of industry pricing structures since they are interfacing to save money. An industry-accepted savings structure, readily available to the customer, will aid both present and future sales. But don't sell the interface short. Take advantage of the opportunity the interface offers.

Interfacing is today's technology. It will be with us for several decades. It could be some time before the next change. What is the *next* revolution? We have moved from keyboarding by typesetters to keyboarding by customers. The coming revolution may be no keyboarding at all but rather voice-activated typesetting. But that has been promised for years. As one salesperson put it, "I won't sell it in my career, and I don't intend to retire for 25 years." Interfacing will be here for some time. Your reputation as an interfacer should be important to you—you may need it for several decades.

Computer Basics

ALTHOUGH MOST OF US NO LONGER immediately think of a mechanical monster when we hear the word "computer," some of us are still not very comfortable in dealing with the machine. First-time computer users sometimes feel as though they have been left alone, defenseless from the onslaught of jargon.

Computers are not difficult to understand. The way they work is based upon applied electronics that has not radically changed since 1946. The first programmable computer (told to do various tasks) was the 1946 ENIAC, and its 18,000 vacuum tubes worked on the same principle that the newest IBM PCjr and Apple Macintosh use.

Digital Computers

Digital computers compute numerically; that is, they use sets of numbers to represent words, keystroke commands, and whatever else is contained in a document. The basic idea to grasp is that computers understand digitally—in terms of *only* two digits: 0 and 1. A computer can be compared to a huge bank of light switches: The lights are either switched on (1) or off (0). The on and off switches are a good analogy because, in fact, that is exactly what the computer does. It "understands" a 0 as a voltage level of 0 volts and a 1 as a voltage level of 5 volts. The most complicated coding is simply a combination of off and on switches, producing the appropriate voltage series.

In 1946, the vacuum tube was the fastest possible switch and thus was used in the ENIAC. By 1948, the transistor had been invented. Transistors require no heating element (unlike a light bulb or a vacuum tube) and therefore can be much smaller than tubes. They also require less voltage. They are cheaper, more dependable, and easier to use. The computer industry converted, along with the space program, television, and transistor radio.

Semiconductors and Chips

The technology continued to develop throughout the 1960s. If you've been around computers at all—or microwaves, refrigerators, calculators, and even digital watches—you have probably heard about *semiconductors*. A conductor is a substance through which electricity flows readily in any direction. Semiconductors are similar to conductors in that they permit electricity to flow through them, but the electrical flow is peculiar. These solids are naturally crystalline, and in that natural state electrical flow is permitted in one direction but moves very weakly in the other (as though the substance was an insulator and not a conductor). Thus the term "semiconductor" logically evolved.

The most common semiconductor is silicon, which, after carbon, is the most common solid on earth. The raw material from which silicon is produced to make most semiconductor circuits is sand! It's no wonder that transistor technology was attractive.

The technologists of the early 1960s created the capability to produce electrical components smaller, cheaper, and quicker. Computers were among their first major projects, and many others, including transistor radios, followed rapidly.

After the semiconductors began to miniaturize electronics, the next development was the *integrated circuit*. These circuits are simply two or more transistors combined, or integrated, with other circuit components (like resistors or capacitors) on the same silicon semiconductor. As tinier and tinier transistors were produced, it seemed logical to make even this lilliputian world more productive. Integrated circuits, or ICs, are now the predominant circuit in all electronics. Because of their silicon base, these circuits are usually called *chips*.

Chips grew in power and complexity but not in size. Technological improvement throughout the 1960s and 1970s meant a progression from the development of extremely complicated chips to the mass production of chips for a wide variety of industrial and commercial applications. As the techniques used to create chips continued to improve, chips with thousands of transistors were created. Each transistor is photoetched onto the silicon substrate from large templates.

About 1970, engineers produced chips capable of much more than simply turning dishwashers on and off. Chips were developed that could actually read information and then make "decisions." This was a breakthrough. These chips were *microprocessors* (see Figure I-1). When the microprocessors were developed, the computer as we use it today was possible. Small desk-top microcomputers are often based upon a single microprocessor chip. So, in a very real sense, the way the microprocessor works is the way our computers work.

Nuts and Bolts: Hardware

Any computer is basically constructed of two parts, *hardware* and *software*. Hardware is the equipment used to process words or numbers; software is the directions the computer follows to process that information. Many experts have different ideas as to what types of hardware are essential. The equipment that you *must* have in the computer you buy, and what is considered peripheral, is debated. Peripheral hardware is usually needed to make a computer handy enough to entice purchase as a business tool,

■ FIGURE I-1. Microprocessor chip: Intel 8080. Photo courtesy Intel Corporation.

but it is not the intrinsically necessary hardware that defines what a computer is.

■ Central Processing Unit

The essential hardware is the *central processing unit* (CPU) and the *main memory*. The CPU is the chip within a computer that does the real work. Common chips used as microprocessors are the Intel 8080 and 8088, the Motorola 68000, the Zilog Z80, and the MOS Technology 6502. Regardless of the chip used, they are all very inexpensive and very powerful. Often referred to as the "brains" of the computer, the CPU processes commands and moves information in strings of 0s and 1s. This chip is no larger than the head of a pencil eraser (see Figures I-2a and I-2b).

Microcomputers, personal computers, minicomputers, and even the largest mainframes all use microprocessor chips. In the larger minis and mainframes, the CPU is constructed of several chips mounted on a single unit known as a board.

How important was the chip to the computer-user revolution of the 1970s? In 1950, it cost about $2.61 to store one character on a computer, in part because of the high cost of the central processing unit. In the 1980s, the cost has dropped to less than one-tenth of one cent per character. While costs have gone down dramatically, capacity has mushroomed.

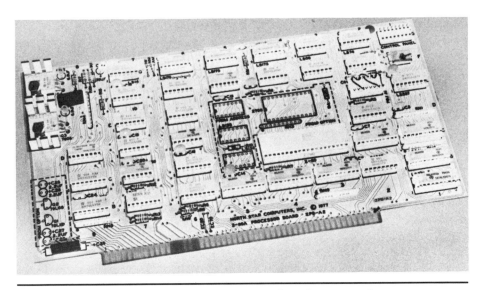

■ FIGURE I-2a. CPU chip. Photo courtesy North Star Computers Inc.

■ FIGURE I-2b. CPU chip against a dime. Photo courtesy Motorola.

■ Main Memory

The main memory is the computer's internal memory. Several technical storage areas make up internal memory, but, in general, the main memory stores the programs and information necessary during a particular computing session. The information is stored electronically on chips in different ways in memory: *RAM* (random access memory) and *ROM* (read-only memory) are the two most often used. (There are also other types of memory: PROM, EPROM, and also EAROM; it can get complicated quickly.)

A computer can do two things with its memory. It can read from it to perform a particular function, or it can store material for later use. These functions differentiate RAM from ROM. The well-known analogy used to describe ROM and RAM are the phonograph record and the cassette tape. A phonograph record has a "memory" that cannot be changed by the user; your Pavarotti record can't be erased to become a Bob Dylan platter. That is the way ROM works. The memory is programmed at the factory and is part of the computer's internal memory. It cannot be edited by the user and is simply part of the way the computer works. The programs are permanent because the systems programs that control the operation of the computer do not change.

RAM is that part of the memory most like an audiocassette. The recording on the tape can be erased and another recording substituted. Similarly, with RAM, new instructions or documents can be written over previous information. RAM is used to store operating programs for the specific jobs you are doing at any particular time, to store data before "dumping" onto external memory, or to temporarily store user-developed programs. The major problem with RAM, unlike cassette tapes, is that RAM is *volatile*— when the machine is turned off, the contents of the memory are lost. If the contents of RAM are needed for future use, you must have some way of permanently storing it.

I/O: Display

The CPU and memory, then, are the essential ingredients in creating a computer. However, in order to construct a computer system that will be useful to you, more hardware is needed. The computer itself does not include any components for creation, permanent storage, or output of information. The first peripherals you will need are the *I/O devices*—input and output equipment.

There are several types of input. The most useful input stations are *on-line*, meaning that the operator is able to communicate directly with the computer. The typical on-line input device is the computer *terminal*. Other possibilities for on-line devices include calculator keyboards or window-display systems. A terminal is a familiar typewriterlike keyboard attached to a television screen. The video monitors offer obvious advantages, but most important is that two-way communication is possible between you and the CPU. The great majority of terminals are currently constructed using a standard keyboard design.

Most terminals come with the computer, especially in the microcomputer market. If you are in the market for more powerful minicomputers, you'll find more options from which to choose. Most minis can be run with a variety of terminals, including but not limited to those sold by the computer's manufacturer. Basically, the terminal is your typewriter pad to talk to the CPU, and there are a variety of schemes to construct terminal/computer combinations.

In the bustling market of microcomputers, for instance, the Apple has a keyboard permanently attached to the video monitor. The Kaypro keyboard is connected to the video monitor/CPU by a cord that plugs in and out. The Osborne has a very small screen attached to the keyboard but offers the option of purchasing a larger screen. The IBM PCjr has a "freeboard," a keyboard that need not be physically connected to the screen. The Sinclair ZX80 has no screen at all but has a keyboard (you use your television set as a video monitor). And the North Star Horizon is a computer without a keyboard or screen. Both must be purchased individually. The keyboard to purchase should be based on your own preference and needs. It will probably be a secondary consideration when making an input decision.

The major I/O decision will be the method used for storage. There are many alternatives here. Your choices will have far-reaching consequences as to how you produce documents and what you expect to do with them. If you wish to interface with typesetters, for instance, there are several storage media that are simply not advisable, although they might be fine for other applications.

I/O: Storage

Suppose you are in the market to buy equipment to communicate with a computer. There are not only decisions about which computer to buy and which way to configure input, but you also have to decide *how* your jobs will be stored: on paper or magnetic media?

■ Paper Media

In the 1970s, most computers used both paper and magnetic storage. For many people, the Hollerith card epitomized their feelings about computers: "Do not fold, spindle, or mutilate." Today, the IBM punch cards are going the way of the dodo. They are rarely used except for data processing because they are bulky and cannot hold very much information. Also, they can be lost or placed in the wrong sequence in a card deck. And, of course, they can't be folded, mutilated, or spindled, or they will jam card readers and sorters.

Punch Cards. *Punch cards* work through a combination of mechanics and electronics. After a *card puncher* transcribes data from a keyboard onto blank cards, the punched cards are stacked and moved to a machine called the card verifier. The verifier makes certain that all the data have been correctly entered. The cards are then mechanically sorted according to whatever sequences or categories you wish: date, salesperson, type of sale, or amount of purchase. Then the electronics begins. The card reader does a specific job very well. Metal brushes or photoelectric cells "read" the cards as they move through the machine, noting when there is a punched hole.

Card processing can seem very fast. Some card readers can operate at speeds of up to 2,000 cards per minute. But that speed, as it turns out, is actually quite slow when compared to other forms of input. For all word processing and for most other applications as well, the days of the punch card are over.

Punched Paper Tape. Another paper medium is *punched paper tape.* Paper tape was more often seen in type rooms of the 1960s and 1970s than in computer centers. It was the first popular way to store information for computerized typesetting. Some typesetters still use paper tape, although using paper media is a bit like using an hourglass—it's quaint, but it really doesn't get the job done as well or as dependably as possible.

The process of getting information from paper tapes to the computer is quite similar to card punching. Paper tapes (see Figure I-3) are punched with holes. Each character on the typewriter keyboard used to create paper tape memory is understood and punched in a particular sequence of six vertical holes. The letter *A,* for instance, is coded as two holes at the top, three positions unpunched, and then one hole at the sixth and final position. The permutations of punched and unpunched positions allow every keystroke to be understood as a different combination of holes (except the space key, which is no hole at all).

Tapes are cheaper than cards, and it's easier to store large amounts of information on tapes because they are less bulky. Once a job is on a tape, it's impossible to fumble it out of order.

There are disadvantages. Tapes are more difficult to edit than punched cards. When a punched card is found to have incorrect data, it's simply thrown away and a new, correct card is produced. The correction process is more complicated with paper tape. To edit a paper tape, the tape must be inserted into a paper tape reader, and a new, corrected tape is made. A second possibility is splicing corrections into the first run tape, but this can create big problems when reading later on. Most typesetting plants that work with paper tape use different colors of tape for different phases of the job. Yellow for first galleys, pink for first corrected proofs, blue for second proofs, and so on. For large jobs, it isn't unusual to see a rainbow of paper

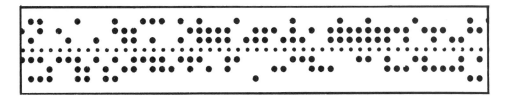

■ **FIGURE I-3. Paper tape is punched with holes that create memory.**

tape streaming through the reader. Tapes can also be easily torn. And remember, don't mutilate, fold, or spindle. For the most part, paper memory has outlived its usefulness.

■ Magnetic Media

After the days of paper tape, the next revolutionary discovery has been magnetic media. Magnetic media are packaged in several ways, but it's all understood by the CPU in the same way.

Magnetic cassettes, tapes, and other forms of storage are similar to the tape used to store audiotapes. The tape is made of plastic with an iron oxide coating on one side. Iron, of course, can be magnetized. When you put data onto a tape or cassette, invisible spots of data are recorded by electromagnetic impulses. Wherever there is an impulse recorded on the magnetized coating, data are stored in memory.

Paper tapes, you recall, are punched in series of six tracks. We've all heard of eight-track audiotapes. In paper tape, remember that the letter *A* was two holes, followed by three unpunched tracks, then finally another hole. For magnetic media, the holes become electronic impulses. The impulses are formed in tracks (seven-track and nine-track are the most popular for computer media) just as in paper tape, and the CPU is capable of reading the impulses sent to it by the tapes because it "understands" the code being used. An *A* is impulse, impulse, no impulse, no impulse, no impulse, impulse. Put into computer vernacular, the letter *A* is understood as 110001 (the 1 being the on, or impulse, switch position; the 0 being off).

One thing is very clear about magnetized storage: It is very fast. The speed of magnetic media depends on how much data are stored on the media (how dense the storage is), and how fast the media can be moved inside the device reading the magnetized surface. The devices that read magnetic tape reels vary from 75 to 200 inches of tape per second, and the character density per inch can range from about 200 to more than 6,000 characters per inch. The slowest reading, then, is about 75×200, or 15,000 characters per second. Top speed is $200 \times 6,000$, or 1,250,000 characters per second! Compare that with the horse-drawn speed of 3,000 characters with paper tape.

Cassettes and Cartridges. Starting with the least powerful alternative, the first option for magnetic storage media are *magnetic cassettes and cartridges*. The cassettes are usable only with the smaller microcomputers sold as home or personal computers. Data are stored on cassette and are read by tape recorders.

There are several major disadvantages with cassette memory in a business setting, and cassettes are very rarely used for professional applications. First, the memory is sequential: if you are using a half-hour tape and the job you want to edit is on the wrong end of the tape, you may have to wait 25 minutes to access the information. Second, the memory is only as good as the system that produces it. If you have a tape recorder that regularly crunches tapes into snarls, your jobs are doomed. The great advantage to cassette memory is its very low cost, but that cost is countered by the dangers of losing important documents.

An alternative that some have used are *digital* cassette recorders, which are capable of recalling documents randomly rather than sequentially. These recorders, however, cost about the same as the diskette systems, so their one advantage—cost—is cancelled.

Cartridges are basically the professional's cassette. They are more reliable than cassette memory and they are capable of retaining more information. One-quarter-inch wide and from 150 to 400 feet long, the cartridge tapes are more often used in business than cassettes, although they still are not popular. The potentially disastrous loss of information continues to be a risk with cartridge systems, so it is unlikely that an interfacer would choose either cassette or cartridge memory. Easier systems are cheap alternatives when compared to the costs of purchasing and implementing interfacing software and hardware. The basic core of a computer system, the storage method, is not the place to cut fiscal corners.

Magnetic Cards. IBM was busy in the 1960s and 1970s. Several ways to store magnetic information were developed by IBM in those years, and the first was the *mag card* system. Mag cards are thin, unprotected sheets of plastic coated with iron oxide. The memory contained on a mag card is read by the IBM-supplied mag card reader, and information is moved from the reader to the keyboard (which looks like an IBM typewriter with several extra features).

The keyboard has no video monitor, but does have the capacity to retain the volatile data that are lost when the machine is turned off. These data can be edited. When all changes are made, the volatile keyboard data can be moved to the mag cards, thus updating them. The mag card systems are forerunners of word processors, but they are not in any sense computers. They allow the operator to move and insert information in much the same way as dedicated word processors. The system is still used in many offices and businesses where many similar documents must be produced with small alterations. (Legal letters are a common application.) It's clear that mag card systems are not intended to be interfacers; they are smart, fast typewriters, but they are not "intelligent" enough to be able to communicate directly with other computerized devices.

Magnetic Tape Reels. Mainframes and the new generation of supercomputers use magnetic tape as a storage medium. These are the computer "eyes" beloved in all those 1950s sci-fi movies. Magnetic tape requires tape reels that look and act very much like motion picture reels. Placed on a *tape drive,* the tape is moved from reel to reel to read data that are then moved to the CPU. A tape drive can cruise at speeds of up to 200 inches per second. Tape damage has been virtually eliminated.

Tape drives can either read data from the CPU or can write information from the CPU onto the tapes. Thus, the drives have a *read-write head,* an electromagnet that applies the magnetic charges to appropriate places on the tapes. In a nine-track drive, there are nine read-write heads, each placing electromagnetic charges onto the tapes (or reading charges from the tape).

Tapes are one of the three basic methods used to store information today. When choosing between tapes and rigid or floppy disks, the basic decision will not be based on how dependable or fast or cheap the magnetic media are. All three systems possess all three qualities. Your decision will indeed probably not even be made by you, but for you, by the manufacturer of the computer you choose to purchase.

Magnetic tape is used in minicomputers for two purposes. First, information can be stored permanently off the computer's internal memory, and thus documents not currently in use do not clutter up the internal storage. Second, when you purchase new software (programs), the software manufacturer usually provides the minicomputer owner with a copy of the programs on magnetic tape. So software is usually loaded onto the computers via magnetic tape. These are good reasons why magnetic tape is so popular.

A nine-track reel of tape that is 2,400 feet long costs about $20. How much would a stack of cards cost that could contain a similar amount of information? A stack of cards capable of holding the same number of characters would be more than a quarter-mile high, requiring more than 2 million punched cards. And that's not all: The tapes, once they are used, can be reused; memory can be erased and new documents can replace out-of-date jobs.

As for disadvantages, magnetic media are not as transparently interpretable as paper memory. If you can read codes, it's possible to edit paper tape or paper card memory very quickly. Magnetic memory requires a printout to decipher errors. More commonly, there are protection problems with magnetic memory.

Any magnetic medium is vulnerable. As Elephant Memory Systems is kind enough to tell us, "fingerprints, dust, coffee spills, cigarette ashes, sneezes, and maybe even dirty looks" can damage it. Magnetic media must be kept away from magnetism, meaning a wide variety of appliances, such as televisions, fans, telephones, typewriters, loudspeakers, and air conditioners. Otherwise the data may be scrambled, or memory may get amnesia and forget everything. And lastly, extremes of cold or heat can cause lost memory. But, overall, the necessary care is more than compensated by the power of those electromagnetic impulses.

■ Rigid Disks

Another significant magnetic medium was also developed by IBM. It is the *rigid disk*, or *hard disk*, or *Winchester system*. Often called "platters," the hard disks are constructed of several aluminum platters coated with iron oxide. The magnetized iron medium is read by read-write heads inside the disk drive, making the rigid disk a self-contained disk storage, reading, and writing system. The disks contain unbelievable amounts of data. The most powerful rigid disks are capable of holding up to 90 megabytes of

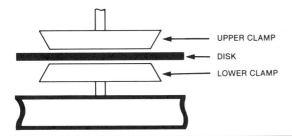

UPPER CLAMP

DISK

LOWER CLAMP

■ FIGURE I-4. Floppy disk drive.

information. By rough count, a 90-megabyte (bytes, kilobytes, and mega-bytes are computer measurements of how big big is) Winchester disk is capable of holding 45,000 pages of typewritten manuscript.

Rigid disks are offered by many microcomputer companies as options. They are also used by minicomputers as a means of increasing the amount of storage available to users. They are expensive, but they are brutes when it comes to storage capacity and speed. The disks rotate at 2,700 to 3,600 rotations per second, or about 150 miles per hour. More important, like magnetic tape, it's possible to interface hard-disk data with typesetters.

■ Floppy Disks

The most familiar magnetic medium is the floppy disk, or diskette. IBM first introduced the floppy disk in the early 1970s for use in its 3740 data entry system. Within ten years, the floppy was king. More people are using floppies, in more applications, and with more computers than any other magnetic or nonmagnetic medium. Floppies are usually 5¼" or 8" in diameter, but the smaller 3½" floppies are becoming increasingly popular (there are other sizes as well). There is no one type of floppy, but all share basic similarities. All are coated with iron oxide, and all are read by being inserted into a box called the *disk drive* (see Figure I-4).

Disk drives contain a read-write head and are usually directly attached to either a microcomputer's or to a minicomputer's terminals but, at times, are independently wired to a terminal. The diskettes are packaged in a square cardboard envelope that protects them from dust, dirt, smoke parti-cles, and whatever else you can think of that might harm the fragile magnetic memory. Once inserted in the disk drive, the read-write head rotates the disk to the area that contains the document demanded by the CPU and reads the document to the CPU.

Diskettes are cheap, reliable, and by far the most popular method used to store typeset documents. Unfortunately, though they are very popular, floppies are not universally understandable. One computer's floppy disk cannot be read by another computer.

Although most phototypesetters do use floppies as storage media, floppies are system-dependent. They do not possess "coherence," an ability to be formatted on one computer and be readable by another. Digital Equipment and IBM have recently funded a multimillion-dollar grant at MIT and Har-

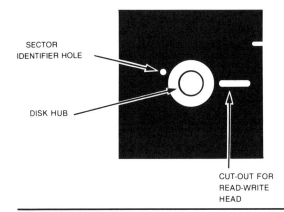

SECTOR
IDENTIFIER HOLE

DISK HUB

CUT-OUT FOR
READ-WRITE
HEAD

■ **FIGURE I-5. Floppy disk.**

vard to research coherence, but this simplification of communications is not close at hand and will be expensive when it is finally developed.

Density: Single-Sided versus Double-Sided. The reason why floppies are system-dependent is their structure. A diskette looks like a 45 rpm record in an envelope, but there are actually several types of diskettes. Floppy disks can be single-sided or double-sided, meaning that iron oxide can be deposited on one side or on both sides of the diskette. The double-sided diskettes require special disk drives with double read-write heads, but can hold twice as much information as their single-sided cousins.

Diskettes are also single density, double density, and quad density. "Density" refers to the amount of data that can be stored on one side of a diskette. Single density disks tend to be slightly more reliable than double density, but single density holds half as much information (meaning perhaps 125 pages of information versus 250 pages). Some diskettes are even dual density, meaning they can function as either single or double density diskettes. Quad density disks are the ones that are double density *and* double-sided. Today, this is the ultimate in storage for diskettes, about 1.2 megabytes, or more than 600 pages of manuscript copy on one diskette.

Sectoring: Soft versus Hard. Beyond simple storage capabilities, there are differences in the way diskettes store jobs. Some diskettes are *hard-sectored*, while others are *soft-sectored*.

Sectoring, which is the segmentation of a disk's space, makes use of a small hole in the disk's envelope known as the sector identifier (see Figure I-5). As anyone knows who has ever used or seen a diskette, the disk has a large hole in its middle (like a 45 rpm record). This hole is the disk hub and allows the disk drive to rotate the disk inside its envelope. The smaller hole, just to the side of the disk hub, allows the disk drive to know exactly where sectors on the disk begin and end.

In soft sectoring, an electronic photocell "notices" the one small hole in the magnetic media and then counts sector marks, which are magnetically recorded and placed to mesh with the tiny sector identifier. This is soft sectoring because the sectors are made possible via software. A computer program in the CPU formats a disk the first time it is used, and the sectors are thereafter recognizable to the CPU.

In hard sectoring, no software is required. Instead, the disk's magnetic film is actually punched with a series of holes. This series marks the beginning of each new sector and is visible through the sectoring identifier (both to the human eye and to the photoelectric cell of the computer). Called hard sectoring because the hardware is physically affected, this method allows more data to be recorded on the disk because space hasn't been taken up by sectoring software. Hard-sector disks do not work in soft-sector disk drives, and vice versa.

Why are there so many different types of floppies? There are several reasons, but most deal with the pecuniary interests of computer manufacturers. Originally, in the early 1970s, an unorganized group of several large manufacturers controlled the computer market. This group wanted to continue to control the market and, furthermore, control their customers.

When a flurry of made-in-the-garage computer vendors began to erupt in the 1970s, the monoliths attempted to make it difficult for new competitors. One tactic was to create diskettes and disk drives that were patented and could not be copied. Once a customer had bought one machine, the customer *had* to continue to buy from the original manufacturer. The restrictive policy worked for a number of years, but in the late 1970s, computer users and maverick computer companies invented several ways to battle the corporate giants.

Those new alternatives made hardware decision making a new game. Suddenly it wasn't important to make certain that your machine could automatically communicate with other devices. You could fake it. The basic fact of today's computer was finally clear: If a computer uses floppies, tapes, or rigid disks as its storage media, you can communicate with other computers. No matter what the nameplate on the computer reads, you *can* interface.

Output: Printers

After typing a manuscript onto a screen, the job is stored on a diskette and is ready to be sent to an editor. Now comes the quandary. The only output is electronic. The only way to view your work is on the video monitor connected to your keyboard. But how can you have your editor do the job of checking for factual errors and typos when your document exists only as a series of lit characters on a television screen?

You could invite the editor over for a glass of wine and an editing session on screen. Or, better, you could send the editor a copy of your diskette and allow him or her to use the diskette to create memory on the publishing company's computer. But any of these schemes necessitate a rather important change in the normal flow of events: changing from editing on paper to editing on a television screen. And some studies have shown that it is in fact easier to neglect typographical errors on a television screen. So what's the solution?

Without hesitation, the answer is a printer. Printers are the specialized machines that do exactly what they advertise. They produce printed copies of your documents. All printers can be categorized into three types: the slow ones, the fast ones, and the very fast ones. Printers can range in price from under $500 to into six figures, so there seems to be a good deal of room for poor decision making here. But reality sets in quickly when you're reviewing your needs and the choices available. The final purchasing decision is usually quite easy.

■ The Pioneers

The first printers were IBM Selectric typewriters converted by IBM to serve as printer/terminals. Using the Selectric connected to an IBM, you could communicate directly with the computer while producing "hard" copy (meaning paper copy). Today, IBM and every other computer company recommend video monitors and keyboards for input. But Selectrics are still being used for output. Many typewriters in the current crop of electronic models can also serve as computer printers.

The advantage of such jerry-rigging is that the typewriters are cheap and can still be used as typewriters. The disadvantages, however, are great enough to warrant the purchase of a bona fide printer. First, typewriters are agonizingly slow printers. The IBM Selectrics printed at the rate of about 15 characters per second, which seems fast when compared to a typist. But 15 characters per second means that the Selectric, or any typewriter converted to printer, takes about 3 minutes to type out a standard 8½″ × 11″ manuscript page. What happens when you want to type a chapter that's 45 pages long?

Because the typewriter is not manufactured to be run hour after hour, day after day, at the rate of 15 characters per second, repairs are often needed even on the best of these typewriters when doing heavy-duty printing. The machines are simply not made to carry this load. If you are printing anything more than an occasional letter, and if your time means anything to you, the converted typewriter ceases to be a feasible option.

■ Letter Quality Printers

If quality is important, there is one class of machines that produces output that looks just like the product of a typewriter. These are the slow machines. They are impact printers, meaning that the image is produced by striking (impacting) ink onto paper. The method used in most letter quality printers is the *daisy wheel* (See Figure I-6). Because the image is still produced mechanically by the petals of the daisy wheel striking ink onto paper, these machines are relatively slow. The general rule of thumb is that the faster the printer is, the more expensive it is. The best-known manufacturers of daisy wheel printers are Diablo, Qume, and NEC. Smith-Corona, the typewriter company, also makes a printer that is selling well, but there are dozens of other suppliers.

Among the more than 200 currently available printers, daisy wheel letter quality printers range in price from $695 (12 characters per second) to more than $4,000 (180 characters per second). Your budget and your needs will have to be balanced. But do you actually need letter quality? Daisy wheel printing may not be necessary. There is a less expensive alternative.

■ **FIGURE I-6. Daisy wheels. Photo courtesy Qume Corporation, a subsidiary of ITT Corporation.**

■ Dot Matrix Printers

Faster, more economical, and quieter than daisy wheels, there are two types of dot matrix printers: impact and, logically enough, nonimpact.

Impact Printers. *Impact printers* require an inked ribbon that is struck by a bank of small hammers to create letters. The letters are "stored" electronically in the printer's computer chips. When the letter *q* is required, the printer recalls the pattern (the matrix) of small dots that would produce a *q* and then orders the hammers to strike those dots correctly (see Figure I-7).

In typesetting terminology, this sort of connect-the-dots technology is called *digital* or *digitized* typesetting. Whether typesetting or printing, the dot matrix method is faster than daisy wheels because less mechanics, and more electronics, are used.

The quality of the dot matrix printer is based upon the number of ham-

dot matrix

■ FIGURE I-7. Dot matrix printing.

mers used. The standard matrix is 7×9 dots per letter, but both fewer dots per letter and more dots per letter are actually being used. The more dots used, the smaller the dots must be, and thus the less visible they are. Printers (or video monitors, which work the same way) are rated in terms of high and low "resolution." Printers that produce images with greater numbers of dots have high resolution, meaning the image is of better quality.

The impact dot matrix printers, like the daisy wheel printers, range in price and ability. A very serviceable printer costs about $600 (125 characters per second), but more expensive models are available at more than $5,000 (up to 400 characters per second with resolutions of up to 96×32 dots per character). For those on a really tight budget, it is possible to purchase slower dot matrix printers (under 50 characters per second) for less than $300. The fastest impact printers, the line printers, can produce copy at the rate of about 2,000 lines per minute.

Nonimpact Printers. The new generation of printing devices are the extremely fast *nonimpact printers*. The most common nonimpact machines are heat-sensitive printers and ink-jet printers. Heat-sensitive papers are produced by chemically treating paper before printing. After purchasing the specially prepared paper, the customer's jobs are, in a real sense, scorched onto the paper. In ink-jet printing, tiny droplets of ink are sprayed in dot matrix patterns to produce letters.

Both of these alternatives have advantages, but for flat-out speed, there's still another way of putting an image onto paper. The most exciting new method is electrostatic printing.

Electrostatic Printers. *Electrostatic printers* are often called "intelligent copiers." The machines can be very expensive—prices range from $20,000 to more than $500,000—but they are revolutionary in scope. A new form of printing, electronic printing, has been created by these hybrids of computer and copier.

Some high-speed nonimpact copiers produce copy at a rate of 20,000 lines per minute by combining electronic images with laser printing. Manuscripts are "copied" by these printers in a special way. No paper original is required. Rather, the original is a computer document sent through an interface to the CPU of the copier. The copier's CPU converts the electronic manuscript into dot matrix patterns, and an invisible electrostatic original is immediately copied.

The price tag of these speed demons will far outreach most word processing budgets, but these printers are enormously cost-effective (and useful) when a few hundred copies of a technical report are needed in one day, or when thousands of pages must be reproduced monthly. For short-run printing of large manuscripts, electronic printing can be an ideal solution.

Choices. So your options run between Radio Shack's CGP at $199.95 and Xerox's 9700 intelligent copier for 2,500 times more. For the majority of us, a good quality printer is available for a reasonable price. Our output, then, is paper, and our method is either the daisy wheel or dot matrix. There are other forms of output, such as computer output to microfilm and microfiche, computer graphics terminal images, and even audio response, but these technologies are important to a limited audience. On the other hand, in an electronic age, nearly all of us still want and need paper copies to work with, and fold—and even mutilate—when we feel like it.

Optional Hardware

When you have purchased the basics, the amount of peripheral equipment available for any computer mushrooms. Many of these options are simple gadgetry, but there are several peripherals that are literally do-or-die accessories.

If your decision is a microcomputer work station dedicated to one user, *a line voltage regulator* is a good purchase. Regulators are inexpensive devices that control "glitches." Glitches, which are death to magnetic media, are surges of power that disrupt the electromagnetic impulses on your media and create havoc out of order. When it happens once, the common reaction is to give up for the day, or week, or forever. For less than $100, the voltage regulators control brownouts and voltage surges and thereby eliminate electrical noise—the static you hear on your AM radio.

Second on your list will be interfacing hardware. You need some way to communicate with whatever or whomever you want to communicate. Depending on the method you choose, different hardware will be needed. You can count on spending at least $500 for interfacing hardware if you are using a word processor and perhaps $5,000 if you are a typesetter.

Then there are the gimmicks and the bells and whistles. You can buy a front panel for your computer—switches and lights and displays. It is possible to flip switches in code and enter data on the computer. But why? A week later, you'll have your first paragraph completed, and the only thoughts you'll have will be 001, 1100, 01011, 111001, and the like.

You can purchase an ergonomically designed work station (that's a desk) to put your terminal on. Or you may want your CRT to swivel on a large lazy Susan, so you can avoid the glare from your overhead lighting. There are cartridges, trays, and binders specifically designed to hold diskettes and other media. A fire safe for protecting copies of your important disks? If static electricity is a problem (and it may be, especially if your computer room has a rug instead of a tile floor), special floor mats are available that conduct static electricity down into the floor instead of up into your CPU. And there are the extra daisy wheels, printer paper, isolators, color graphics monitors, light pens, and voice and speech synthesizers (the first allows you to speak to your computer, and the second lets it talk back—neither are necessary and neither work well).

Of course, hardware alone can do nothing. What you need now is the human element of the computer equation. The computer is a dummy without directions. Those directions, called programs, are the *software.*

Software

There are actually two types of software. Computer professionals often distinguish between *programs,* which are sets of instructions developed to be used in your computer, and the *documentation,* which are manuals and technical data sheets telling you how to use the programs.

The first rule regulating computer usage and computer purchases in the 1980s is that the hardware works. The software may or may not. Software development is not a mechanical science; software quality is ultimately dependent on the skill of the programmer. The programs you are using can be elegant or klutzy (as the programmer calls it, a "kluge"). Both kinds will work, but the elegant software will be easier to use, understand, and learn. If you're stuck with poor software, computer usage can be a chore instead of a savings of time and labor.

What do the programs actually do? The answer to that question depends on what type of programming software is being used. There are several types, and they are all necessary. Complicating matters, you'll first have to purchase software that tells the hardware not what to do, but how to *understand* what to do.

■ Operating System

The *operating system* (OS) is a permanent fixture of the computer. For the Apple Macintosh, engineers have perfected the technique of permanently implanting the operating system on ROM chips (which means that this memory cannot be erased—called *firmware*).

The value of intransigent operating systems is simple. The OS is the organized collection of directions that tell the computer how to process jobs, understand the various keystrokes, and communicate with peripherals like keyboards, printers, and the like. If you had to tell the CPU how to work every time you turned the computer on, you'd not only become very frustrated, you'd also waste time. In the early days of mainframe computers, computer operators had to load CPU instructions *every* time a new job was begun, clear the CPU of any data before beginning another job, and then start over.

With OS programming, the computer has a boss. The OS manages the computer's time and processing schedule so that more than one job can be run at one time. These master control programs are the roads all other programs follow. They needn't be worried about; they're silent partners that do their job without prodding or coding.

There are two types of operating systems: those contained on disks in disk operating systems (DOS) and those software programs loaded on the CPU by other means. Because of the blind devotion of the operating system, it might seem unimportant to you which operating system your computer uses. But the operating system chosen has substantial consequences. Most importantly, programs that perform functions such as word processing and data processing are often written to be used on *one* operating system. Thus, if you know which programs you want to use, *your first priority will be to buy a computer that uses the OS you need to operate that software.*

What's Available? Several very popular operating systems are available. The best known for use with the widely adopted 8080 chips is Digital Research's CP/M. CP/M was ready to go when diskette microcomputers were first hitting the market, and it is very inexpensive. Its popularity is based in part on the fact that users can "support" (or use) several languages with CP/M and, in part, on the rather secondary fact that it was at the right place at the right time. In the 1970s, when microcomputers were first beginning to change the computer environment, CP/M was ready. You can use several computer languages (more on languages later) with CP/M: BASIC, FORTRAN, Pascal, APL, COBOL, and C are among the most recognizable. But CP/M is certainly not alone.

MS-DOS is the most important competitor on the microcomputer market. It's used in the IBM Personal Computer and all of the clones of the PC. Radio Shack has produced its TRSDOS for use with its TRS computers; OASIS, manufactured by Phase One Systems, is a widely used operating system designed for the Z80 chip; FLEX, by Technical Systems, is the best known OS for the M68000. The list could go on. The best of the rest (and all have features that make them specifically desirable) include Apple-DOS, Cromix, CP/Net, HDOS, Midas, MP/M, and Xenix.

In the world of the large minicomputers, the operating systems include UNIX, developed by Bell Labs in the late 1960s and then sold to the general public by AT&T because of the operating system's power and easy interactivity. UNIX was first designed to be used on Digital Equipment Corporation equipment. The PDP series has since been replaced by the very popular VAX line of computers, but UNIX continues as a successful operating system. Digital itself produces its own operating system for the VAX computers, VMS. At Data General, the Nova microcomputers are run with MP/OS, an operating system that can be upgraded to Eclipse, the operating system that runs the machine described in Tracy Kidder's best-selling *The Soul of a New Machine*.

IBM, of course, manufactures its own operating systems for use with its computers (just as every other computer manufacturer does). One byword of today's hardware and software market is "IBM-compatible," referring to hardware and software that can be supported by IBM operating systems.

There are several OS managers from which to choose. The tough job is deciding which software you wish to use and then finding the operating system that will run that software. Once that's done, you'll probably never think about your operating system again.

The Binary System

As you type a program or use a word processing software package to create manuscripts, you type on your keyboard and see letters appearing on your screen. But the computer understands letters in a very different way than you do. Computers don't speak English, they speak in a coded language called *binary,* a language that has only two characters. The characters aren't even very interesting: 0 and 1.

Binary language is one of those subjects that contribute to the mysteries of the machine. It is not difficult to understand, but binary code looks imposing and unintelligible. The two digits of binary are understood by the computer, not as numbers, but as the state of an electronic impulse: on or off, yes or no, there or not there. Computers interpret in binary because they are fast idiot savants. They know how to determine whether there is electronic current, but that's all they know.

So the binary code is used to express letters, numbers, and eventually complicated concepts to the computer (see Figure I-8). This is how it works.

BINARY NUMBER

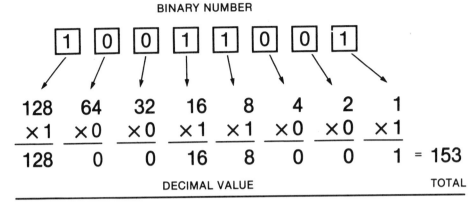

■ FIGURE I-8. How binary code works.

Numbers are expressed in powers of two, just the way numbers in the decimal system are expressed in powers of ten. Thus, remembering that we're now in binary, the number 10 means (reading from right to left) zero plus two to the first power, or zero plus two, or expressed in the decimal system, 2. The number 01 means one, plus two to the power of zero (which is zero). So the total is 1. Because we're not used to dealing with binary, at first examples seem to be complicated. But it's really just another way of expressing numeric values.

Numbers are always expressed in powers of two. So how could you express a decimal number like 70 in binary? Begin at the beginning, which in this case is the largest power of two less than 70, 64 is two to the sixth power ($2 \times 2 \times 2 \times 2 \times 2 \times 2$). You must still account for the remainder of six after you have decimally subtracted 64 from 70. Six, of course, is two to the second power (2×2, or 4) plus 2 to the first power (2). So, in binary, to express the decimal number 70 you will have to include in a series of 0s and 1s the codes for two to the sixth, second, and first powers.

Your value for two to the zero power: 0.

Your value for two to the first power: 1.

Your value for two to the second power: 1.

Your value for two to the third power: 0.

Your value for two to the fourth power: 0.

Your value for two to the fifth power: 0.

Your value for two to the sixth power: 1.

That should be all you need to express 70. Starting from the bottom of your list of 0s and 1s, the binary number for decimal 70 (remember to read from left to right, with the leftmost number being two to the sixth power) is 1000110.

Unfortunately, one computer's binary system is not another's, because as it turns out, binary is not the translation. It's the dictionary. Each computer manufacturer creates different coding sets, so binary patterns mean different things in different manufacturers' "languages." Since translations are different, one machine can't talk immediately to another. That's why interfacing is necessary. We have to make one machine's numeric codes understandable to another's.

User Programs

When the CPU is ready to process information, you can then actually use the computer for what it was intended—to process some sort of information.

You'll need software for this. This software, the user programs, are either written by you or purchased from software manufacturers. Your user programs are written in English, but it's a peculiar form of English. It's written in one of the strange dialects of English known as *computer languages.*

■ Computer Languages

There are hundreds of computer languages, but the most popular are those that are easiest to learn. BASIC is one of the standards of what are called the *high-level programming languages.* These are the easy-to-use (or at least relatively easy-to-use) languages that are based on English. Other popular high-level languages include FORTRAN, C, COBOL, FORTH, and Pascal. The single most important grain of truth to understand about computer languages is that *today it is not necessary for a computer user to learn a computer language.*

Languages are for programmers. If you want to program, fine. But if you simply want to be able to "turn a key" and have the computer work for you, that's not only possible, it's often the most profitable alternative. Programming can be fun, but it's not for everybody. There are literally hundreds of software programs on the market. It is more than likely that one of these "canned" programs will be suitable for your application. User programs can be purchased in source code (English) or in machine code (binary). The latter cannot be easily edited by the buyer and are usually cheaper. The source code programs can be edited.

Software + Hardware = Results

After you have loaded the operating system, you'll begin by connecting terminals to the box that houses the CPU (which most of us call the computer). You begin to type on the terminal. Let's say you type the letter X. On the screen, you see the letter X appear. But what did the computer actually do?

First, the pressure you created by striking the keystroke X was a switch. That switch sent an electronic signal to the CPU because the operating system directed it to do so. The X has been understood by the computer as a series of binary digits. In this case, the series of binary digits (0s and 1s) is 10001000. After the CPU correctly understands the electronic signal for X as 10001000, it then sends a signal to the monitor in front of you, and the screen glows to create a pattern of small dots that make up the letter X.

By the way, shorthand for binary digit—to contract a long string of syllables—is *bit.* Each 1 and 0 used to express the code in binary is one bit. Different computers can process different numbers of bits at the same time. The typical microcomputer these days is an 8-bit machine because it uses an 8-bit microprocessor chip. These chips, then, can process 8 bits at a time. And, to explain the other computer buzzword most often used, a *byte* is a collection of 8 bits. So 10001000 is 8 bits, 1 byte. Computer storage is most often calculated in thousands of bytes, called *kilobytes,* or in millions of bytes, called *megabytes.*

The 16-bit machines are rapidly becoming the standard for the microcomputer market. And on the minicomputer and mainframe computer fronts, computer engineers have already developed chips that are 16-bit, 32-bit, and so on. The advantages of bigger bit machines is that the faster information can be processed, the faster you (and the computer) can work. The faster it works, the more powerful it is.

But where did 10001000 come from? In this case, 10001000 is a peculiar form of binary. It's a *binary coded decimal,* or BCD for short. This bit is not really expressing a value in binary at all. It's actually a decimal number that has had each of its two decimal digits converted to binary. So the number actually is 1000 1000. Converting that binary string to decimal, the number we forge out of 1000 1000 is 8 8. So, as our story gets close to a solution, first, why does X mean a decimal 88?

Remember the numeric codes? Programs can be written in English, but they can't be read by the CPU in English. They must first be converted into numeric codes, which then can be interpreted to be understood by the CPU in binary. The reason for the numeric codes is that the CPU must have some way of understanding X. The letter X has to be converted into a number before it can be converted into binary. Binary codes are only numbers! When the translations are made, the pattern of translation is usually 8 bits at a time, although there are some codes that translate with 5- and 6-bit code sets.

Whichever dictionary is used, the conversion is always from an English character on the keyboard to a numeric code understood by the CPU to mean a certain binary code, then to a numeric code, and finally to an English character on the terminal screen. But recall that the *numeric codes are not standardized.* Therein lies the problem.

■ ASCII and EBCDIC

If the computer world were perfect, there would be one universally accepted numeric code as a go-between for binary and English and it would probably be ASCII, the American Standard Code for Information Interchange (pronounced "Askey"; see Figure I-9). Known internationally as CCITT Alphabet Number 5, this 8-bit code was originally developed to be used for telegraphs and teletype machines. ASCII has been around for a while. In the 1950s, teletypes were used as terminals for computers, replacing the front panels of switches and lights that seem nostalgic now. Since the teletypes were in place, as was the conversion code, ASCII was the obvious choice.

There have been several other codes that represent letters and other characters in data transmission, but these have restricted uses. Morse code and Baudot, used in American networks serving the deaf, didn't create translation problems because they were too clumsy to be used. But then came news from IBM—a new code named EBCDIC (see Figure I-9).

Binary	Decimal	Octal	Hexadecimal	ASCII	EBCDIC	TTS
00000000	000	000	00	NUL	NUL	Tape Feed
00000001	001	001	01	SOH	SOH	Thin Space
00000010	002	002	02	STX	STX	E
00000011	003	003	03	ETX	ETX	3
00000100	004	004	04	EOT	PF	Elevate
00000101	005	005	05	ENQ	HT	PF
00000110	006	006	06	ACK	LC	A
00000111	007	007	07	BEL	DEL	$
00001000	008	010	08	BS		Space Band
00001001	009	011	09	HT	RLF	Add Thin
00001010	010	012	0A	LF	SMM	S
00001011	011	013	0B	VT	VT	Em Space
00001100	012	014	0C	FF	FF	I
00001101	013	015	0D	CR	CR	8
00001110	014	016	0E	SO	SO	U
00001111	015	017	0F	SI	SI	7
00010000	016	020	10	DLE	DLE	Return
00010001	017	021	11	DC1	DC1	'
00010010	018	022	12	DC2	DC2	D
00010011	019	023	13	DC3	DC3	-
00010100	020	024	14	DC4	RES	R
00010101	021	025	15	NAK	NL	4
00010110	022	026	16	SYN	BS	J
00010111	023	027	17	ETB	IL	Bell
00011000	024	030	18	CAN	CAN	N
00011001	025	031	19	EM	EM	,
00011010	026	032	1A	SUB	CC	F
00011011	027	033	1B	ESC		Quad Left
00011100	028	034	1C	FS	IFS	C
00011101	029	035	1D	GS	IGS	En Space
00011110	030	036	1E	RS	IRS	K
00011111	031	037	1F	US	IUS	QR
00100000	032	040	20	SP	DS	T
00100001	033	041	21	!	SOS	5
00100010	034	042	22	"	FS	Z
00100011	035	043	23	#		)
00100100	036	044	24	$	BYP	L
00100101	037	045	25	%	LF	VR
00100110	038	046	26	&	EOB	W
00100111	039	047	27	'	ESC	2
00101000	040	050	28	(		H
00101001	041	051	29	)		Em Leader
00101010	042	052	2A	*	SM	Y
00101011	043	053	2B	+		6
00101100	044	054	2C	,		P
00101101	045	055	2D	–	ENQ	0
00101110	046	056	2E	.	ACK	Q
00101111	047	057	2F	/	BEL	En Leader
00110000	048	060	30	0		O
00110001	049	061	31	1		9
00110010	050	062	32	2	SYN	B
00110011	051	063	33	3		Upper Rail
00110100	052	064	34	4	PN	G
00110101	053	065	35	5	RS	;

■ FIGURE I-9. Conversion charts for several computer codes.

Binary	Decimal	Octal	Hexadecimal	ASCII	EBCDIC	TTS
00110110	054	066	36	6	UC	Shift
00110111	055	067	37	7	EOT	Lower Rail
00111000	056	070	38	8		M
00111001	057	071	39	9		.
00111010	058	072	3A	:		X
00111011	059	073	3B	;		1
00111100	060	074	3C	‹	DC4	V
00111101	061	075	3D	=	NAK	Quad Center
00111110	062	076	3E	›		Unshift
00111111	063	077	3F	?	SUB	Delete
01000000	064	100	40	@	SP	
01000001	065	101	41	A		
01000010	066	102	42	B		
01000011	067	103	43	C		
01000100	068	104	44	D		
01000001	069	105	45	E		
01000010	070	106	46	F		
01000011	071	107	47	G		
01000100	072	110	48	H		
01000101	073	111	49	I		
01000110	074	112	4A	J	¢	
01000111	075	113	4B	K	.	
01001000	076	114	4C	L	×	
01001001	077	115	4D	M	(	
01001010	078	116	4E	N	+	
01001011	079	117	4F	O			
01001100	080	120	50	P	&	
01010001	081	121	51	Q		
01010010	082	122	52	R		
01010011	083	123	53	S		
01010100	084	124	54	T		
01010101	085	125	55	U		
01010110	086	126	56	V		
01010111	087	127	57	W		
01011000	088	130	58	X		
01011001	089	131	59	Y		
01011010	090	132	5A	Z	!	
01011011	091	133	5B	[	$	
01011100	092	134	5C	\	*	
01011101	093	135	5D	]	)	
01011110	094	136	5E		;	
01011111	095	137	5F	—	¬	
01100000	096	140	60	`		
01100001	097	141	61	a	/	
01100010	098	142	62	b		
01100011	099	143	63	c		
01100100	100	144	64	d		
01100101	101	145	65	e		
01100110	102	146	66	f		
01100111	103	147	67	g		
01101000	104	150	68	h		
01101001	105	151	69	i		
01101010	106	152	6A	j		

■ FIGURE I-9 (cont.)

Binary	Decimal	Octal	Hexadecimal	ASCII	EBCDIC	TTS
01101011	107	153	6B	k	,	
01101100	108	154	6C	l	%	
01101101	109	155	6D	m	__	
01101110	110	156	6E	n	>	
01101111	111	157	6F	o	?	
01110000	112	160	70	p		
01110001	113	161	71	q		
01110010	114	162	72	r		
01110011	115	163	73	s		
01110100	116	164	74	t		
01110101	117	165	75	u		
01110110	118	166	76	v		
01110111	119	167	77	w		
01111000	120	170	78	x		
01111001	121	171	79	y	\	
01111010	122	172	7A	z	:	
01111011	123	173	7B	{	#	
01111100	124	174	7C		@	
01111101	125	175	7D	}	'	
01111110	126	176	7E	^	=	
01111111	127	177	7F	DEL	"	
10000000	128	200	80			
10000001	129	201	81		a	
10000010	130	202	82		b	
10000011	131	203	83		c	
10000100	132	204	84		d	
10000101	133	205	85		e	
10000110	134	206	86		f	
10000111	135	207	87		g	
10001000	136	210	88		h	
10001001	137	211	89		i	
10001010	138	212	8A			
10001011	139	213	8B			
10001100	140	214	8C			
10001101	141	215	8D			
10001110	142	216	8E			
10001111	143	217	8F			
10010000	144	220	90			
10010001	145	221	91		j	
10010010	146	222	92		k	
10010011	147	223	93		l	
10010100	148	224	94		m	
10010101	149	225	95		n	
10010110	150	226	96		o	
10010111	151	227	97		p	
10011000	152	230	98		q	
10011001	153	231	99		r	
10011010	154	232	9A			
10011011	155	233	9B			
10011100	156	234	9C			
10011101	157	235	9D			
10011110	158	236	9E			
10011111	159	237	9F			

■ FIGURE I-9 (cont.)

Binary	Decimal	Octal	Hexadecimal	ASCII	EBCDIC	TTS
10100000	160	240	A0			
10100001	161	241	A1			
10100010	162	242	A2		s	
10100011	163	243	A3		t	
10100100	164	244	A4		u	
10100101	165	245	A5		v	
10100110	166	246	A6		w	
10100111	167	247	A7		x	
10101000	168	250	A8		y	
10101001	169	251	A9		z	
10101010	170	252	AA			
10101011	171	253	AB			
10101100	172	254	AC			
10101101	173	255	AD			
10101110	174	256	AE			
10101111	175	257	AF			
10110000	176	260	B0			
10110001	177	261	B1			
10110010	178	262	B2			
10110011	179	263	B3			
10110100	180	264	B4			
10110101	181	265	B5			
10110110	182	266	B6			
10110111	183	267	B7			
10111000	184	270	B8			
10111001	185	271	B9			
10111010	186	272	BA			
10111011	187	273	BB			
10111010	188	274	BC			
10111011	189	275	BD			
10111110	190	276	BE			
10111111	191	277	BF			
11000000	192	300	C0			
11000001	193	301	C1			
11000010	194	302	C2			
11000011	195	303	C3			
11000100	196	304	C4			
11000101	197	305	C5			
11000110	198	306	C6			
11000111	199	307	C7		G	
11001000	200	310	C8		H	
11001001	201	311	C9		I	
11001010	202	312	CA			
11001011	203	313	CB			
11001100	204	314	CC			
11001101	205	315	CD			
11001110	206	316	CE			
11001111	207	317	CF			
11010000	208	320	D0		}	
11010001	209	321	D1		J	
11010010	210	322	D2		K	
11010011	211	323	D3		L	
11010100	212	324	D4		M	

■ FIGURE I-9 (cont.)

Binary	Decimal	Octal	Hexadecimal	ASCII	EBCDIC	TTS
11010101	213	325	D5		N	
11010110	214	326	D6		O	
11010111	215	327	D7		P	
11011000	216	330	D8		Q	
11011001	217	331	D9			
11011010	218	332	DA			
11011011	219	333	DB			
11011100	220	334	DC			
11011101	221	335	DD			
11011110	222	336	DE			
11011111	223	337	DF			
11100000	224	340	E0			
11100001	225	341	E1		R	
11100010	226	342	E2		S	
11100011	227	343	E3		T	
11100100	228	344	E4		U	
11100101	229	345	E5		V	
11100110	230	346	E6		W	
11100111	231	347	E7		X	
11101000	232	350	E8		Y	
11101001	233	351	E9		Z	
11101010	234	352	EA			
11101011	235	353	EB			
11101100	236	354	EC			
11101101	237	355	ED			
11101110	238	356	EE			
11101111	239	357	EF			
11110000	240	360	F0		0	
11110001	241	361	F1		1	
11110010	242	362	F2		2	
11110011	243	363	F3		3	
11110100	244	364	F4		4	
11110101	245	365	F5		5	
11110110	246	366	F6		6	
11110111	247	367	F7		7	
11111000	248	370	F8		8	
11111001	249	371	F9		9	
11111010	250	372	FA			
11111011	251	373	FB			
11111100	252	374	FC			
11111101	253	375	FD			
11111110	254	376	FE			
11111111	255	377	FF			

■ FIGURE I-9 (cont.)

Many computer professionals feel that the creation of a competitive code set was an action by the major manufacturer of computers to write the rules of the game. Some computers use EBCDIC; some use ASCII. Both "sides" are intransigent. So it's a fact of interfacing and computer life—we have two codes.

■ The Problems

If there were only two codes, interfacing between EBCDIC-based equipment and ASCII-based equipment would be quite simple. With translations between the competitive codes, you're ready to go. But there's also the New International ASCII of 1978 to confuse matters further. Even a third alternative would not be a terrible problem. The major obstacle is our keyboards.

Take a look at any typesetting keyboard: em space, line space key, perhaps precedence uppercase and lowercase keys, an insert space, and, of course, a quad left key that automatically pushes words to the left margin. Most typesetting keyboards will have either those specific, or similar, keystrokes. Now, look at a word processing keyboard. No quad left key here, but there's a control, a line feed, a backslash, and perhaps an escape key. None of these is on the typesetter keyboard.

Constructing translations of keys that don't exist on one keyboard is one major difficulty. But there's a second stumbling block. Whether ASCII or EBCDIC is used, there are no punishments for manufacturers that do not strictly adhere to the industry standard. Furthermore, because each keyboard is different, ASCII standard is actually something of a fiction. Virtually every hardware manufacturer uses a different (sometimes slightly different, sometimes radically different) version of ASCII. So, even if the typesetter and the word processor are both compiling with ASCII, they will not immediately be understandable to each other. Even if ASCII is nominally shared, it isn't.

■ Standard Practice

The manufacturer of your hardware determines what code set will be used with your equipment. But whichever version of either code set you use, all operations at the level of binary and machine code are relatively similar. Let's go back to our example at the keyboard. You type the word "about." After looking at the ASCII chart (Figure I-9), you can determine the BCD (binary coded decimal) for the first letter, *A*. To do that, you'll have to convert *A* into the decimal figure given to it on the ASCII chart. That number is 65.

But, looking more closely at the chart, you see other available numbers: 41 and 101. In this case, 41 is the hex code number for *A*. Hex code is short for *hexadecimal,* meaning based on 16. Hex, again, is simply another way of expressing a number of objects, just like binary and decimal. In the case of hex, you use powers of sixteen, not ten or two. The other number is 101. This is an *octal* code. Octal code is yet another counting system, this time using powers of eight.

For most interfacing applications, you will use hex code. There are several good reasons for this, but the major reason is that hex can express up to 256 characters using only two digits or a digit and a letter. Decimal can only express 100: from 00 to 99. Hex, though, can add to this 100 numbers by starting with 1A, 2A, 3A, and so on. The 16 characters used in determining hex codes are 0, 1, 2, 3, 4, 5, 6, 7, 8, 9, A, B, C, D, E, and F. When all possible permutations of those characters are constructed, you have 256 combinations. And that is more than enough to give every character on any keyboard its own two-character hex code. If you're going to translate every keystroke as something, you need a different code available for each character. Decimal and octal simply don't have enough characters to do the job, so hex is therefore the system of choice.

So rather than translating the word "about" into decimal code, let's use hex for the time being. As you'll see later, there are equivalents for decimal and hex, so that it's not really critical which code set is used, as long as you use the sets correctly.

Continuing with Figure I-9, the hex code for A is 41. In binary code, we are now going to do something a little strange. I know that some people say doing anything in binary code is a little strange. But, by inventing yet another type of notation, interfacers can use binary coded hexadecimals (remember BCD, binary coded decimals?) to refer to hex codes like 41. So A equals hex code 41. Hex code 41 becomes binary 0100 (meaning 4) plus 0001 (meaning 1). Put these 0s and 1s together, and we have the accepted binary code for A in ASCII: 01000001. You'll notice that it takes 8 bits, or 1 byte, to represent a single character.

But look again, there's something even more magical happening here. Compute the value of 01000001 in decimal codes, recalling that this apparently obtuse string of zeros with a couple of 1s thrown in is in binary. The number, then, is equal to 1 to the zero power plus 1 to the seventh power. Checking out the arithmetic, that's 64 plus 1, or 65. What's the significance of 65? Check the letter A in Figure I-9 and you'll see the decimal value: 65! It works.

What that means is that you can think of ASCII binary codes in either straight decimal equivalents, *or,* if you prefer, in terms of what I've called binary coded hexadecimals. It doesn't matter, because 01000001 will mean A, whether A means 41 (in hex) or 65 (in decimal). You can go either way.

Finally, continuing with our example "about," we must translate the letter B. Hex code for B is 42, which translates into 0100 0010, or 01000010. Next is the letter O. This one is slightly different than our ABC's. The hex code for O is 4F. Because F is part of our hex code, we can't translate this as a binary coded hexadecimal, as the collection of two sets of four binary codes. This is where the table of equivalents comes in handy. Our solution is to retreat to decimal coding. The decimal code for O is 79. So, rather than converting 4F (a hex) into binary, just convert 79 (a decimal) directly: 79 is 64 + 8 + 4 + 2 + 1, so our binary code for O becomes 01001111. Since we know by our earlier example that decimal 79 is indeed equivalent to hex 4F, we can be sure we've arrived at the right sequence for binary. Remember: If this is confusing, don't worry about it. The computer does this for you.

The reason you do need to know about hex coding is that there will be times during your interfacing when translations will have to be made in hex. If you know the basics, with a little practice and this book open to the table of hex and binary equivalents, you'll have some problems but you'll be able to master the required arts.

About? We have the *U,* hex code 55, or binary 0101 0101, and then the *T,* hex code 54, or binary 0101 0100. Now the big moment. We can express one word in binary. The word "about," in ASCII, works itself into binary reality:

A	*B*	*O*	*U*	*T*
01000001	01000010	01001111	01010101	01010100

Putting this string together, "about" is:

0100000101000010010011110101010101010100

Pity the poor programmers who had to work this way in the Paleolithic age of computers. It's easy, looking back, to see why programs are usually given in English source code rather than binary machine code, and why binary code programs can't be edited. But binary does work. Because computers are the machines that they are, binary is the only way that they work.

Computers are standardized. All use binary. Human beings, being the autonomous creatures that we are, are not standardized, and neither are our plans to use and interpret computer codes. So we don't have a standard, even when it would be to our benefit. Given the number of keyboards currently in use and the number of different manufacturers of computer systems, and even the existence of totally new keyboard layouts, the standardization of an ASCII, or any other, code set seems impossible. Therefore, we must learn to use hex so we can translate the various versions of ASCII and EBCDIC we've created. The computer is ready to conform to a single, universal standard, but we're not.

Typography Basics

KEYBOARDING IS THE FIRST STEP toward producing interfaced documents. A second step, equally important, is typography—the design of pages that are *correctly* typeset to be easy to read and attractive. In order to produce a job that meets minimum typographic standards of readability and appropriateness, there are rules that should be followed when preparing any document for typesetting. To understand those rules, several sets of terms must be defined.

■ Typesetting Measurements

A *pica* is the basis of a typesetter's system of measurement. Roughly one-sixth of an inch, the pica is further divided into *points*. There are 12 points to the pica, 72 points to the inch.

Some typesetters use other systems of measurement, such as the newspaper's *agate* or the European *cicero*. But points and picas are the only system used in 95 out of 100 type houses. Any graphic arts supply store carries several types of pica rulers and printer's gauges.

■ Typesetting Parameters

Line length is the length of a typeset line, measured from one margin to the other. Measured in picas, line length is often signified in typesetting specifications by circling the appropriate pica length.

Type size is the size of the type. Measured in points (larger type is measured in picas, but if the type is 4 picas, it's called 4-line, not 4-pica), type size is determined by measuring from the top of an ascender to the bottom of a descender. *Ascenders* are parts of letters that rise above the height of a lowercase *x* (such as *l, f, t, h,* and *k*). *Descenders* are those parts of letters that fall below the baseline—an imaginary line that all the letters rest on. Examples of descenders are *p, q,* and *y*.

Line space is the space between typeset lines. Line space is measured in points, from one baseline to the next. Type size and line space are often specified with a slash: 10/12 means 10 point type with a 12 point line space.

Finally, *type style* (also known as the typeface or font) is the complete set of characters available in a particular design. There are hundreds of typefaces available, but text faces are usually divided between *serifs* and *sans serifs*. Serifs are identified by the short strokes that close off the tops and bottoms of each letter. Sans serifs, as the name suggests, have no serifs. The serif faces are more sedate and, until several years ago, were believed to be more readable than the sans. Recent research indicates that correct typographic standards are much more important to readability than the sans serif/serif controversy.

■ Type Spacing

Spaces are used in typesetting to produce lines that are even at both margins. The typesetter's central processing unit is programmed to "read" the available number of spaces in each line and then make end-of-line and spacing decisions based on the amount of room taken up by the type. All available space is distributed evenly among the spaces.

There are two standard spaces, both of which are based upon the *em system of measurement.* The *em* is a square of a particular type size—an 18 point em is an 18 point square. An *en* is half an em.

When indenting paragraphs, a combination of ems and ens should be used. If five spaces (as in word processing) is used, each paragraph will be indented unequally because the size of a space is determined for each line by the typesetter CPU. The standard indent is usually 2 ems. If you are using a very short line length, the standard indent may be reduced to an em plus an en, or even 1 em. The important fact to remember is *always to use ems and/or ens for standard indents.*

■ Typographic Patterns

Justified lines are even on both the right and left margins. This is the standard mode for most modern typesetters. If you do not want your typesetting to be justified, you must access one of the patterns below.

Ragged right typesetting is even on the left margin but uneven on the right. Because the eye needs an even left margin for easy reading, justified and ragged-right composition are the two most popular alternatives for text type.

Ragged left is the opposite of ragged right. Here the left margin is uneven (ragged) and the right is even. Like *centered composition,* this is best used for headlines. Interfaced copy, because it usually consists of long textual material, is rarely the place for ragged left.

Flush left lines are those that are pushed to the left margin, such as with the last line of a paragraph or a headline. Most typesetters require a flush left code to override the automatic justification feature of the photo unit. Without the flush left code, the last line will be justified regardless of how many words it contains.

Rules of Composition

The standard rules of composition are not stringently followed by all typographers for all jobs. But if you are not a type professional, the rules should be followed. The result will not win awards for innovative typography, but it will be competent and readable typesetting. The rules are divided according to the typesetting parameters with which they are involved. A recap of these guidelines is provided at the end of this discussion.

■ Line Length

Research regarding how we read has pointed to very specific recommendations concerning optimum line lengths. The most readable line length for any type size is two and one-half times that type size. Ten point type, then, is most readable set 25 picas long.

Lines that are too short result in choppy reading that's tiresome; lines that are set too long are even worse. If you have ever read a single line twice, it's because the line was typeset at too long a measure. When a line is set at more than three and one-half times the type size, our eye loses its peripheral anchor at the left margin. Scanning back to the left, we begin to read the same line over again because the eye has "lost its place."

Set a line length one and one-half to three times the type size when setting any long body of type. If the final page size is 8½″ × 11″ and the job is a long document, consider a two-column format. Double columns usually are more readable because the reader needn't scan across the entire page, then back, and then across again. Constant eye movement is tiresome, and most readers will not bother with text that is difficult to read. Remember that when setting for a two-column page you must allow for space between the columns of the page. Leave from 1½ to 3 picas for the gutter when determining the line length.

■ Type Size

A commonsense rule for type size is to use sizes that are large enough to be read. Ten point and 12 point are the most popular sizes for text. Display type is set in larger sizes (above 14 point) and should be used to call attention to titles, chapter heads, etc. Do not follow a 72 point display line with 8 point text type. A rule of thumb is to use display faces one and one-half to two and one-half times the type size. When using 10 point type, use 14 point or 18 point for minor heads and less important display. Use 24 point, and possibly 30 point, for chapter heads and more significant headlines. A display line of 48 points or 60 points will overpower 10 point text type and may appear out of place.

The fact that 5 point type exists is not a good reason to use it. "Fine print" type is rarely used. Use 7 or 8 point type for footnotes. Five point type is too small to be legible.

■ Line Space

When allowing for space between lines of text type, use a line space of 1 or 2 points above the type size. Lines that are "aired out" more than 2 points may appear disjointed. If you are setting 10 point type, use a line space of 11 or 12 points.

The extra space between the lines is known as *lead*. Lead is used to incorporate white space into the page design. The white space eliminates the possibility of a very black page. "Gray" type is the easiest to read; dense typesetting is much more difficult for the reader.

Never specify a line space smaller than the type size in text type. That will result in lines of type touching each other, making it both visually unappealing and difficult to read.

When moving from display type to text type, if you wish the display type to be positioned close to the text, specify a line space two times the size of the type *to which you are moving*. If your display line is 30 point type and your text is 12 point type, a 24 point line space after the 30 point typeset line is appropriate. Remember to change your line space to 13 or 14 points when you begin to type your 12 point type.

■ Type Style

When you have chosen a particular family of type to be used in text type, the job should, in most cases, be completely set with that family. You may move, for instance, from Helvetica to Helvetica Italic for emphasis, but do not move from Helvetica to Cooper Black. Italics and bolds should be used only for emphasis; regular type versions are easier to read than other variations.

It is not unusual to use a different typeface for display. Sans serifs are often used for headlines, with a serif for the text; but the reverse is also possible. Remember that the serifs tend to be the most readable faces, and regular versions are always more readable than bold, italic, condensed, or expanded versions.

A Recap of the Rules

1. Specify a line length close to two-and-one-half times the type size used in text.

2. Use 10 or 12 point type size for text.

3. Use display type that is one and one-half to two and one-half times the size of the text type.

4. When footnotes are required, use 7 or 8 point type. Never use a size smaller than 7 point if avoidable.

5. When line spacing text, use a line space 1 or 2 points above the type size.

6. When line spacing display, set a line space of at least twice the size of the type to which you are moving.

7. In general, use one family of type exclusively for text type in a job.

8. If you are using a double-column format, remember to allow for a gutter of 1½ to 3 picas between the columns.

9. Use em or en spaces for indents.

10. Use justified or ragged right composition for text. Reserve centered and ragged left for display type.

Glossary:
Word Processing
and Typesetting Terms

AA. Author's alterations. Changes charged to the customer by the type-setter.

ACK/NAK. Affirmative acknowledgment/negative acknowledgment. A system used in the transmission of data to make certain that blocks of data have been successfully received.

ASCII. American Standard Code for Information Interchange. The standard code set, established by the American National Standards Institute, for transmission of data.

Acoustic coupler. A device used in telecommuncations. A standard telephone fits into the coupler, and data are telecommunicated through standard telephone analog signals.

Agate. A system of measurement, $1/14$ of an inch, used in determining newspaper ad space.

Alphanumeric. A set of alphabetic or numerical characters, usually used as shorthand for quicker input.

Analog. A property, such as temperature or voltage, that varies continuously over time. Also, computers or computerized signals that operate based on such properties.

Architecture. The organizational structure of a computer system.

Ascenders. Parts of letters that rise above the height of a lowercase (small) x. Ascenders are used when measuring type size.

Assembler. A program that converts data into binary code.

Asynchronous transmission. Data transmission that is not regulated by a timing source. The beginning and end of blocks of data are signalled by start and stop bits.

Automatic answering. A feature of several modems. When receiving a telephone message, the phone modem automatically answers the telephone call and begins to receive information. *See also* Modem.

Automatic dial. A feature of several modems. An operator types a telephone number on screen and the connected modem automatically dials the number to begin the telecommunications session.

Backup. Copies of programs or data safely stored in the event that originals are mistakenly destroyed.

Baseline. The imaginary line that all letters rest on.

Baud. A measure of the rate at which data are transmitted. Baud rate is expressed in bits per second—300 baud is 300 bits per second.

Binary. A numbering system with a base of two. Binary uses only the digits 0 and 1.

Binary coded decimal. A number coding system in which binary digits (0 or 1) represent one decimal digit.

Bisynchronous transmission. A shorthand term for binary synchronous; usually referred to as synchronous.

Bit. Abbreviation of binary digit, either 0 or 1.

Black boxes. Early media converters that are not programmable by the user.

Body type. Type that measures from 6 to 14 point. Also known as text type.

Bold. A heavy version of a regular typeface.

Bus. Wire circuits that provide a communications path between the CPU and the output plugs (such as the RS-232).

Byte. A group of bits (usually 8) representing a character.

CP/M. Control Program for Microcomputers. An operating system for 8080, 8086, and Z80 single-user computers. One of the two standard operating systems of the 1980s.

CPU. *See* Central processing unit.

CRT. *See* Cathode ray tube.

Canned programs. Programs purchased from a software house, ready for use by the purchaser of the software.

Card puncher. A machine used to punch holes in Hollerith cards as a storage medium.

Cathode ray tube. An electronic tube on which information is displayed. Together with the keyboard, the CRT is part of the terminal.

Central processing unit. The "brains" of the computer, the circuitry of the word processor. Controls the interpretation and execution of instructions.

Character display. A measure of the number of characters shown on a terminal screen at one time. Minimum character display for word processing is 80 characters (horizontally) and 24 lines (vertically).

Chip. A silicon wafer on which integrated circuits are etched. In a microcomputer, a complete central processing unit may be stored on one chip.

Cicero. The basis of a system of measurement used by European printers and typographers. There are 13 points in one cicero; 6 ciceros to the inch. The American system is based on points and picas.

Code sets. Different systems used to interpret binary codes. Because there are different systems, translations are necessary to allow communications. ASCII and EBCDIC are the two main code sets.

Compiler. A program that converts high-level languages (such as BASIC or FORTRAN) into binary codes.

Computer language. *See* Language.

Computer unit. The central processing unit of a computerized typesetting machine. Controls end-of-line and h&j decisions.

Continuous transmission. Transmission of data that is not paced by time or on-off codes; the transmission continues until all data is sent.

Control codes. A keyboard character, or sequence of characters, that initiates, stops, or modifies a particular function.

Conversion service. A company that converts information stored on a computer from one media to another; for instance, from magnetic cartridges to magnetic diskettes.

Copyfitting. A method used to determine how much space will be required to set a given amount of copy in a given typeface and size.

Counting keyboard. In typesetting, a keyboard that adds up the space remaining on a line as each character is typed. The operator must make the end-of-line decision based on that information.

Crash. A failure, either of hardware or software, that causes computer processing to stop.

DC1/DC3. Synonym for X-On/X-Off. In telecommunications, a system that allows the receiving computer to signal the sender to stop transmission momentarily. When the receiver is ready, another signal is sent to begin transmission again.

DOS. Disk operating system. An operating system contained on a disk and loaded onto the computer, not stored permanently on ROM chips. The most common disk operating systems are CP/M and MS-DOS.

Daisy wheel printer. A printer with fonts consisting of single-character spokes radiating from a central hub. An impact printer.

Data bits. In data transmissions, the bits that actually carry information to be stored. Parity, stop, and start bits are not data bits.

Data processing. Performance of specified operations on data. Number crunching.

Debug. Eliminating errors, either from a program or from a communications routine.

Dedicated. A word processor or terminal that is permanently assigned, either by software or by a user, to one task.

Delimiter. A code used in constructing translation tables. The delimiter signals the beginning or the end of a single translation.

Descenders. Parts of letters that fall below the baseline. Type size is measured from the top of an ascender to the bottom of a descender.

Digital. Information that is coded in binary numerics.

Digital typesetting. Third-generation typesetting. Film fonts are no longer used. The computer unit stores digital codes, and letters are produced by the computer in the form of microscopic dots or lines.

Digitized typesetting. *See* Digital typesetting.

Direct connect modem. A null modem, the wire connecting two machines during hardwiring.

Direct entry typesetting. Two forms of typesetting. The first-generation direct entry typesetters set a letter immediately after a key is struck on the keyboard. Later machines store jobs in memory for typesetting directly to the photo unit.

Direct-impression typesetting. Typesetting with typewriter technology. Also known as typewriter composition and strike-on typesetting.

Direct interface. *See* Direct interfacing.

Direct interfacing. Interfacing methods involving a direct electrical connection between the two machines being interfaced (hardwiring and telecommunications).

Discretionary hyphen. A hyphen that corrects automatic hyphenation logic problems. Discretionary hyphens are placed between appropriate syllables and used only if necessary (thus they are discretionary).

Disk. A flat, circular magnetic storage medium. The disk is rotated, like a phonograph record, in the disk drive. Disks are either rigid or floppy.

Disk capacity. The amount of information that can be stored on a magnetic disk at one time.

Disk drive. A device equipped with a read-write head that allows information to be stored on or read from a disk.

Diskette. A floppy disk. A cheap storage medium, usually either 8″ or 5¼″ square, used in most microcomputers. Used as a secondary storage device in some minicomputers.

Display type. Type more than 14 point in size.

Documentation. Manuals and other instructions that provide explanations and system guidelines.

Dot matrix printer. A nonimpact printer that prints characters by using a matrix of small dots. The quality is poorer than from daisy wheel printers.

Double density. Floppy disks that are able to store double the amount of data as single-density disks.

Downtime. The amount of time a computer is inoperative due to failures. Usually expressed as a percentage of the total time the computer is used.

Dual disk drive. Two disk-drive capability in a computer. Dual drive makes editing and backup much easier when word processing.

Duplex. Modems that are capable of both sending and receiving information at the same time. Also known as full duplex.

EBCDIC. Extended Binary Coded Decimal Interchange Code. The code set used by IBM to represent data.

Electronic manuscript. A document sent to a typesetter or printer in electronic, rather than paper, form.

Electrostatic printer. Expensive copying devices that are able to convert telecommunicated data directly into paper copies. Machines that "copy" from electronic originals.

Em indent. An indent the width of an em. *See also* Em space.

Em space. A fixed space equally as wide as the type size being used.

En indent. An indent the width of an en. *See also* En space.

En space. One-half an em space.

Family. All the available typefaces and type sizes based on a single design.

File. A collection of data treated as a unit.

File length. The maximum size of a document permitted by the software being used. Some word processing programs allow file lengths of only 5K, or $2\frac{1}{2}$ pages; others allow lengths up to the disk capacity (which may be 200 or more pages).

Filmstrip. In typesetting, a plastic strip containing negatives of each character in an alphabet.

Firmware. Programs that cannot be edited by the purchaser.

Floppy disk. *See* Diskette.

Flush left. A type pattern in which material is set even on the left margin but uneven on the right margin. The opposite of flush right.

Font. A complete set of all characters in one typeface in one size. Includes letters, numbers, punctuation marks, and symbols.

Font drum. A round cylinder on which are attached letter negatives. The cylinder revolves, bringing the appropriate letters before a flashing light source. The flash of light exposes photographic paper and phototypesetting is the result.

Formats. An interface coding system that requires the customer to insert format codes, such as F1, when an agreed-on combination of typesetting parameters is needed. F2 is another combination of parameters, and so on.

Frequency modulation. Conversion of digital signals into binary signals (audible tones) of varying cycles per second; conversion into signals based on time.

Front-end system. A minicomputer programmed to control typesetting terminals and output units.

Full duplex. A modem capable of sending and receiving information at the same time. *See also* Duplex.

Galley. Long sheets of typesetting.

Global search and replace. In word processing, a feature that allows an operator to specify a string of characters that will first be found and then automatically be replaced by the word processor.

Half-duplex. A modem capable of receiving and sending information, engineered to do only one of the two functions at any one time.

H&j. Hyphenation and justification. Decisions made by the computer unit of most phototypesetters.

Hard disk. A magnetic disk permanently encased in a hard material. Also known as rigid disk.

Hard returns. In word processing, return codes that are mandatory. Examples include returns at the end of paragraphs. Compare soft returns.

Hard-sectored. Magnetic media physically sectored in some way, usually with holes punched in the media. *See also* Soft-sectored.

Hardware. Mechanical, electronic, and magnetic components of any computer system.

Hardwiring. Connecting two computers with communications cable and sending information through the cable.

Hexadecimal codes. Usually abbreviated "hex," a system of numbering based on 16. The 16 "digits" of this system include 0 through 9 and A through F.

High-level programming languages. Languages that permit the programmer to work in succinct English codes rather than complicated binary instructions; examples include FORTRAN, BASIC, C, and COBOL.

Hollerith cards. Paper storage medium. Cards are punched with patterned holes readable by paper punch readers.

Hot type. Type produced from molten metal. Some typesetting professionals refer to phototypesetting as cold type.

Hyphenation logic. The program of a phototypesetting machine that determines where hyphens will be placed.

I/O. Input/output. Input devices include terminals and key punch machines. Output devices include printers, disk drives, and the CRT.

Impact printer. A printer, usually letter quality, which prints characters by striking individually inked letters from a ball or daisy wheel font onto paper.

Indirect interface. *See* Indirect interfacing.

Indirect interfacing. Interfacing methods that do not involve a direct electrical connection between the two machines being interfaced (OCR and media conversion).

Input device. Any device capable of creating data (usually the keyboard).

Integrated circuit. Synonym for chip. A silicon circuit containing thousands of tiny transistors on a single wafer.

Interface. Any hardware or software device that allows information to be shared between two computerized machines. Indirect interfacing methods (involving intermediate translating devices) include optical character recognition and media conversion; direct interfacing methods are hardwiring and telecommunications.

Justified. Even margins on both sides of a typeset column.

K. Abbreviation for kilobyte. A kilobyte is two to the tenth power or 1,024 bytes.

Kerning. Adjusting space between letters.

Keyboard. The part of the terminal where characters are typed to create a document. Similar in appearance to the typewriter.

Keystroke. Striking one character on a keyboard. If that character is transmitted electronically, it need not be rekeyed.

Kilobyte. *See* K.

Language. A system of commands understandable by the CPU. There are several types of languages: binary, machine code, high-level languages such as BASIC and C, and assembly languages.

Laser typesetting. A typesetting technology that could eliminate phototype and substitute the "burning" of paper by laser light.

Lead. The difference between the type size and the line space. In common notation, 10/12 means a type size of 10 and a line space of 12, or 2 points of lead.

Letter space. Space between letters set in type. Especially important to control when setting display type.

Line by line/X-On. A data transmission method that requires a receiving computer to send a signal permitting the sender to transmit a line. A signal is sent before each line.

Line length. The length of a typeset line, measured in picas.

Line space. Measured in points, the length from one baseline to the next baseline.

Line voltage regulator. A device that controls electrical current surges. By stopping surges and other irregularities before they reach the CPU, the regulator eliminates possible losses of data.

Lines per minute. A speed rating given to all phototypesetters. Expressed in terms of the number of lines set in 1 minute, 8 point type, 11 picas wide.

MS-DOS. Microsoft's Disk Operating System. Along with CP/M, one of the two standard disk operating systems for microcomputers.

Machine language. A language understood and used directly by the computer.

Mag cards. Magnetized cards, used by IBM and other electronic typing systems, that are capable of storing information for later retrieval.

Magnetic cassettes and cartridges. Magnetic memory media similar in appearance to audio and videotape cassettes and cartridges.

Magnetic media. Any form of storage using a magnetic surface to retain data. Magnetic media include cartridges, cassettes, disks, and tapes.

Main memory. The circuits of a computer in which data are stored.

Mainframe. Powerful computers that are usually dedicated to data processing or networking.

Massaging. Adding keystrokes, editing, or repairing errors in a telecommunicated file.

Measure. Synonym for line length.

Mechanicals. The proper term for the process of putting together the elements of the page into a single image. Often called pasteups.

Media. Forms of permanent storage of information. Includes paper tape, magnetic tape, magnetic cassettes and cartridges, magnetic diskettes, and Hollerith cards.

Media conversion. An indirect interface in which media are converted from one (unintelligible) format into another (intelligible) format by an intermediate device.

Media converter. Hardware that converts magnetic media into usable information. Programmable converters allow the purchaser to program the device to convert from many different computers.

Megabyte. Approximately one million bytes or one thousand kilobytes; precisely, 1,048,576 bytes.

Memory. Part of a computer capable of storing binary coded information.

Menu. A list of commands displayed on screen.

Microchip. *See* Integrated circuit.

Microcomputer. The least powerful computer, usually priced at less than $10,000, containing a microprocessor and I/O units.

Microprocessor. The basic core of any computer. The elementary chips that control how the computer works.

Minicomputer. Intermediate priced (and powered) computers sold for between $30,000 and $300,000. Minis allow multiuser networks to share the CPU.

Mnemonics. Symbolic names for instructions, codes, or phrases. Used to aid operator memory.

Modem. Acronym for modulator-demodulator. A device that is capable of converting and interpreting signals received through telephone lines.

Monitoring lights. A feature of several modems. Lights that inform the user of the current telecommunications situation (on, off, sending, receiving, etc.).

Mouse. A handheld device that controls a menu on screen.

Multiplexing. Simultaneously transmitting several messages over a single data transmission line.

Nanosecond. One-millionth of a second.

Networks. Computer systems that allow several terminals to exchange data through the sharing of a common CPU.

Nibble. Four bits. One-half of a byte.

Nonimpact printer. A printing device that creates letters or images without striking paper. The dot matrix and ink-jet printers are examples.

Nonproprietary operating systems. Operating systems, such as CP/M and MS-DOS, that are not controlled by one hardware manufacturer.

Null modem. The communications cable used in hardwiring.

OCR. Optical character recognition.

Octal. A numbering system with a base of eight.

Off-line. An intelligent terminal capable of operating without being in direct communication with a more powerful computer.

On-line. Terminal or other device that is in direct communication with the CPU.

Operating system. An organization of software that controls the overall logic and operation of the computer.

Optical character recognition. A technology that produces devices capable of reading typed characters and converting those characters into magnetic data.

Optical scanning. The method used in OCR to "read" characters. Pages are scanned for specific patterns. When patterns are identified, letters and numbers are created in memory.

PE. Printer's errors. Mistakes made by the typesetter.

Paced transmission. Transmission of data which is controlled by on/off signals or by time.

Paper tape. The first form of typesetting memory. Holes are punched in strips of paper, which are read by paper punch readers.

Parallel port. A plug at the back of a computer capable of transmitting more than one bit at a time; transmission is parallel along several tracks.

Parallel transmission. Data transmissions that send 8 bits at a time.

Parity. A system used to detect errors in data transmissions. Parity is assigned as either odd or even. Each bit is checked to make certain that the parity (total number of 1 data bits) is odd or even, as specified. If parity is not achieved, an error has occurred.

Parity bit. The bit used to establish odd or even parity. If parity is even, and the number of data bits is odd, the parity bit is assigned a value of 1. If the number of 1 data bits is even, the parity bit is 0.

Pasteups. *See* Mechanicals.

Peripherals. The various input and output devices, storage units, and other hardware forming the computer system. Anything except the CPU, RAM, and ROM.

Phase modulation. Conversion of digital signals into binary signals (for example, audible tones) of varying wavelengths.

Photodisplay unit. A phototypesetter that produces optically spaced display lettering.

Pica. A unit in a system of measurement used by typesetters. One pica is 12 points. There are approximately 6 picas in 1 inch.

Point. A measurement of line space and type size. There are 12 points to the pica. One point is 1/72 of an inch high.

Point-to-point. Data transmission directly from one computer to another, without intermediate connectors.

Port. An output plug through which the communications cable is connected to the S-100 bus and CPU.

Programs. Software. Instructions that tell the CPU to perform a specific task.

Protocols. The rules and parameters that govern the exchange of information between computers.

Punch cards. *See* Hollerith cards.

Punched paper tape. *See* Paper tape.

Quads. A piece of type metal used in filling out lines and spacing between words. The terminology has carried over to phototypesetting.

RAM. Random access memory. Memory that can be changed by the user.

ROM. Read-only memory. Memory that can only be read, and not changed, by the user.

RS-232 port. A standard plug with 25 pins, used to connect computers and I/O devices.

Ragged left. A pattern of lines that are ragged on the left and even on the right margin. Opposite of ragged right.

Ragged right. A pattern of lines that are ragged on the right margin and even on the left. Opposite of ragged left.

Read-write head. That part of the disk drive that rotates the magnetized surface and then either reads or writes magnetic memory onto the disk.

Rigid disk. A hard disk. A disk, typically used in microcomputers, capable of storing large amounts of information. The disk is permanently encased.

S-100 bus. The standard bus used in many microcomputers. Circuits that move information from the CPU to the RS-232 port.

Sans serif. Typeface without serifs.

Satellite keyboarding. Keyboarding by terminals that are connected to the computer only through telecommunications.

Script. A typeface that looks like handwriting. Letters touch when typeset. Those typefaces based on handwriting in which letters do not touch are known as cursives.

Semiconductor. A solid, such as silicon, capable of conducting certain sorts of electrical currents.

Send/receive option. An option available on several typesetters that allow the typesetting machine to both send information to a computer *and* to receive information back from the word processing computer.

Serial interface. An interface based on serial transmission. *See also* Serial transmission.

Serial transmission. Data transmission that sends 1 data bit at a time.

Serif. Short cross-stroke in the letters of most typefaces. Faces with serifs are known as roman or, simply, serif. Serif typefaces are often used in body type.

Set solid. Typesetting in which the type size and line space are the same. 10/10 is type set solid.

Setting. Producing type, either by hand, by casting, by photography, or by typing.

Shared-logic system. A configuration of terminals and other I/O devices that share the same CPU and can thus share information.

Sign-on. A document that permits a user to use a computer. Sign-on documents often contain passwords that are required for user access to the computer.

Simplex. A modem that either sends or receives information but cannot do both during one transmission.

Slave keyboards. Keyboards having limited memory and processing power; dedicated solely to producing keystrokes to be manipulated by a more powerful front-end computer. *See also* Front-end system.

Soft returns. Returns inserted in word processing documents by the software. Returns at the ends of individual lines of copy to allow the operator to begin the next line.

Soft-sectored. Magnetic media sectored by magnetic pulses instead of physically punched holes. *See also* Hard-sectored.

Software. Programs. Instructions created to order the CPU to perform certain tasks.

Spacebands. Spaces between words.

Specs. The measurements, such as line space, line length, type size, and font number, which are necessary for typesetting. Shorthand for specifications.

Standalones. Computers that are capable of operation without connection to any other computer.

Start and stop bits. Bits at the beginning and end of asynchronous transmission, notifying the receiving computer that a character has begun and ended.

Straight matter. Simple textual material. *See also* Tabular material; Technical matter.

Strike-on typesetting. *See* Direct-impression typesetting.

Strikeouts. A word processing feature that allows slashes or dashes to be typed over the material—"striking it out."

Strikeovers. A word processing feature that allows more than one character to be printed over the same position; useful for constructing math symbols and foreign language accents.

Subscripts and superscripts. Smaller numbers and letters appearing below (subscripts) and above (superscripts) normal numbers and letters; necessary in mathematical and scientific typesetting.

Supercomputer. A powerful computer, such as the Cray 1, capable of millions of operations per second. Much more powerful than the mainframes, these computers are usually used as the hub of a network.

Superscripts. *See* Subscripts and superscripts.

Synchronous transmission. Data transmission that is regulated by time. Also called bisynchronous or, simply, synch.

System degradation. A problem created when too many input devices are connected to a single CPU. The system operation slows down (degrades) as more devices join the network.

TTY. Abbreviation for teletypewriter. An obsolete but still used term for asynchronous transmission.

Tabular material. In typesetting, tables and charts.

Tape drive. A mechanism capable of reading and writing information onto magnetic tapes.

Technical matter. Difficult typesetting composed of scientific or mathematical material.

Telecommunications. The transmission of information through telephone lines.

Terminal. A keyboard connected to a television screen (CRT).

Text type. *See* Body type.

Throughput. The amount of work performed by a computer during a given period of time.

Time-sharing. Dividing a computer's time among several users, thus decreasing the costs for each. There are companies that offer time-sharing services, meaning the user buys computer time from the vendor.

Translation tables. Sets of equations that control the translations of data sent from one computer to another.

Type. The proportionally spaced letters produced, in different typefaces and sizes, by composition machines.

Type designer. Graphic designer who creates typeface designs.

Type house. A company that specializes in typesetting.

Type size. The length from the top of an ascender to the bottom of a descender. Measured in points.

Type style. *See* Typeface.

Typeface. A single style of type.

Typesetter. A person who sets type, either by keyboarding or by hand. Also a machine that sets type.

Typewriter composition. *See* Direct-impression typesetting.

Typography. Creating pages with type.

U&lc. Upper- and lowercase. Capital letters and small letters, the typical way in which type is set for body copy.

UDK. User-defined keys. *See also* User programmable keys.

Unattended/attended mode. An option offered by typesetting and interface hardware manufacturers that allows an interface to be conducted either with the help of personnel (attended) or without (unattended).

Understrikes. A word processing feature that allows a line to be printed under words or phrases; underscoring.

User-defined keys. *See* User programmable keys.

User groups. Clubs and organizations devoted to a specific operating system, computer, or word processing program.

User programmable keys. Keys on a terminal that can be programmed by the user to mean any string of characters (or program) desired. Also called UDK.

VDT. Video display terminal. A combination of a CRT (cathode ray tube) and terminal.

Variations. Different weights and stresses of a regular typeface. Bold, italic, condensed, and expanded are several variations.

Volatile memory. Information that is lost whenever power to the computer is interrupted.

White space. Along with art and type, the third element in any design. The blank areas of the page.

Winchester system. *See* Hard disk.

Word processing. Using a computer to create, store, retrieve, and edit text.

Word space. The space between words. In most typesetting systems, word space is used to justify. The computer unit of the typesetter puts more or less space between words, as necessary, to justify each line.

Word wrap. In word processing, the ability of the computer to end a line automatically (with a soft return) and then wrap around to the next line for additional keyboarding.

X-height. The height of the lowercase x of the alphabet. Different typefaces have different x-heights.

X-On/X-Off. Synonym for DC1/DC3.

Index

Specific brands of microcomputers, word processors, telecommunications devices, and typesetting machines, as well as brand name software programs and companies that manufacture any of the above, are indexed where there is substantive discussion in the text. Passing references are not indexed.

ACI. *See* Advanced Communications Interface
ACK/NAK capability, 125
Acoustic couplers, 28, 91, 131
ADC. *See* Applied Data Communications
Advanced Communications Interface, 103
Altertext disk reader, 82–83
AM Comp/Edit Telecom interface, 105–106
AM Varityper typesetters, 105–106
Analog signals, 132
Antares, 83–84
AppleDOS, 55, 56
Apple Lisa, 58, 103, 104
Apple operating systems, 56
Apple word processing software, 53
Applied Data Communications, 84
ASCII, 119, 121–123, 186–192
error checking in, 125–126
Asynchronous transmission, 123–124
checklist for, 128
compared with bisynchronous, 124
Automatic answering, 134
Automatic dialing, 134

Backup copies, 65
Baud rate, 124–125, 132

Binary coded decimal, 186
Binary system, 183–184
Bisynchronous transmission, 123–124
checklist for, 129
compared with asynchronous, 124
Bits, 121–127, 185–186
Black boxes, 79–80
Block and file moves, 48–49
Book manufacturers, interfacing for, 35–36
Byte, 47, 186

CAC. *See* Computer Assistance Center
Canned programs, 185
Card puncher, 170
Cathode ray tube, 9
Central processing unit, 10, 167–168
Character display, 48, 66
Chips and semiconductors, 165–166
Code conversion charts, 187–191
Code insertions, 140–143
Code sets, 119, 121–123, 186–192
Coding deletions, 137
Coding guidelines, 69
Comp/Edit Telecom, 105–106
Composition, rules for, 197–198
Compugraphic typesetters, 95–96, 101–103
Computer Assistance Center, 102

Computer languages, 185
Computers. *See* Mainframe computers; Microcomputers; Minicomputers; Word processors
Continuous transmission, 127, 130
Control codes, 127
Conversion service, 79
   see also Media conversion
Cost savings, 6–7, 18–20
   from coding options, 142–143
   for customers, 34–35, 38, 155
   with in-house typesetting, 114, 154
   for materials, 21
   from telecommunicating, 28
CP/M, 56, 57, 182–183
CPS 1000 typesetter, 105
CPU. *See* Central processing unit
Cromwell Context, 84–85
CRT. *See* Cathode ray tube
CRTronic typesetter, 99
CW/CI interface, 95–96

Daisy wheel printers, 178–179
Data bases, 65
Data bits, 123–127
Data Communications Interface, 103
Data processing, 2
DCI. *See* Data Communications Interface
DC1/DC3, 127
Debugging, 69, 158
Dedicated word processors, 8, 11
Delimiter, 149
Digital computers, 165
Digital typesetting, 15, 97, 179
Direct connect modems, 131
Direct entry typesetters, 95–96
Direct interfacing, 27–30, 81–82
   options compared, 93
   see also Hardwiring; Telecommunications
Disk
   density of, 176
   floppy, 15, 175–177
   hard, 174–175
   single- and double-sided, 176
   soft- and hard-sectored, 176–177
Disk capacity, 48
Disk drive, 64–65, 175
Diskette, 15, 175–177
Disk operating system, 55–57, 182–183
Documentation, for word processors, 49, 61

DOS, 55–57, 182–183
Dot matrix printers, 179–181
Downtime, 10
Dual disk drive, 65

EBCDIC, 119, 121–123, 186–192
   error checking in, 126
EditWriter typesetters, 101–102
Electrostatic printers, 180
Em and en indents, 138, 196

File length, 47–48
Floppy disk, 15, 175–177
Font drum, 14
Formats for coding, 142–143
Frequency modulation, 132
Front-end systems, 80, 84, 98
Full duplex modems, 132

Global search and return, 49

Half-duplex modems, 132
H&j programs, 138
Hard disk, 174–175
Hard returns, translating, 138–139
Hardware, 11–13, 166–169
   checklist for, 64
   optional, 181
   selection, 54–57
Hardwiring, 27–28, 30, 38–40, 88–91
   applications of, 90–91
   problems with, 90
Headers and footers, 50–51
Hexadecimal code, 121, 192–194
High-level programming languages, 185
Hyphenation, coding for, 146
Hyphenation logic, 146
Hyphens and dashes, translating, 137

IBM-compatible computers, 52, 56
IBM-compatible software, 183
IBM PC, 52, 57
ICI. *See* Intelligent Communications Interface
Impact printers, 179–180
Indents, 196
   translating, 138, 139

Indirect interfacing, 22, 24–27, 80
  options compared, 93
  see also Media conversion; Optical
    character recognition
In-house graphics facilities, 38–40
  interfacing in, 39, 154
  selling typesetting, 114, 154, 162–
    163
In-house typesetting, 39–40, 109–117,
    153–154
  benefits of, 113–114
  equipment costs, 111–112
  first year cost estimate for, 40
  guidelines for transition to, 115–116
  personnel costs, 112
  personnel for, 110–111
  physical plant for, 110
  printing costs, 112–113
  production control for, 111, 114
  questions for equipment vendors,
    116–117
  suggested development, 153–154
Input devices, 41–43, 169–170
Input problems, 136–140
Integrated circuits, 166
Intelligent Communications Interface,
    101–102
Interfacing, 3, 5–8
  becoming a competitive necessity, 34,
    35, 157
  choice of method, 86–92
  choosing equipment, 92–94
  code problems, 121–123, 192
  customer criteria for, 37–38
  deciding on, 75–79
  direct, 27–30, 81–82, 93
  economic considerations, 18–20
  implications of, for typesetting com-
    panies, 155
  indirect, 22, 24–27, 80, 93
  for in-house graphics facilities, 38–
    40, 14, 154, 162–163
  input choices for, 41–43, 169–170
  input problems with, 136–140
  investment worksheet for, 22, 23
  market for, 159
  marketing strategy for, 159–162
  operating system problems, 56–57
  for printing companies and book
    manufacturers, 35–36
  for quick printers, 36–37
  reasons for, 5, 18–22
  satellite keyboarding for, 35–36
  selling services, 158–162

software checklist for, 58–59
  time-saving advantages of, 21–22
  translation checklist for, 150
  type quality improvements from, 20–
    21
  with typesetters, 98–106
  for typesetting companies, 33–37,
    157–158
  for typesetting customers, 37–38
  typesetting problems with, 140–141
Interfacing manual, 69, 71–73
Interfacing options, compared, 30, 93
  see also Hardwiring; Media conver-
    sion; Optical character recognition;
    Telecommunications
Investment work sheet, for interfacing
    costs, 22, 23
Itek Converter library, 85
Itek typesetters, 103–105

Justification, 138, 196

K. *See* Kilobyte
Kaypro 4, 57–58
Keyboard, 20, 66, 170
  satellite, 35–36
Keystroke savings, 6, 8, 16, 18–19,
    135–136
Kilobyte, 47–48, 186
Kurzweil OCR scanner, 24, 42, 87

Laser typesetting, 15, 97
Leaders, coding for, 146
Letter quality printers, 178–179
Line by line/X-On, 127, 130
Line length, 195, 197, 198
Line space, 196, 197–198
Line voltage regulator, 181
Linotron and Linoterm typesetters, 99–
    100
Lisa. *See* Apple Lisa

Mag card system, 1, 9, 173
Magnetic cassettes and cartridges,
    172–173
Magnetic memory, 8, 15, 172–174
Magnetic tape, 8, 173–174
Mainframe computers, 11, 12, 13
Main memory, 169
Mark IX typesetter, 105

MASS-11, 53–54
Mathematical symbols, translating, 138
MCS. *See* Modular Composition System
MediaCom 5000, 25, 26, 81–82
Media conversion, 25–27, 30, 31, 79–86, 104–105
  cost of, 26–27
  deciding on, 79, 86
  equipment for, 79–80, 81–85
Megabyte, 186
Memory
  disk, 15, 174–177
  magnetic, 8, 15, 172–174
  main, 169
  paper tape, 15, 171–172
  random access, 64, 169
  read-only, 169
  for typesetters, 14
  for word processors, 8, 9
Menu, 46, 49
Mergenthaler typesetters, 99–101
Microchips, 13
Microcomputers, 13, 26, 57–58
  Apple, 58, 103–104
  choosing, 42–43
  IBM PC, 52, 57
  as input stations, 20, 41–43
  Kaypro 4, 57–58
  minimum technical specifications for, 63–66
  operating systems for, 55–57
  see also Word processors
Microprocessors, 166, 167
Microsoft Word, 52
Minicomputers, 2, 11, 12–13, 41
  choosing, 43
  software for, 53–54
Mnemonics, 135–136, 144–147
Modems, 3, 28–29, 91, 119, 131–134
  null, 27, 90
  selecting, 133–134
  testing, 134
  types compared, 131
Modular Composition System, 103
Monitoring lights, 134
Mouse, 58
MS-DOS, 55–56, 57, 183
Multiplexer networks, 2, 4, 97

Networking
  satellite, 35–36
  telecommunications for, 2–3

Networks
  information, 5
  multiplexer, 2, 4, 97
  point-to-point, 2, 3
Nonimpact printers, 180
Nonproprietary operating systems, 65
Nontransparent transmission, 127
Null modem, 27, 90

OCR. *See* Optical character recognition
OCR readable typeface, 24
Octal code, 192
Omnitech 2000 typesetter, 100–101
On-line information data bases, 65
On-line input, 169
Operating systems, 55–57, 65, 182–183
Optical character recognition, 22, 30, 31, 42
  advantages of, 24–25
  applications of, 25
  equipment for, 86–87
  problems with, 24, 42
  from type buyers' viewpoint, 87–88
Optical scanning. *See* Optical character recognition
Output devices. *See* Typesetters

Paced transmission, 127, 130
Pagination, 50–51
Paper tape memory, 15, 171–172
Parallel port, 65
Parallel transmission, compared with serial, 88–89
Parity bits, 123–124, 125–126
PCS. *See* Personal Composition System
Perfect Writer, 52–53
Personal Composition System, 103
Personal computers. *See* Microcomputers
Phase modulation, 132
Photoscanning typesetters, 97
Phototypesetting, 14, 97–98
  see also Typesetting
Point-to-point networks, 2, 3
Ports, 28, 65, 89–90, 91
Printer commands, 50
Printers, 177–181
  choosing, 180–181
  typewriters used as, 178
Printing companies, interfacing for, 35–36
Processing speed, 63
Programmable converters, 79–80

Protocols, 119–130
  ACK/NAK capability, 125
  baud rate, 124–125, 132
  checklist for establishing, 120
  code sets, 119, 121–123
  number of data bits, 126–127
  number of stop bits, 126
  paced or continuous transmission,
    127, 130
  parity, 125–126
  transmission types, 123–124
  transparent or nontransparent mode,
    127
Punch cards, 170–171
Punched paper tape, 15, 171–172

Quadritek typesetter, 104
Quick printers
  interfacing for, 36–37
  typesetting by, 37
Quotation marks, translating, 139–140

Radio Shack operating systems, 56
RAM. *See* Random access memory
Random access memory, 64, 169
Read-only memory, 169
Read-write head, 173–174
Returns, translating, 138–139
Rigid disk, 174–175
ROM. *See* Read-only memory
RS-232 port, 29, 65, 89–90, 91

Satellite keyboarding, 35–36
Self-diagnostic tests for modems, 134
Semiconductors and chips, 165–166
Send/receive option, 130
Serial interface, 29
Serial transmission, 29–30
  compared with parallel, 88–89
Service, for computers, 62
Shaftstall media converters, 25, 26, 80,
    81–82
Shared-logic system, 10–11
Sign-on document, 130
Simplex modem, 132
Slave keyboards, 20
Soft returns, 138–139
Software
  desirable extras, 50–51
  essential features, 46–50
  for minicomputers, 53–54

operating systems. *See* Operating
  systems
  purchasing checklist, 47
  selection of, 45–46, 47, 51
  for telecommunications, 91–92
S-100 bus, 89–90
Spacing, 196
  coding for, 145
  translating, 137
Special characters, coding for, 146
Standalone systems, 8, 10, 11, 42–43
  see also Microcomputers
Start bits, 123–124
Stop bits, 123–124, 126
Storage, 170–177
  choosing, 174
  magnetic media for, 172–174
  paper media for, 170–172
  see also Memory
Straight matter, 44, 76, 143–144
Supercomputers, 11
Synchronous transmission, 123–124
  checklist for, 129
  compared with asynchronous, 124
System degradation, 11

Tabs, coding for, 145
Tabular material, 44
Tape drive, 173
Technical matter, 44, 143–144, 162
Technical specifications for word pro-
    cessors, 63–66
Telecom, 105–106
Telecommunications, 2–3, 28–30, 31,
    91–92
  advantages of, 29–30, 31
  cost advantages of, 92
  serial, 29–30
  software for, 91–92
  translation tables for, 30, 91–92
Terminal/computer combinations, 170
Terminals, 9–11, 169–170
Time-sharing, 11
Trade groups, 18
Training, 18, 62–63
Translation
  from ASCII to EBCDIC, 121, 187–191
  input problems, 136–140
  typesetting problems, 140–144
Translation checklist, 150
Translation tables, 30, 91–92, 122
  coding alternatives for, 142–143
  coding deletions in, 137

creating, 144–147
mnemonics for, 135–136, 144–147
for typed input, 137–140
writing, 148–149
Trans/Media 500, 84
Transparent transmission, 127
TRSDOS, 55, 56
Type font coding chart, 70
Type houses, interfacing for, 34–35
Type quality, 20–21
Typeface, 196
Typesetter commands, coding for, 145–146
Typesetters, 95–106
choosing, for interfacing, 106–107
Compugraphic, 101–103
digital scanning, 15, 97
direct entry, 95–96
interfacing with word processors, 5–8
Itek, 103–105
laser scanning, 15, 97
memory for, 14
Mergenthaler, 99–101
photographic, 14, 97–98
Typesetting
compared with typewriting, 20–21
development of, 13–15
in-house. See In-house typesetting
by quick printers, 37
steps in, 19
of technical matter, 143–144
technical parameters in, 143
Typesetting codes, mnemonics for, 136
Typesetting companies
advantages from interfacing, 157–158
implications of interfacing for, 155, 157
interfacing for, 33–37
marketing interfacing capability, 158–162
pricing guidelines for, 162–163
selection of, by type buyers, 151–153
Typesetting customers
cost savings for, 34–35, 38, 155
interfacing for, 37–38
Typesetting measurements, 195
Typesetting parameters, 195–196
coding for, 145
Typesetting problems, troubleshooting, 140–144

Typesetting users
alternatives for, 41
groups of, 40–41
Type size, 195, 197, 198
Type style, 196, 198
Typewriters, as printers, 178

UDK. See User-defined keys
Unattended/attended mode, 130
UNIX, 183
User-defined keys, 50
User groups, 62
User-programmable keys, 50
User programs, 185

Varityper typesetters, 105
VDT. See Video display terminal
Video display terminal, 9
Volkswriter, 52

Winchester system, 174–175
WordCom SI, 86–87
Word processing, 2, 8–13
employee preparation for, 68–69
options compared, 11, 13
shared-logic option for, 10–11
site preparation for, 68
standalone option for, 1, 10, 11, 42–43
support systems for, 61–63
time-sharing option for, 11
troubleshooting input problems, 136–140
Word processing conventions, 137–140
Word processors
choice of, 11–13
dedicated, 8, 11
installation of, 68–73
interfacing with typesetters, 5–8
vendor considerations, 66–68
see also Microcomputers
WordStar, 52–53
Word wrap, 49

X-On/X-Off, 127